AMERICAN EDUCATION

Its Men

Ideas

and

Institutions

The First
State Normal School
In America

The Journals
of
Cyrus Peirce and Mary Swift

ARNO PRESS & THE NEW YORK TIMES
*New York * 1969*

Reprint edition 1969 by Arno Press, Inc.

*

Library of Congress Catalog Card No. 76-89213

*

Manufactured in the United States of America

Editorial Note

AMERICAN EDUCATION: *Its Men, Institutions and Ideas* presents selected works of thought and scholarship that have long been out of print or otherwise unavailable. Inevitably, such works will include particular ideas and doctrines that have been outmoded or superseded by more recent research. Nevertheless, all retain their place in the literature, having influenced educational thought and practice in their own time and having provided the basis for subsequent scholarship.

Lawrence A. Cremin
Teachers College

The First
State Normal School
In America

The Journals
of
Cyrus Peirce and Mary Swift

LEXINGTON COMMON IN 1926 — THE FIRST BUILDING USED BY THE NORMAL SCHOOL, 1839–1844, IS AT THE EXTREME RIGHT

THE FIRST STATE NORMAL SCHOOL
IN AMERICA

THE JOURNALS OF
CYRUS PEIRCE AND MARY SWIFT

WITH AN INTRODUCTION

By ARTHUR O. NORTON

PROFESSOR OF THE HISTORY AND PRINCIPLES OF EDUCATION IN
WELLESLEY COLLEGE, LECTURER IN THE HARVARD
GRADUATE SCHOOL OF EDUCATION

CAMBRIDGE
HARVARD UNIVERSITY PRESS
LONDON : HUMPHREY MILFORD
OXFORD UNIVERSITY PRESS
1926

PRINTED BY
WRIGHT AND POTTER
BOSTON, MASS., U. S. A.

"LIVE TO THE TRUTH"

THIS BOOK IS DEDICATED TO THE MEMORY OF

FATHER PEIRCE

IN GRATEFUL APPRECIATION OF HIS PIONEER SERVICE
TO THE CAUSE OF STATE NORMAL SCHOOLS

BY THE

ALUMNAE ASSOCIATION OF THE STATE NORMAL SCHOOL
FRAMINGHAM, MASSACHUSETTS

ACKNOWLEDGMENTS

The Committee intrusted with the publication of the journals of Cyrus Peirce and Mary Swift extends its thanks —

To the Alumnæ of the State Normal School at Framingham for their loyal support.

To the Hon. Charles E. Stone of Waltham for permission to print the journal of Cyrus Peirce, for photographs, and for the loan of much additional material.

To Miss Kate G. Lamson for permission to publish the journal and the photographs of her mother, Mary Swift Lamson.

To contributors to the publication fund: Mrs. William Gould of Santa Barbara, California, who gave in memory of four pupils of Father Peirce, — her sister, Annie Faulkner, and her cousins, Eliza, Elvira, and Harriet Rogers; the Framingham Clubs of New York and Boston; and Miss Myra I. Billings.

To Professor Arthur O. Norton of Wellesley College for the Introduction, and for the compilation and editing of additional documents concerning the early history of normal schools in Massachusetts.

To Mr. Theodore W. Noon and Mr. Frederick G. Livingood of the Harvard Graduate School of Education for the index to the journals.

> SOPHIA FAULKNER CAMPBELL, 1867
> MARY HOWARD FOWLER, 1873
> MARY C. MOORE, 1872
> ANTOINETTE B. ROOF, 1886
> HARRIET B. SORNBORGER, 1891
> KATHARINE H. STONE, 1879
> HENRY WHITTEMORE, *Principal*, 1898–1917
> > *Committee of the Alumnæ Association of the*
> > *State Normal School at Framingham, Mass.*

The writer of the Introduction would add that the Committee of the Alumnæ Association has not only underwritten the fund for the publication of this volume, but it has also supervised the transcription of the journals, and has carried out the laborious task of comparing the printed text, point by point, with the original manuscripts. Moreover, it has shared the not inconsiderable labor of selecting the illustrations and securing the necessary photographs therefor.

The tasks of the present writer have been, first, to collect and study the sources for the history of the normal school at Lexington; second, to share with the Committee the work of securing illustrations, including the two rare maps of Lexington; third, to select from the mass of documents the few which are placed at the end of this volume; and fourth, to write the Introduction. Some hints, only, of the labor involved in the first of these tasks appear in the pages of this volume. Notes and bibliography are reduced to a minimum, since the book has already been expanded much beyond the original plan.

To name all who have aided in this research is impossible; the writer can only extend thanks in general to many who have contributed information and suggestions. Particular mention must be made of Mr. J. H. Edmonds of the Massachusetts Archives, Mr. Julius H. Tuttle of the Massachusetts Historical Society, Mr. Edwin B. Worthen of the Lexington Historical Society, Hon. Charles E. Stone of Waltham, Miss Kate G. Lamson and Mr. John Albree of Boston.

To Lady Francis Campbell, Chairman of the Committee on Publication, and to the Secretary of the Committee, Miss Mary C. Moore, the writer owes deepest thanks for invaluable contributions of fact; to the Committee as a whole, and to the Alumnæ of the school, his gratitude for their patience. What he owes to his wife she will understand.

ARTHUR O. NORTON.

WELLESLEY, MASS., April 19, 1926.

TABLE OF CONTENTS

LIST OF ILLUSTRATIONS

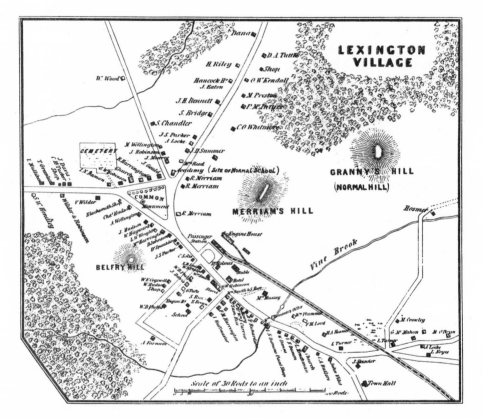

LEXINGTON VILLAGE (MAP OF 1853)
Location of Normal School, 1839–1844

THE FIRST STATE NORMAL SCHOOL IN AMERICA

THE JOURNALS OF CYRUS PEIRCE AND MARY SWIFT

INTRODUCTION

By ARTHUR O. NORTON

I. PRELIMINARIES

I

The journals of Cyrus Peirce[1] and his pupil, Mary Swift, first published in this volume, record the beginnings of the State Normal School which is now located at Framingham, Mass. This institution is distinguished as the pioneer among the 167 state normal schools and state teachers' colleges which are now established in the United States — the first of its type, indeed, on the American Continent. It was opened on July 3, 1839, at Lexington, in the building [2] which was erected in 1822 for the short-lived Lexington Academy, and which (several times remodeled) still stands at the northeasterly corner of Lexington Common, over-looking the first battleground of the American Revolution. In 1844 the school was moved to West Newton,[3] and thence, in 1853, to the commanding site which it now occupies on the hill at Framingham, some twenty-five miles west of Boston.[4] It is one of the three public normal schools which were created by the Massachusetts [State] Board of Education in 1838, and which were opened in succession — the first at Lexington as above noted, the second at Barre (Sept. 4, 1839), the third at Bridgewater (Sept. 9, 1840) —

---

[1] The name is pronounced "Purse."

[2] See frontispiece; also illustrations opposite pp. xlviii, liv and 70; also maps opposite pp. xiii and xxxiii.

[3] Illustration opposite p. 138.

[4] Illustrations opposite pp. 168, 198, 268, 274.

to serve, respectively, the northeastern, the central, and the southeastern areas of the state. The establishment of these schools was one of the first of the far-reaching educational reforms which were brought about during the eventful years 1837–1848 by the distinguished Secretary to the Board of Education, Horace Mann.

II

A bitter controversy raged about these institutions during their early years, and especially during the years 1839–1842. They had been established after a fourteen-year campaign by the friends of public education, to meet the desperate need of competent teachers for the district schools of the state. Similar institutions had long been successful in Prussia, and they had been established recently in France. Their success in Massachusetts was uncertain; hence they were set up at first merely as a three-year experiment.

A powerful group of enemies in the state and in the Legislature were determined to abolish these schools without delay, and lost no time in moving to the attack. Misrepresentation and abusive attacks in the newspapers, and propaganda in the Legislature, were employed against the normal schools. In Horace Mann's phrase, "Ignorance, bigotry and economy were arrayed against them." For various reasons a particular attack was directed against the school at Lexington. It was generally agreed, afterward, that Cyrus Peirce's success in developing there a course of professional training for teachers played an important part in the victories which were won for the normal schools in the Legislatures of 1840 and 1842.

The victory was of more than local importance. The policy of maintaining state normal schools was under vigorous discussion in other states. Friends and foes of this policy watched keenly the progress of the experiment in Massachusetts. Henry Barnard, at that time an educational leader in Connecticut, and afterward the chief historian of American education, recorded his belief that, had Peirce failed at Lexington, the cause of normal schools in the United States would have failed, or would have been indefinitely postponed.

III

The sources for the early history of the school, in manuscript and in print, include scores of documents. Most of these are in the carefully kept collection of the Alumnæ Association, at Framingham. Others are in the State Archives, and in the library of the Massachusetts Historical Society, in Boston. Many more have been discovered and assembled recently by the writer of this introduction.

Among them all, the journals of Cyrus Peirce and his pupil, Mary Swift, which have long been in the collection in Framingham, are unique in their detailed account of the work of the school during its first two years. By the authority and with the support of the Alumnæ Association they are now published.

The text as printed in this volume omits matter amounting to about twelve printed pages from the journal of Mary Swift. The omissions are duly indicated. The text is also divided into chapters, not found in the original manuscripts. A few insertions are indicated by brackets. Otherwise, the copy is exact.

Other important documents, now inaccessible and little known, are quoted or reprinted in their entirety, to throw further light on the early years of the school at Lexington. Two of these, of great value, are Peirce's own description of the school in 1841 (page 1*ff.*), and his statement in 1851 of the aims which guided his work (page 278*ff.*). These documents should be compared closely with James G. Carter's remarkably comprehensive and clear-cut "Outline of an Institution for the Education of Teachers," first published in 1825 (page 227*ff.*), and with the preliminary outline published by the Board of Education in 1839 (page 261*ff.*).

Abundant illustrations and two maps give reality to persons, places, school equipment, and manuscripts concerned.

IV

The purpose of this introduction is to indicate in outline the historical setting for these documents. Some suggestion is made, in the following pages, of the scope and spirit of

the great revival of public education in Massachusetts between 1825 and 1850, of which the work at Lexington formed
a part.   Many of the leading figures of that historic movement appear for a moment in the pages of these journals:
Horace Mann, Edmund Dwight, Governor Edward Everett,
and members of the Board of Education, — especially Jared
Sparks, first Professor of American History at Harvard and
later President of that University; Robert Rantoul, Jr., a
distinguished lawyer, and a leader in many movements for
popular education; George Putnam, a leading clergyman of
his time.   Among these, too, are representatives of the campaign for free public schools in other states: Henry Barnard
of Connecticut, and James Wadsworth of New York.   Both
men were afterward concerned in establishing normal schools
in their own states.

For our present purposes, however, these are minor actors.
In this volume, Cyrus Peirce and a little group of girls in
their teens hold the center of the stage.   The action passes
mainly in the town of Lexington in 1839–1841, and especially in the building at the corner of the Common.   Here, as
Peirce wrote many years later, "began in 1839 a new battle,
against ignorance and bad teaching."   The girls who as
students sorely tried Peirce's patience, and who as teachers
afterward demonstrated, in schoolrooms far and wide, the
value of the professional training which he gave them, were
the Minute Men of the new war.   One of them wrote afterward, "We were told so often that the responsibility for the
success of the enterprise rested for the time being upon our
shoulders, that we felt that we *must* succeed."

Six of the twenty-five who gathered at Lexington during
the first year lived to see normal schools in every state in
the Union, and an army of more than one hundred thousand
students each year following the path which they first traced
in 1839.

II. THE JOURNALS

I

Cyrus Peirce (affectionately known in the annals of the
school as "Father" Peirce) was the Principal of the institution at Lexington (1839–1842) and at West Newton

(1844–1849). Mary Swift, then seventeen years old, was one of the twenty-five young women who enrolled as students in 1839–1840, and who were afterwards distinguished, individually as teachers, and collectively as "the first class of the first State Normal School in America."

The two journals — one by the teacher, the other by the student — give an account of the daily life and work of the school during the years 1839–1841 and 1839–1840, respectively. Along with records of local and temporary interest they furnish information of the first importance to students of the early history of American state normal schools; they record the work of the classroom from day to day, — the lectures, the recitations, the experiments, the discussions, the questions, and the methods of teaching, together with comments and criticisms on the work, the pupils, and the instructor, chiefly by the instructor himself. The result is a surprisingly detailed account of the exact matter, method, and progress of this pioneer experiment of the state of Massachusetts in the professional training of teachers for its public schools. Although much has been written concerning the early history of normal schools in Massachusetts, there has always been of necessity a certain vagueness as to the exact character of the professional training which they offered. The facts are now revealed in hitherto unknown detail, in the case of one of these institutions, by the journals here published.

II

The general theory of professional training for teachers, so far as the new normal schools were concerned, was repeatedly stated in the writings of the period. Its leading ideas may be summed up as follows:

1. The purpose of such training is to prepare teachers for the ungraded district schools of the state. (At that time there were practically no other public schools in Massachusetts. The first public high school was established in Boston, 1821, and even in 1840 less than twenty others had been opened in the state. Nearly all were very small. A few communities had schools graded as primary, intermediate or grammar, and high schools; but these were the

rare exceptions. The ungraded district school was the type.)

2. The studies included in professional training for teachers are —

(1) A thorough review of the "common branches" — spelling, reading, writing, grammar, geography, and arithmetic — required by law to be taught in the "common schools."

(2) Advanced studies (except ancient languages) so far as time permits.

(3) The physical, mental, and moral development of children.

(4) The science and art (*i.e.*, principles and methods) of teaching each of the "common branches."

(5) The art of school government; *i.e.*, the organization of the day's work; rewards, punishments, and discipline in general.

(6) Practice in teaching and governing a "model or experimental school."

The journals tell us in detail the manner in which this program was carried out, day by day, at Lexington.[1] As may be expected, they differ markedly in character.

III

Peirce's journal is invaluable for its critical estimates of the progress of the work, and for other information; but it is in no sense an attempt at a systematic record of the day's work. Such a record ("my other journal," page 63 *ff.*) Peirce apparently did keep, beginning probably in 1840. It was for the benefit of the students, and it was read to the entire school from time to time. This journal is unfortunately lost. The surviving document is his private journal. It includes lists of visitors to the school, the names of new students, a brief statement of subjects discussed during the day, comments on the quality and progress of the work, on the methods of teaching adopted, on the progress of the model school, and on the successes and failures in his own and the students' work. On many days, especially during the hurry

[1] See also Peirce's extremely important description of his methods of "teaching the art of teaching," published by Henry Barnard early in 1841 (pp. l–lv).

of the first five months, Peirce made no entry at all. Taken by itself it would lack much of the significance which it gains from the journal of Mary Swift.

The reader of Peirce's journal will observe regretful notes of his own impatience, and a tone of increasing despondency and discouragement as the experiment progresses. Overwhelming labors, anxiety over the success of the school, and increasing ill health explain these characteristics. It must be remembered that Peirce was carrying the entire burden of the experiment, except for occasional assistance from his wife. He organized and administered the school, carried on its correspondence, taught all the subjects of the curriculum (ten subjects in a term, and seventeen different subjects in the course of the first year!), developed the methods and material of the purely professional side of the work, established the "model or experimental school" of about thirty children, and acted as demonstration teacher and critic of student teaching therein. Because funds for assistance were lacking, he even acted as janitor of the building. His heart was in the success of the new institution, and for that success he counted no labor too arduous and no service too menial. His program included, at times, eight hours a day in the classroom, divided equally between the normal school and the model school. His day's work began well before dawn, and it ended toward midnight.

Failing health led him to ask urgently for release at the end of the fifth term (Dec. 22, 1840); but it was met by the more urgent appeal of Horace Mann to remain at his post. The question of continuing the normal school experiment was soon to come before the Legislature. A powerful party sought to abolish the schools. Mann felt that a change of the Principal at Lexington might be disastrous to the cause. Peirce, although desperately in need of relief, consented to stay. He wrote, "truly I would rather die than that the EXPERIMENT should fail through my unfaithfulness or inefficiency." In spite of growing exhaustion he continued until August, 1842. Meanwhile (March 2, 1842) the Legislature voted to continue the experiment. The battle for the normal schools was virtually won. Peirce then retired, so broken in health that further teaching seemed out of the question.[1]

Under these circumstances it is not remarkable that his private journal is brief and incomplete, that despondency and discouragement mark its later entries, and that the entries cease entirely near the end of the sixth term (March, 1841). The wonder is that Peirce kept the journal at all. It does not represent fairly the teacher who during these years was impressing upon his students — girls of sixteen, seventeen, and eighteen years — lifelong habits, enthusiasms, and ideals, and a professional outlook as teachers.

IV

The journal of Mary Swift is in marked contrast to that of Cyrus Peirce. It is a matter-of-fact, copious, and systematic "account of the business of the school and of the studies in which we are engaged." Many entries in Peirce's journal are so brief as to be almost meaningless without the surprisingly complete narrative of his pupil for the corresponding day. She often reports at length the work of days for which Peirce makes no entry whatever. Her journal contains probably the only existing notes of Peirce's lectures on school government and on the art of teaching; and though it was interrupted by two illnesses of the writer (the first half of November, 1839, and the whole of February, 1840) the existing record leaves no doubt whatever as to the nature of Peirce's course. The professional spirit which pervaded all the work of the school — even the review of the common branches — is clearly apparent from this journal.

The description of classroom work from day to day is the most important part of Mary Swift's record, but by no means all. There are glimpses of life in Lexington, and of its hospitable inhabitants, in 1840. A two-story wooden church with box pews, and a pulpit eight feet above the floor, stood on the Common, near its southerly apex, in 1839. On Sundays there were meetings "all day," — *i.e.*, in the morning and the afternoon. Mary Swift was a regular attendant at these meetings. After the custom of

---

[1] See his letter to Horace Mann, quoted in part on p. 78.

the time she took notes on the sermons and recorded them in her journal. She describes the fair (probably a church fair) at "Mt. Independence," — a hill in East Village, two miles down the post road to Boston, — and the fifty-mile view from the observatory on the hilltop. She mentions briefly tea at Mrs. Benjamin Muzzey's beautiful new house, the kindness of various persons to her during her long illness in February, and a call at "the old Clarke house," — now known as the Hancock-Clarke house, and visited by thousands of tourists annually, — where she "obtained Gov. [John] Hancock's Autograph." She refers to walks on the Lincoln, Concord and Burlington roads, and out to the fine estate of "Esquire Phinney" on Spring Street, two and one-half miles to the southwest of the village (see map, opposite page xxxiii). Her mention of the stage to Boston, eleven miles distant, reminds us that the railway had not yet arrived in Lexington.[1]

Two events — the Harvard Commencement and the Middlesex County School Convention — described by Mary Swift are of peculiar interest. Her account of the Harvard Commencement of August 28–29 (pages 97*ff*.) is one of the best now extant. With the rest of the audience she sat patiently through five hours of orations, dialogues, discussions, and other exercises by the graduating class. Her judgment as to the best of the twenty-five numbers on the program is the same as that of one of the oldest living graduates, who reported the same meeting. Her notes on the Middlesex County School Convention (Dec. 28, 1839) at Waltham, six miles from Lexington, are perhaps the only records now remaining of that gathering. Her outline of the lecture, "Special Preparation a Pre-requisite for Teaching," which Horace Mann delivered at this meeting, shows close attention to the main points. With equal care she described the visit, between meetings of the convention, to the cotton factory near by on the Charles

---

[1] In 1839 the railway was still a novelty in Massachusetts. The first (Boston to Newton) was opened in 1834. In 1839 five short lines, completed or under construction, radiated fanwise from Boston to Salem, to Lowell, to Fitchburg, to Worcester, and to Providence. Travel was still mainly by horseback, carriage, or stage-coach; freight traffic was mainly by canals and rivers, or by four, six, or even eight-horse wagons over the turnpikes. At this time Lexington, a natural halting place for through traffic, between Boston and northwestern Massachusetts and Vermont, contained no less than ten taverns.

River.[1]   She reported also (page 124) the excellent address of Governor Edward Everett on "Normal Schools," in the Lexington meeting-house above described.

As a whole, her journal reveals a serious, accurate observer, and a systematic, copious writer. It is a remarkable achievement for a girl of seventeen years.

V

A few pages must be given to the visitors to the school, and persons other than students who are mentioned in the journals. The number of visitors was large, especially during the first year (see Index, under Visitors). To identify these persons, and to follow their careers and relationships, so far as records permit, is a fascinating study. At first mere names on the page, they gradually emerge from the past as substantial and lively personalities, individual to the last degree.

The residents of Lexington in 1840 and thereabouts may be traced in the pages and portraits of Charles Hudson's too rare "History of Lexington," in the equally rare "Proceedings of the Lexington Historical Society," and in the collections of that society. Many members of this old and settled community appear for a moment in the pages of the journals, — Davises, Fiskes, Harringtons, Lockes, Phinneys, Merriams, Munroes, Muzzeys, Parkers, Tidds, Wellingtons, and others. One would gladly pause to make the acquaintance of these families, many of whom had been settled in Lexington for more than a century, and some for nearly two centuries. In 1840 some of those who had been awakened by Paul Revere in his midnight ride in 1775, and a few of the Minute Men themselves, were still living.

The two clergymen then settled in the town — Rev. Dr. Charles Follen of East Village, and Rev. O. A. Dodge of Lexington Village — are mentioned several times. Both were greatly interested in the success of the school; both

---

[1] This factory, established about 1813, first brought together in a single building all the processes of manufacturing cotton cloth, and used water power on a large scale for the operation of the machinery. It heralded the transformation of Massachusetts from a seafaring and agricultural state to a manufacturing state. This transformation was going forward rapidly in 1839. The growth of large centers of population in place of the then prevalent even distribution of the inhabitants in rural townships and villages resulted. This, in turn, raised the problem of graded city schools.

died before the end of its first year. Dr. Follen and his young son Charles, Jr., a pupil in the model school, perished in the burning of the steamer "Lexington" in Long Island Sound, on the eve of the dedication of his church, as related in the journals (pages 25, 196). Rev. Mr. Dodge, "the best friend of the normal school in all this vicinity," went to Boston in spite of serious illness, in the winter of 1840, to defend the institution against the attack made upon it in the Legislature. The exertion undoubtedly hastened his death.

Certain of the visitors from out of town brought news of the intellectual movements and social reforms which were then rising into prominence. Phrenology, the Peace Movement, Non-Resistance, Temperance Reform, and Transcendentalism were represented by talks from various men. The abolition of slavery was not publicly discussed at the normal school; it was too explosive a topic at that time.

"Mr. Felch" lectured on Phrenology, — the 'science' of determining the abilities and character of individuals by 'feeling the bumps on their heads.' It was supposed to be peculiarly valuable for teachers as a means of quickly understanding their pupils; and it may be described as an early and very crude form of mental and moral test. Its fallacies were soon detected, and it was thrown aside by all but quacks; but in 1840 many distinguished men on both sides of the Atlantic expected much from the new 'science,' and it was much discussed at Lexington. Mr. Felch's lecture "began at half-past six and lasted until ten," after which "he examined the heads of many of the scholars" (pages 18, 151).

Caleb Stetson held a "conversation" on Non-Resistance. Samuel J. May, brother-in-law of A. Bronson Alcott, friend, biographer and successor of Peirce at Lexington, spoke on Peace (page 49).

A. Bronson Alcott, of the neighboring town of Concord, discussed Transcendentalism before the somewhat mystified young ladies of the normal school. "He spent the morning defining it," wrote one of them demurely, "but I have not yet learned what it is." Alcott "gently rebuked" Cyrus Peirce for impatience with his pupils. "This may not have been very agreeable," wrote Peirce (page 50), "nevertheless it may have been strictly Just." Alcott is well known as a member of the distinguished group at Concord which included Ralph Waldo Emerson, Henry D. Thoreau and Nathaniel Hawthorne. He is best known, perhaps, as the father of the four "Little Women" who were afterward immortalized by his daughter Louisa. The school world of 1830–1840 knew him, however, as one of the most progressive teachers of the time. His novel private school in Boston (1834–1839) is described in Elizabeth P. Peabody's "Record of Mr. Alcott's School."

Others came to Lexington with a more professional interest in the new experiment:

Dr. William A. Alcott, cousin of Bronson Alcott, and a member of the State Board of Education, was among these. He was the author of many educational works, including "Confessions of a Schoolmaster," and a prize essay on "Schoolhouse Architecture."

Dr. Samuel G. Howe, founder of schools for the blind and for the feeble-minded in Boston, is mentioned several times in the journals. Howe's schools have grown into the great Perkins Institution for the Blind at Watertown, and the equally noted Massachusetts School for the Feeble-Minded (now the Walter E. Fernald State School) at Waverley. Dr. Howe promptly sent one of his teachers to Lexington for training, and called Mary Swift to his staff soon after she left the school. Her work with Laura Bridgman and others is noted on page xxxi. The Lexington-West Newton-Framingham Normal School has been represented with great distinction by its graduates, in work for the blind, to this day.

Governor Edward Everett — formerly Professor of Greek at Harvard, afterward its President, still later a Senator of the United States, and Ambassador to England — thought it worth his while to give much attention to the training of teachers. His address on "Normal Schools," reported by Mary Swift (page 124*ff*.) and published in Barnard's "American Journal of Education," is still a classic of its kind.

Horace Mann is perhaps the most widely known of the group today. His name is given to uncounted schools, public and private, in the United States; his statue shares with that of Daniel Webster the place of honor before the Massachusetts State House; his bust is in the Hall of Fame. On the centennial of his birth (1896) over seven hundred books and articles by and about him were listed in an incomplete bibliography. His twelve annual reports as Secretary to the Board of Education have been read far beyond the bounds of the United States, and some of them have been translated into foreign languages. Their flaming sentences embody a high vision of what the public schools may be and do in a democracy.

The list must close. A collection of the published biographies, the writings, and the writings about the persons who pass across the stage at Lexington would number some thousands of titles. The daily routine of the school passed amid the stir of great reforms. "It was the day of ideals in every camp. . . . A great wave of humanity, of benevolence, of desire for improvement, — a great wave of social sentiment, in short, — poured itself among all who had the faculty of large and disinterested thinking."[1] Many of these idealists and reformers were among the visitors.

Among all the movements of the day none was counted more important than universal education. Even the hitherto neglected blind, deaf and feeble-minded were to be included in its scope. *And the professional training of teachers was the main objective of the campaign for universal education.* Perception of the vital importance of this work attracted many visitors to Lexington. Through skilled teachers even the prophecy of Isaiah was to be fulfilled: "Then the eyes of the blind shall be opened, and the ears of the deaf shall be unstopped . . . and the tongue of the dumb shall sing."

III. THE WRITERS OF THE JOURNALS

I

The writers of these journals deserve larger notice than can be given here. Cyrus Peirce (1790–1860), the youngest of twelve children, was born in the town of Waltham, Mass.,

---

[1] John Morley, "Life of Richard Cobden," p. 61.

on the farm which had been occupied by his ancestors since 1650. Peirce's father was one of the Waltham Minute Men; he served in the Lexington-Concord fight and at Bunker Hill, in 1775. The old farmhouse, built about 1740, and shaded by great elms planted about 1800, is still in use (see illustration).

Peirce early displayed a fondness for study; accordingly, he was prepared for college at Framingham Academy, and under private tuition. He graduated from Harvard College in 1810, and from the Harvard Divinity School in 1815. During the years 1818–1826 he was the pastor of the Unitarian Church in North Reading, Mass.

His life work, however, was teaching. He was a "born teacher." As an undergraduate he taught with great success a district school in West Newton during the long college vacations which then came in the winter. On graduation from college he was called to a private school in Nantucket Island, where he remained for two years. After leaving the Divinity School he returned for three years to the position in Nantucket. During this period (1816) he married Harriet Coffin, a member of a well-known family in that island. She was everywhere and always "a most intelligent, devoted, effective helpmeet." They had no children. To the students at Lexington and West Newton she was always "Mother Peirce." After his pastorate at North Reading, and four years in a private school in North Andover, Peirce was recalled (1830) to Nantucket, where he served in private and public schools until summoned by Horace Mann, in 1839, to the pioneering work at Lexington.

In 1842 he resigned, broken in health by the labor and the anxiety which attended the development of the new institution. At the time he felt that his teaching was over; but after two years of rest he was recalled to his post. The school had been moved to larger quarters in West Newton; competent assistants and better equipment were provided. Under these conditions Peirce served five years more, when failing health compelled his final retirement from this work. He died in 1860.

As a student Peirce was distinguished by qualities which

BIRTHPLACE OF CYRUS PEIRCE, WALTHAM, MASSACHUSETTS
(Photographed in 1924)

he showed afterward as a teacher. The following char-
acterization is given by one of his college classmates:

> The uniform success of Cyrus Peirce, in whatever he undertook,
> was owing to his singular fidelity and perseverance. No one
> could have been more faithful, patient, persevering, than he was.
> Whatever the subject of study might be, his mind took hold of it
> with a tenacious grasp, and never let go, until he had reached a
> satisfactory result. In this particular, I have never known his
> equal. The action of his intellect was rather slow, but he investi-
> gated thoroughly and reasoned soundly. I therefore always con-
> sidered his statement of facts, unquestionably true; and his
> opinions as entitled to special regard. His very studious, as well
> as reserved habits, kept him much of the time in his room. At
> recitations, from which he was never absent, no one gave better
> evidence of a faithful attention to the exercises, in whatever
> department they might be. He always showed, when "taken
> up," that he had "got his lesson." Yet, owing to his great mod-
> esty, his slow utterance, his entire lack of the faculty of "showing
> off," he did not pass for half his real worth as a scholar. He was
> thorough in whatever he undertook. He was inquisitive and
> candid. The exact truth was his object; and he patiently re-
> moved every obstacle in the way of his attaining what he sought.[1]

As a teacher Peirce was successful, first of all, as a disciplinarian. He maintained excellent order in his schools, —
a thing to be wondered at in those days. As a beginner
he secured order after the usual fashion of the day, — a
liberal use of the rod. As a more experienced teacher, however, he abandoned flogging, and used moral suasion with
equal success. In this he joined the progressive party of
the time. The subject of corporal punishment was then
under violent debate. The older masters maintained not
only that the rod, the ferule, and the strap were essential
to order, but also that even a discussion of the question
was objectionable because of its bad effect on the discipline
of their schools. Peirce's final, and sensible, attitude on
this question is summed up in his discussion of school government at Lexington (pages 117*ff.*).

Peirce's success, however, was due to far higher qualities

---

[1] "Memoir of Peirce," by Samuel J. May. Barnard's "American Journal of Education," IV, 275.
May was Peirce's friend and successor (1842–1844) at Lexington.

than those of a mere disciplinarian. He insisted on and secured from his pupils "excellence in whatever they undertook to learn or do. . . . Thoroughness, exactness, fidelity in all things, intelligence in every exercise, and an exalted tone of moral sentiments were the admirable characteristics which were acknowledged to be conspicuous in Mr. Peirce's school."

These characteristics he succeeded in impressing on his students to a remarkable degree.

When Mr. Mann first visited his school in Nantucket, he was charmed by the evidence of power that the whole management and all the recitations of the school evinced; and when he spoke of it afterward to gentlemen of the place, one of the most respectable citizens said to him that he had lived 40 years on the South Shore, and could always tell Mr. Peirce's scholars, whenever he met them in the walks of life, by their mode of transacting business, and by all their mental habits, which were conscientious, exact, reliable. . . . Those who were conversant with his modes of instruction, and of appeal to the sense of intellectual and moral duty in his pupils can pick them out, even now, from other teachers. This characteristic of the school was handed down many years through the influence of his early pupils.[1]

Still more, Peirce inspired his pupils, and, in spite of temporary discouragements, gave them self-confidence. Two of his pupils in Nantucket afterward wrote the following accounts of his influence on them:

I shall always look back to the time passed in Mr. Peirce's school, as one of the best and happiest periods of my life. He inspired me with new views, new motives, a new thirst for knowledge; in short, he opened an almost new terrestrial world to me; and, over and above all, he was the one who awoke in my mind a deep interest in religion. Exact, cheerful obedience to all the laws of God, he made appear to me a most reasonable service. My understanding was convinced, my feelings were enlisted, and, by judicious management and careful nurture, he led me onward and upward, until I sincerely think, I obtained, through his ministration, "that hope which is an anchor to the soul, based upon the rock of ages." I shall, therefore, always love and respect Cyrus Peirce, as my spiritual guide and father.[2]

---

[1] "Life of Horace Mann," by his wife, Mary Peabody Mann.
[2] Barnard's "American Journal of Education," IV, *275ff.*

It is twenty-three or four years since I was one of Mr. Peirce's pupils, in Nantucket. His name has ever been, and ever will be, fragrant in my recollection. His was the first school that I really loved to attend; and he was the first teacher for whom I felt a positive affection. . . . Mr. Peirce was eminently successful in discovering whether a pupil comprehended what he was endeavoring to learn, or the language of the lesson he was reciting. Under his method of teaching, I first began to understand what I was about at school. He would not allow us to conceal our ignorance, or seem to know what we did not. He would probe us through and through, and expose our superficialness. Because I began to understand my text-books, I began to feel the exhilarating love of learning for its own sake. I had been to school all my days before; but it had been, until then, a mechanical work to me. I can distinctly recollect this blessed change in my mental condition. It was a new birth. A dispensation of intellectual and moral life and light came upon me. Mr. Peirce seemed to me to *see through* a boy, — to read his thoughts, — to divine his motives. No one could deceive him; and it always seemed exceedingly foolish, as well as mean, to attempt to deceive him, because he was so evidently the best friend of us all. I can see him now, — moving rapidly but without noise about the school-room, always alive to the highest good of every one; quickening our pulses, every time he approached us, by some word of encouragement; inspiring us with the determination necessary to attain the object at which he pointed.

Mr. Peirce was very skillful in discovering the mental aptitudes of a pupil, and drawing him out in the direction in which he was most likely to attain excellence; thus exhibiting a boy's powers to himself, making him conscious of the ability to be somebody, and do something.[1]

Rev. Samuel J. May, Peirce's friend, biographer, and successor at Lexington, adds as his personal estimate:

Mr. Peirce's profound reverence for truth is the basis of his character as a man and a teacher, — truth in everything, — the whole truth, the exact truth. Never have we known another so scrupulous. His reverence for truth was ever active, ever working in him, and renewing itself, day by day, in some higher manifestation, or some deeper expression. Although he frequently, if not every day, closed his school with the admonition, — "my

---

[1] Barnard's "American Journal of Education," IV, 275*ff.*

pupils, live to the truth," — yet it never seemed like a vain repetition; it always appeared to come fresh from his heart, as if it were a new inspiration of his longing for them to become all that God had made them capable of being.[1]

Of the quality of Peirce's pioneering work at Lexington there is abundant testimony from competent critics. Horace Mann, Samuel G. Howe, George B. Emerson are among these. Mann's visit to the school is thus described in his own journal:

Sept. 14. (1839) On Thursday [Sept. 12] I went to Lexington, where I spent the whole day in Mr. Pierce's school; and a most pleasant day it was. Highly as I had appreciated his talent, he surpassed the ideas I had formed of his ability to teach, and in that prerequisite of all successful teaching, the power of winning the confidence of his pupils. This surpassed what I have ever seen before in any school. The exercises were conducted in the most thorough manner: the principle being stated, and then applied to various combinations of facts, so that the pupils were not only led to a clearer apprehension of the principle itself, but taught to look through combinations of facts, however different, to find the principle which underlies them all; and they were taught, too, that it is not the form of the fact which determines the principle, but the principle which gives character to the fact.[2]

It is interesting to compare with Mann's record the corresponding entries in the journals (pages 7, 110). The letters of Samuel G. Howe, Principal of the Perkins Institution for the Blind, and George B. Emerson, first Principal of the first American public high school (Boston, 1821–23) and later head of a most successful private school for girls in Boston, are further evidences of Peirce's remarkable power as a teacher.[3] There is no doubt that his high standards led him to underestimate his own success, and hence to feel needlessly the discouragement which is often evident in his journal.

---

[1] Barnard's "American Journal of Education," IV, 275*ff.*
[2] "Life of Horace Mann," by his wife, Mary Peabody Mann.
[3] See pp. 271, 274.

MARY SWIFT (MRS. EDWIN G. LAMSON) IN 1909, AGE 87

(Her last photograph)

II

Mary Swift (1822–1909) had been one of Peirce's pupils in Nantucket; she was one of the first to enter the normal school at Lexington. Her journal and the certificate given her by Cyrus Peirce (pages 81*ff.*) speak sufficiently for the character of her work there. Soon after she left the school in 1840 she was called by Dr. Samuel G. Howe to teach in the Perkins Institution for the Blind in Boston. She continued for three years the education of the blind deaf-mute, Laura Bridgman, whose training had been begun by Dr. Howe with a success which attracted world-wide attention. In this work Mary Swift's journal-keeping habit persisted, and her record took shape in an important book, the "Life and Education of Laura Bridgman." She shared in the education of Oliver Caswell, another blind deaf-mute. She also helped to prepare two blind boys for college. In the 1840's all this was pioneering work of the first importance. Many years later she inspired Helen Keller, one of the most famous of blind deaf-mutes, to learn to talk.[1]

For nine years she served on the Board of Trustees of the Lancaster, Mass., State Industrial School for Girls, and on the School Committee of the town of Winchester. In 1858 she began the movement which resulted in the organization of the Young Women's Christian Association in Boston in 1866, and for forty years thereafter she was an active worker for that organization. In 1847 she married Mr. Edwin G. Lamson of Boston. Four children were born of this marriage, one of whom, Miss Kate G. Lamson, has been of much assistance in the preparation of this sketch. Mary Swift Lamson was a leading spirit in the remarkable group of twenty-five girls who first gathered at Lexington, 1839–1840. Their class reunions continued until 1895. Nearly all of them were married in due season, but the interest in the profession of teaching with which Peirce inspired them, in their single year at Lexington, continued to the end of their days. In 1902 at a great gathering of the alumnæ of the school in Framingham, Mary Swift Lamson delivered the valedictory of her class, — of whom six members were still living, — and gave an all-too-modest account of their serv-

---

[1] Keller, "Story of My Life," p. 59.

ices. In 1903 she edited the records of the class, thus, in
a sense, completing the journal which she began in 1839.
She died in 1909, at the age of eighty-seven.

IV. HISTORICAL SETTING

To read these journals with understanding it is necessary
to bear in mind the circumstances under which they were
written. They form a chapter in the history of the great
revival of public education in Massachusetts during the
second quarter of the nineteenth century; apart from this
historic movement much of their meaning is lost.[1] The
origins and general history of the Lexington-West Newton-
Framingham Normal School,[2] the life and work of Cyrus
Peirce,[3] and the subsequent careers of Mary Swift and
her classmates[4] should be studied also by way of introduction. Within the pages here available a brief outline
only is possible. The incredible labors by which Peirce
established the normal school at Lexington on a firm basis
have already been mentioned (page xix). The inspiring educational reforms of the time, and the patriotic and devoted
service of a few leaders to the cause of public education,
claim our attention.

The two broad facts to be recalled in connection with the
revival of education above mentioned are (1) the disin-
tegration and decline of the free public schools in Massachusetts during the half century from 1775 to 1825; (2)
the reorganization, revival, and expansion of public education in the state from 1825 to 1850. The dates are, of
course, merely approximate.

I

Between 1775 and 1825 the system of public schools
inherited by the new Commonwealth from colonial times

---

[1] "Horace Mann and the Common School Revival," by B. A. Hinsdale, New York. Scribners,
1898.

[2] "Historical Sketches of the Framingham State Normal School." Published by the Alumnæ Asso-
ciation, Framingham, 1914. See also "Normal Schools," Henry Barnard, Hartford, Conn., 1851, and
Barnard's "American Journal of Education," General Index, under Normal Schools, Lexington, West
Newton, Framingham, Cyrus Peirce, Edmund Dwight, Horace Mann.

[3] "Memoir of Cyrus Peirce," by Samuel J. May. Barnard's "American Journal of Education," Vol.
IV, pp. 275ff.

[4] "The First State Normal School in America: Records of the First Class." Edited by Mary
Swift Lamson. Published for the Class, 1903.

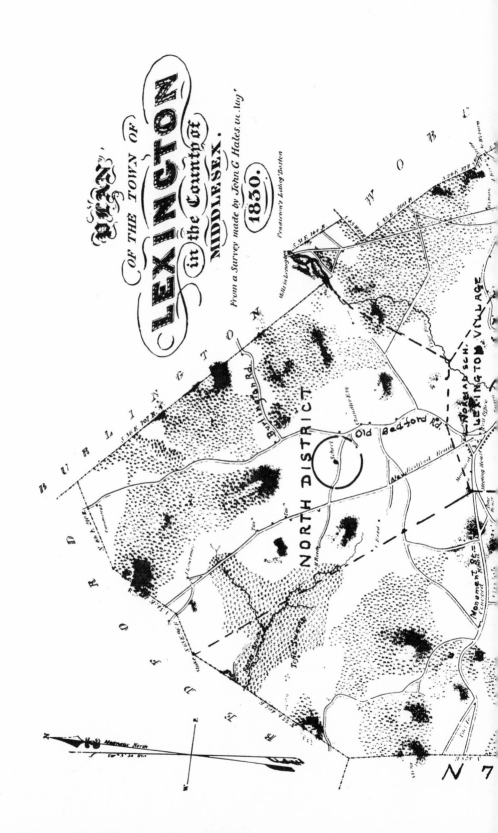

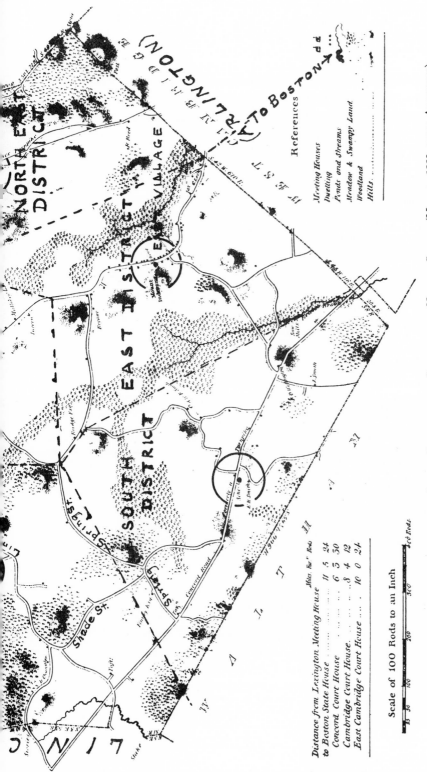

References

Meeting Houses
Dwelling
Ponds and Streams
Meadow & Swampy Land
Woodland
Hills

Distance from Lexington Meeting House

	Miles.	Fur.ⁿ	Rods
to Boston State House	11	5	24
Concord Court House	6	5	30
Cambridge Court House	8	4	12
East Cambridge Court House	10	0	24

Scale of 100 Rods to an Inch

LEXINGTON: THE TOWN, THE VILLAGES, THE SCHOOL DISTRICTS AND SCHOOLS, THE NORMAL SCHOOL (MAP OF 1830, WITH ADDITIONS)

showed little or no improvement; in some respects it grew worse. Schools multiplied in number with the increase in population, but they did not improve in quality; they were merely more of the same kind. Incompetent teachers, low salaries, meager school appropriations, and public apathy toward the public schools prevailed throughout the state, forming a vicious circle of cause and effect from which there seemed to be no escape. During these fifty years Massachusetts produced not a single leader of marked importance in the field of public education.

The state Legislature not only did nothing for the public schools, but actually passed a series of laws (1789–1824) which lowered the minimum state school requirements much below the level set by the colonial school law of 1647! There was no state school officer of any kind. County school officers did not and do not now exist. Extreme local self-government in school affairs prevailed. Each of the 300 towns (*i.e.*, townships) into which the state was divided supported its own schools by town tax. In theory, each town also managed its schools through a town (township) school committee. In most cases, however, the town was divided into districts;[1] each school district had a separate committee which managed the local school quite independently of, and sometimes in defiance of, the town school committee. The "system" of free public schools in Massachusetts during this unfortunate half century is more accurately described as a leaderless chaos of between 1,500 and 2,500[2] one-room, ungraded district schools, each in charge of a "prudential committee" elected by the voters of the district. This committee — frequently one-man — chose the teacher, selected the textbooks, and otherwise managed the school, often regardless of the town school committee. Scores of these districts contained less than twenty pupils each. It was a case of local self-government pushed to absurdity. With no official leader for public education in the state, concerted action to improve the schools was impossible. Few district committees would

---

[1] The map of Lexington (facing this page) illustrates the division of a town into its districts.

[2] The number is estimated. The division of towns into school districts continued for many years. The first actual statistics, in 1837, showed about 3,000 districts, distributed among 306 towns and the three incorporated cities (Boston, Lowell, Salem) of the state. At that time there were only 14 public high schools (often called "town schools") in the state.

have welcomed advice from any state — or even from any township — official in the management of their schools.

Meanwhile, in scores of communities throughout the state, leading citizens set up academies and other private schools to which they sent their children for a better training than the wretched public schools could afford. In these communities the public schools, neglected by the community leaders, tended to sink to still lower levels. This tendency continued until 1840 or later.

II

A competent leader in the field of public education appeared at the beginning of the second period (1825–1850). In 1824–1825 James G. Carter, a Harvard graduate of the Class of 1820, — an experienced teacher, who had earned his way through academy and college, — published a pamphlet and a series of newspaper articles in which he called attention to the alarming decadence of the public schools, and suggested plans for "a thorough radical reform." The state government, according to Carter, should cease to lower educational standards, as it had been doing during the preceding forty years, and should adopt a constructive policy toward public education, beginning with a revision of the antiquated school laws. *Most important of all, the state should undertake to train and certify teachers for the schools in a state institution — a professional school — devoted solely to this one purpose.*

In masterly fashion and brilliant style Carter reviewed the history of public education in New England, analyzed the existing defects of the "system," pointed out the deplorable inefficiencies of the teachers, and sketched "An Outline of an Institution for the Education of Teachers."[1] This outline afterward earned for Carter the title of "Father of Normal Schools in Massachusetts."

Carter's work marked the beginning of a twelve-year period of agitation for educational reform in Massachusetts. An increasing group of educational leaders joined in the movement. It took form and gathered headway

---

[1] For the entire document see pp. 227–245.

with a more or less definite program, in which the improvement of teachers, better methods of teaching and school management, better schoolhouses, and better school equipment held a central position. In 1826 Carter, finding the projected state institution for the education of teachers impracticable, proposed to establish a private seminary for teachers at his home in Lancaster, and to secure state aid therefor. His bill for this purpose was defeated in the Senate (1827). The project was allowed to drop for the time, but it was not forgotten.

During these years (1825–1837) many private academies in the state advertised "the preparation of teachers for the common schools" as one of their attractions. An "English Department or Seminary for Teachers," limited to men, was established in 1830 at Andover Academy in charge of Samuel R. Hall, a most competent man, who had conducted a private seminary for teachers near Concord, Vt., since 1823, and who had published in 1829 a widely read little book entitled "Lectures on Schoolkeeping." The Andover experiment had but limited success, owing chiefly to lack of financial support. Only about one hundred prospective teachers completed the course between 1830 and 1842, when the project was abandoned. Long experience made it clear that other academies of the state — private institutions with very limited resources — could neither meet the cost of a course of professional training for teachers, nor furnish to the public schools the needed supply of such teachers.

While the plan of a state institution for the training of teachers was in abeyance some cautious beginnings were made in revising the state school laws, as Carter had suggested in 1824. Extreme caution was necessary. There was a perpetual difficulty in finding the proper balance between control by the state government and local self-government by the towns. This question played no small part in the subsequent history of the normal schools. The towns resented state interference in their local affairs. They remembered the attempted despotisms of George the Third of England, and they had before their eyes the spectacle of the Prussian and the French monarchies of the times.

As a result they were thoroughly suspicious of centralization of power in state officials. The Legislature, it must be remembered, was made up of representatives from the towns. Naturally these representatives were cautious about enacting state laws which seemed to interfere with self-government in their own districts. They were still more cautious about creating state officials who had power to intervene in town affairs. The citizens of the state were but slowly educated to the idea that some further centralization of power in the state government was for the good of the towns. Certain steps were taken, however, in the school laws of 1827, 1834, and 1837.

In 1827 the towns of the state were required to send to the Secretary of the Commonwealth annual statistical reports concerning their schools. Thus, for the first time in its history, the state government undertook to collect information as to the actual condition of public education in the entire Commonwealth.

In 1834 a State School Fund was created, and its income was distributed among the towns. This step, at any rate, made clear the fact that the state government might actually do good in entering town school affairs. Meanwhile the campaign for a "state seminary for the education of teachers" was given renewed emphasis: first, by the desperate need of competent teachers for district schools throughout the state; and second, by the spread of information (especially by the lectures of Charles Brooks, 1835–1837) as to the remarkable success of the Prussian state seminaries for teachers of the elementary schools (*Lehrerseminare*) reorganized under the Prussian school law of 1819. The value of these institutions in meeting the need for competent teachers in the elementary schools had been fully recognized in France, and similar institutions (*écoles normales primaires*) had been organized in that monarchy under the law of 1833.

In 1837 the American Institute of Instruction, the most influential association of teachers in New England, presented a strong memorial to the Legislature requesting the establishment of such an institution in Massachusetts; but at the moment the Legislature took no action on the

request.[1] In the same year, however, the Massachusetts
Board of Education was created, and this paved the way
for the establishment of the normal schools.

III

Since the Board of Education played a vital part in this
achievement, and in the subsequent battle (1840) to prevent the new normal schools from being abolished by the
Legislature, a few lines must be devoted to its origin and
functions. During the preceding years — especially since
1835 — a few leaders had perceived that even in the hated
monarchies of Prussia and France the centralization of
power in state school officials had resulted in vast improvements in the public elementary schools. The Prussian
village schools were recognized as the best of their kind in
the world; the teachers were trained as for a profession,
and they made teaching their life work. As a group they
were, in this respect, at least, in striking contrast to the
rapidly shifting body of young women and young men who,
with no other training than that given by the district
schools themselves, taught most of the district schools of
Massachusetts. The contrast led to the question whether
some centralization of power in state school officials in
Massachusetts might not overcome the evil effects of the
excessively decentralized district system, and make for
improvement in the pitifully inadequate district schools.

The power of Prussian and French state school officials
was too despotic to be tolerated for a moment in the free
townships of Massachusetts. It seemed possible, however,
to evolve a state Board of Education without these powers,
but with sufficient authority to take action for the good of
the schools throughout the state.

In 1837 James G. Carter was a member of the Legislature,
and chairman of the Committee on Education. In this
position he secured the enactment of the law creating the
Massachusetts Board of Education. It was signed by
Governor Edward Everett on April 20, 1837. The Board
was composed of nine persons, — the Governor, acting as

---

[1] See pp. 246–252.

chairman *ex officio*, and eight persons appointed by him.
It had few powers, but great opportunities. It was required to collect information as to the actual state of the
schools, to diffuse throughout the state information as to
the best methods of education, to report annually to the
Legislature, to suggest to that body measures for improvement of the schools, and to appoint a Secretary who was in
effect the executive agent of the Board. The law of 1837
completed the first phase of the movement for state-wide
school reform begun by Carter in 1824. The phase of
discussion was ended, the phase of action was now to begin.

The Board chose as its Secretary Horace Mann (1796–
1859), a graduate of Brown University, a lawyer by profession, long a member of the Legislature and then President
of the Senate, an eloquent speaker and writer, an ardent
believer in the chief social and humanitarian reforms then
under discussion. These included the improvement of the
public schools, the education of the blind, the deaf and the
feeble-minded, the abolition of slavery, temperance reform,
prison reform, and the state care of the insane. Among
these the cause of free public education held a chief place.
Few persons in Massachusetts saw as did Mann the responsibilities and opportunities of the new post.

IV

At this point it is necessary to recall the unpleasant fact
that many of the passing generation were more than doubtful as to the wisdom of universal education. They still
held to the theory of the aristocratic republic, while many
leaders of the generation which was rising to power in the
1820's adopted democratic and humanitarian views. The
older group believed "that classes are essential, — one to
work, the other to improve; . . . that one portion of mankind is to be refined and cultivated, the other to suffer, toil
and live and die in vulgarity." They were skeptical "on
the subject of attempting to enlighten and improve the
masses," and they lamented "that the good old days of the
aristocracy had gone by when no upstart could ever obtain
ingress into their ranks." The younger generation held to

HORACE MANN

Secretary to the Massachusetts Board of Education, 1837–1848

(From a pen drawing)

the theory of "the improvability — the accelerating improvability — of the race." They believed in the right of every individual in the race to a fair start in the battle of life; they held that the preservation of democracy in government, as well as the rights and liberties of the individual, depended on the diffusion of education among the masses. They believed ardently that free public schools, "good enough for the richest, open to the poorest," were the best means of achieving these ends.

To them the battle for the public schools was but a continuation of the war for liberty and democracy which began with the opening shots of the American Revolution on Lexington Common.

Wisdom and knowledge, as well as virtue, diffused generally among the body of the people, being necessary for the preservation of their rights and liberties . . . it shall be the duty of legislatures and magistrates, in all future periods of this commonwealth, to cherish the interests of literature and the sciences, and all seminaries of them; especially . . . public schools and grammar schools in the towns.

So run the words of the Constitution of 1780, written by men to whom the battles of Lexington, Concord and Bunker Hill were only five years in the past.

How else can we so worthily or sincerely show either gratitude or admiration for the deeds of our ancestors as by improving and transmitting to others the various blessings they achieved for us. In our day, things are to be done, though not such things as they did. They did what the circumstances of that age demanded: the exigencies of our age demand the performance of appropriate acts quite as imperatively as theirs did. Our imitation of their example, as adapted to our times, is the only legitimate proof of our admiration, or the true measure of our gratitude.[1]

So wrote Horace Mann in his journal on the sixty-second anniversary of Bunker Hill. To the educational leaders of the 1820's and later the words of the Constitution were the orders for their own battle in behalf of the public schools. Their attitude is well summed up by sentences from Horace Mann's journal, and from his letters, on accepting the office

---

[1] "Life of Horace Mann," by Mary P. Mann.

of Secretary of the newly created Massachusetts Board of
Education:

> Henceforth, so long as I hold this office, I devote myself to the
> supremest welfare of mankind on earth . . . I no longer write
> myself attorney, counsellor or lawyer. My law books are for
> sale. My office is "to let". . . The ·interests of a client are
> small compared with the interests of the next generation. Let
> the next generation, then, be my client . . . God grant me an
> annihilation of selfishness, a mind of wisdom, a heart of benevo-
> lence! . . . Here stands my purpose, ready to undergo the hard-
> ships and privations to which I must be subjected, and to en-
> counter the jealousy, the misrepresentation and the prejudice
> almost certain to arise . . . I know one thing, — if I stand by the
> principles of truth and duty, nothing can inflict upon me any per-
> manent harm. . . . If I do not succeed in the task I will lay claim
> at least to the benefit of the saying, that in great attempts it is
> glorious even to fail.[1]

To miss the spirit which animated the leaders of the
campaign for the public schools is to miss the whole meaning of the movement. They were devoted to a sacred
cause, — the cause of democracy and humanity. Without
the free public schools great masses of the population must
remain in ignorance. But, as the founders of the Republic
had repeated again and again, in one form or another, an
ignorant people cannot be a free people: "If a nation
expects to be ignorant and free in a state of civilization it
expects what never was and never will be" (Jefferson).
"Knowledge will forever govern ignorance; and a people
who mean to be their own governors must arm themselves
with the power which knowledge gives" (Madison). "The
instruction of the people in every kind of knowledge that
can be of use to them in the practice of their moral duties
as men, citizens, and Christians, and of their political and
civil duties as members of society and freemen, ought to be
the care of the public, and of all who have any share in the
conduct of its affairs, in a manner that never yet has been
practiced in any age or nation. . . . Laws for the liberal
education of youth, especially of the lower classes of the

---

[1] "Life of Horace Mann," by Mary P. Mann.

people, are so extremely wise and useful, that to a humane and generous mind, no expense for this purpose would be thought extravagant" (John Adams). The list of these utterances can be greatly extended. In a word, ignorance is the foe of democracy. The "new battle against ignorance" which Cyrus Peirce began at Lexington was in the truest sense a battle for democracy.

More than this, it was a battle for life, liberty, and the pursuit of happiness for individuals. Human minds and hearts are stunted and deformed by ignorance, as human bodies are by starvation; they are crippled and mutilated by ignorance, as human bodies are by the wounds of war. "From the beginning of time" (said Horace Mann) "in every other nation that has ever existed [the masses] have usually been subjected to a systematic course of [mental] blinding, deafening, crippling. As an inevitable consequence of this, the minds of men have never yet put forth one-thousandth part of their tremendous energies." In this new nation, dedicated to human liberty, these things ought not so to be. For the good of the masses, and even for the selfish interest of the more fortunate, "wisdom and knowledge, as well as virtue," should be "diffused generally among the body of the people."

The public schools, "open to the poorest; good enough for the richest," were the only effective weapons for the new warfare. To the betterment of these institutions Horace Mann, Cyrus Peirce and other leaders of the revival devoted themselves with ardor, and at the personal sacrifice of time, money, and health. Overwhelming labors, hardships, privations were their portion as Mann foresaw. Their spirit was still the spirit of the men who fought out the American Revolution: "In our day things are to be done, though not such things as they did." When Mann learned that the cautious Legislature had fixed his salary at $1,500, and that two-thirds of this would be required for his traveling and office expenses as Secretary to the Board, he wrote in his journal (April 18, 1838), "Well, one thing is certain: if I live and have my health, I will be revenged on them; I will do them more than $1,500 worth of good."

V. The Great Achievement: State Normal Schools

"*In our day things are to be done . . .*". There was no doubt as to *what* was to be done. The needed reforms had been widely discussed (and some of them had been begun) since Carter's criticism of the schools in 1824. In 1837 the Board of Education and its Secretary, Horace Mann, found the program of action ready to their hands. To detail the condition of the public schools at that time, and to describe the sweeping reforms brought about between 1837 and 1848, would be to write a book. Things were done. In twelve years of astonishing labor, marked by stormy controversies and bitter opposition from many who should have been the friends of the movement, Mann and his too little known fellow workers roused the public as never before to the support of the public schools. Hundreds of the three thousand little district schoolhouses in the state were repaired; hundreds more, "not tenantable by any decent family out of the poorhouse or in it," were replaced by better buildings. School taxes were increased; town school committees were stimulated to action. Blackboards — little used in 1837! — were introduced. School libraries, maps, and globes were multiplied — though even in 1848 most schools still lacked them. These and many more things were done in those epoch-making years. But the greatest achievement, as Mann rightly believed, was the establishment of state normal schools. "Without these, all other labors and expenditures would have yielded but a meagre harvest of success. . . . In the school, an accomplished teacher is the one thing needful. . . . Present, he supplements all deficiencies. Without him, the best-appointed school is a lifeless organism, waiting for a soul to enter and inhabit it, and put in action its vast powers of beneficence. Common schools will never prosper without Normal Schools."[1]

The desperate need of trained teachers for the district schools has been mentioned (page xxxiii). (page xxxiii) A few details

[1] Report, 1848, pp. 27, 28.

may now be added. Except in the three cities (Boston, 80,000; Lowell, 18,000; Salem, 15,000) each school in the state had usually two teachers each year. A woman — frequently a girl of seventeen or eighteen — taught the summer term of about four months, at an average salary of $5.38 per month, and board; a man — frequently a youth under twenty — usually taught, or tried to teach, the winter term of ten or twelve weeks, at an average salary of $15.44 per month and board. The youth undertook the task at some peril; not seldom the winter school was broken up by unruly "big boys," — often older than the teacher himself, — who came for the express purpose of "putting the teacher out." In 1837 about 400 of the 2,800 country winter schools were thus closed. The 5,600 teachers employed each year in the rural district schools of the state were a rapidly shifting group, busy most of the year in other occupations. Most of them had no education beyond the spelling, reading, writing, English grammar, geography and arithmetic which they had themselves studied in the district schools. Many teachers were deficient even in these branches. School committees reported that they often accepted such candidates because no others were to be had at the "salaries" paid.[1] As for "the science and art of teaching" and "school government," most teachers had never heard of such studies. After a survey of the situation Mann estimated that, of the 6,000 teachers who were employed each year in the district schools, *including* the cities, not over 200 regarded teaching as a permanent vocation. Some of these, by long experience, or by being "born teachers," were of great excellence. Cyrus Peirce was one of them. But the lack of competent and fairly permanent teachers was the greatest single defect of the system of free public schools.

The establishment of a state "institution" or "seminary" for the training of teachers had been urged with increasing force since Carter's "Outline" of 1825. The thing was now to be done.

In its first report to the Legislature (Feb. 1, 1838) the Board of Education stated: "The subject of the education

---

[1] For the quality of these teachers see the Memorial of the American Institute of Instruction, p. 246*ff*.

of teachers is of the very highest importance in connection with the improvement of our schools. . . . The Board cannot but express the sanguine hope, that the time is not far distant, when the resources of public or private liberality will be applied in Massachusetts for the foundation of an institution for the formation of teachers, in which the present existing defect [of trained teachers] will be amply supplied."

A few weeks later Edmund Dwight — a wealthy merchant of Boston, who was greatly interested in public schools, and who was a member of the Massachusetts Board of Education — invited Horace Mann and a number of others to meet at his house on March 9, for a conference on the project of securing state aid for the training of teachers. Momentous consequences followed this conference. Without Dwight's gift of $10,000, many years must have passed before the state Legislature could have been induced to appropriate any money for "Teachers' Seminaries." And without these institutions, as has been shown above, no enduring reform of public education was possible. One can easily understand Mann's exultation over the event of the evening at Mr. Dwight's, as recorded in his journal.

March 10. [*1838*] . . . [After giving a lecture (possibly the one on "Special Preparation a Prerequisite to Teaching") to the Society for the Diffusion of Useful Knowledge he] went to Mr. [Edmund] Dwight's where a number of gentlemen were assembled to discuss the expediency of applying to the Legislature for a grant to aid in the establishment of Teachers' Seminaries. Considerable was said on both sides, but mostly on the *pro* side. But, after they had mainly dispersed, Mr. Dwight gave me authority to propose to the Legislature, in my own way, that $10,000 should be forthcoming from himself or others; and that at any rate he would be responsible for that amount to accomplish the object, provided the Legislature would give the same amount for the same cause. On Monday, it is my intention to make a descent upon the two honorable bodies, and see if they cannot be so rubbed as to emit the requisite spark. This looks well.

March 13. I had the satisfaction of sending the following communication to the Legislature: —

To the President of the Senate and the Speaker of the House of Representatives.

GENTLEMEN: — Private munificence has placed at my disposal the sum of $10,000 to promote the cause of popular education in Massachusetts.

The condition is, that the Commonwealth will contribute the same amount from unappropriated funds in aid of the same cause; both sums to be drawn upon equally as needed, and to be disbursed, under the direction of the Board of Education, in qualifying teachers for our common schools.

As the proposal contemplates that the State in its collective capacity shall do no more than is here proffered to be done from private means, and as, with a high and enlightened disregard of all local, party, and sectional views, it comprehends the whole of the rising generation in its philanthropic plan, I cannot refrain from earnestly soliciting for it the favorable regards of the Legislature.

> Very respectfully,
> HORACE MANN,
> *Secretary of the Board of Education.*

This appears to be glorious! I think I feel pretty sublime! Let the stars look out for my head! . . .

The events which followed are detailed in Mann's account, and are not here repeated (see page *253ff.*). The Legislature, after a favorable report from its Committee on Education, appropriated the money by resolve, and the document was signed by Governor Edward Everett on April 19, 1838. It was the anniversary of the battle of Lexington, — "a fact in regard to the date [wrote Mann] which those who are curious in coincidences may hereafter remember."

In the light of subsequent history there can be no doubt that this date marks the beginning of a new epoch in American education, — the epoch of the professionally trained teacher in the elementary school. The far-reaching consequences of the beginning in Massachusetts can be traced in the spread of normal schools to other states, in the slow rise of teaching to the status of a profession, and, most of all, in the happier and better education of millions of children. To indicate the part which Massachusetts, and especially the graduates of her normal schools, played in this development would be to write a volume. Such a book would do long-deferred justice to the skilled services of the women who — in country district schools, in crowded mill cities, in seaports thronged with immigrants speaking every language under the heavens — taught well and faithfully spelling, reading, writing, English grammar, geography, and arithmetic. No one who has seen the children of many nations and languages in our public schools can doubt that these teachers, more than any other agency, have given us our greatest bond of national union, — a common speech.

VI. THE NORMAL SCHOOL AT LEXINGTON

More than a year passed, after the vote of the Legislature, before the training of teachers was actually begun. During the interval, the Massachusetts Board of Education and its Secretary spent much time in the necessary preparations. The questions which were raised, the discussions which followed, and the decisions which were made are detailed in Mann's account (see page 257). The Board decided, after discussing other plans, to establish three "institutions for the qualification of teachers," each for an experimental term of three years. The name *normal schools* (from the French, *écoles normales*) was chosen (June 1, 1838) to mark their special character as professional schools for the training of teachers. They were to be under the direct control of the Board of Education, and to be located, respectively, in the northeastern, the central, and the southeastern parts of the state.

Regulations and a course of study for the projected normal schools were adopted by the Board on Dec. 28, 1838. On the same date the first of the three locations was definitely fixed at Lexington. (Barre was chosen for the second, March 13, 1839; Bridgewater for the third, May 28, 1840.) A prolonged search for a principal for the school at Lexington resulted in the fortunate choice of Cyrus Peirce, whose acquaintance the reader has already made.

The vacant academy building at the corner of Lexington Common was leased, and remodeling was begun. As funds ran short, Mann sold his law books, and gave the proceeds toward the completion of the work. Thus, in Peirce's phrase, "the implements of warfare, barracks and camp-ground" were prepared for the "new battle against ignorance and bad teaching."

Apparently Mann, with a keen sense of the dramatic fitness of things, had hoped to open the school on April 19. Unavoidable delays made this impossible. The opening was announced for July 3, 1839. Mann's journal records both the event and his prophetic vision of what was to follow:

July 2. — To-morrow we go to Lexington to launch the first Normal school on this side the Atlantic. I cannot indulge at this late hour of the night, and in my present state of fatigue, in an expression of the train of thought which the contemplation of this event awakens in my mind. Much must come of it, either of good or of ill. I am sanguine in my faith that it will be the former. But the good will not come itself. That is the reward of effort, of toil, of wisdom. These, as far as possible, let me furnish. Neither time nor care, nor such thought as I am able to originate, shall be wanting to make this an era in the welfare and prosperity of our schools; and, if it is so, it will then be an era in the welfare of mankind.

July 3. The day opened with one of the most copious rains we have had this rainy season. Only three persons presented themselves for examination for the Normal School in Lexington. In point of numbers, this is not a promising commencement. How much of it is to be set down to the weather, how much to the fact that the opening of the school has been delayed so long, I cannot tell. What remains but more exertion, more and more, until it *must* succeed?

Something of the toil, effort and wisdom — of the "more exertion, more and more," — which Cyrus Peirce devoted to the success of the cause has already been indicated. His own description of the school eighteen months later forms a fitting close to this introduction, and an essential prologue to Peirce's journal. It was written in reply to a letter from Henry Barnard, who had visited the school in March, 1840, and who referred to it as "the most interesting educational experiment now making on this side of the Atlantic."

[To Henry Barnard]

Lexington, January 1, 1841.

Dear Sir: — I very cheerfully comply with your request to communicate to you information in regard to the Normal School in this place. I will take up the points on which you have desired information, in the order you have named them.

1. *Direction and Inspection.* — The school is under the immediate direction and inspection of a Board of Visiters, chosen from and by the Board of Education. The administration of the school has, in fact, been almost entirely under the direction of the Principal. Of rules and orders regulating the terms of admission, the course and term of study, etc., etc., I have received nothing more than what is published in the number of the Common School Journal for February, 1839, to which I refer you. [See page 261*ff*.]

2. *Building.* — The Normal School is an edifice fifty feet in length, and forty in breadth, two stories high, with suitable out-buildings, pleasantly situated in the angle of two roads near the old battle-field, enclosed in a yard of convenient dimensions, which is ornamented with trees and shrubbery. In the basement are a kitchen, diningroom, washroom, and woodhouse, together with storerooms; on the ground floor, are a parlor and bedroom for steward, a sittingroom for the young ladies, (boarders,) and one schoolroom; in the second story are five dormitories with a schoolroom; and in the attic, four dormitories. The house will accommodate about twenty boarders; — the two schoolrooms will seat from seventy-five to eighty scholars; the lower room is now used for the model school. There is access to the schoolrooms from the main body of the building, as well as from without.

This building is private property, now held as security, by the trustees of the ministerial fund in this place, by whom it is leased to the Board of Education for a moderate rent. When the Board of Education were seeking a suitable location for a Normal School in this section of the Commonwealth, said trustees offered this building for their accommodation; and they, together with other friends of education in this place, pledged themselves to raise $1,000

LEXINGTON COMMON (Left foreground)　　NORMAL SCHOOL　　THE "OLD" BEDFORD ROAD

(From a drawing by Electa N. Lincoln of the Class of 1843)

in behalf of the school. The building and premises may be worth from $5,000 to $7,000.

3. *Revenue.* — A portion of $10,000 from private munificence, and of an equal sum granted by the Legislature, is, I believe, the entire amount of funds. Scholars pay their own board, ($2 per week,) and meet all incidental charges, such as for fuel, cleaning, etc. Class-books are mostly supplied by private munificence. Tuition is gratis.

4. *Inventory.* — All the furniture of the boarding-house establishment belongs to the steward, who has the use of the building gratis, furnishes it at his own risk and expense, and gets his pay from his boarders; — he cannot, however, charge more than $2 per week for board, including washing.

The school has two stoves for heating, two maps, a pair of globes,[1] an apparatus for illustrating the most important principles of natural philosophy and astronomy, a small library of about 100 volumes, chiefly works on education and for reference, — all worth from $600 to $800.

5. *Maintenance.* — Reference to what I have said under numbers 3 and 4.

6. *Teachers.* — The Principal is the only teacher at present in the school; he is paid by a fixed salary. The model school is taught by the pupils of the Normal School.

7. *Number of pupils.* —The whole number that has been in the school is forty-one; the greatest number at any time, thirty-four. In the model school, thirty has been the usual number.

8. *What is required of applicants for admission.* — For an answer to this, allow me to refer you to the School Journal, as before.

9. *Studies pursued, and text-books, art of teaching, etc.* — For the *full* course contemplated, I refer you to the Journal, as above. The branches that have been actually taken up are the following, viz: all the common branches *particularly* and *fully;* together with Composition, Geometry, Algebra, Physiology; Natural, Intellectual, and Moral Philosophy; Natural History, Botany, Political Economy, Book-Keeping, Vocal Music, and the *art of Teaching.* The books used in the school are Worcester's Dictionary, and

---

[1] See illustration opposite p. 94.

Worcester's Fourth [Reading] Book, Abbot's Teacher, Russell's First Lessons [in Enunciation], Testament, Grund's Geometry, Colburn's Sequel [to Intellectual Arithmetic] and Algebra, Wayland's Moral Philosophy, Newman's Political Economy, Hitchock's Book-Keeping, Combe's Constitution of Man, Combe's Physiology, Brigham's Mental Excitement, Smellie's [Philosophy of] Natural History, Comstock's Botany, Abercrombie's Mental Philosophy, Combe's Moral Philosophy, Story's Constitution of the United States, Newman's Rhetoric, Hayward's Physiology, Day's Algebra; Scientific Class-Book by [Walter R.] Johnson, for the various branches of natural philosophy.

You ask for a full account of my manner of instruction in the *art of Teaching.*[1] This it is not easy to give. From what I say, you may get some idea of what I *attempt,* and of the *manner* of it. Two things I have aimed at, especially in this school. 1. To teach *thoroughly* the principles of the several branches studied, so that the pupils may have a *clear* and *full understanding* of them.[2] 2. To teach the pupils, by my own *example,* as well as by *precepts,* the *best way of teaching the same things* effectually to others. I have four different methods of recitation. 1st, by question and answer;[3] 2d, by conversation;[4] 3d, by calling on one, two, three, more or less, to give an analysis of the whole subject contained in the lesson; and 4th, by requiring written analyses, in which the *ideas* of the author are stated in the *language* of the pupil.[5] I do not mean that these are all practised at the same exercise. The students understand that, at all the recitations, they are at perfect liberty to suggest queries, doubts, opinions. At all the recitations we have more or less of discussion. Much attention is paid to the *manner* in which the pupils *set forth, or state* their positions. I am ever mingling, or attempting to mingle, at these exercises, theory and example; frequently putting the inquiry to them, not only, "How do you understand such and such a statement?" but, "How would you express such and such a sentiment, or explain such a principle, or illus-

---

[1] This section contains Peirce's best account of his method of "teaching the art of teaching." After reading the journals it is well to turn back to this account for a fuller study. It is well also to turn to the page references in notes 2 to 5 below for illustrations of the points made.

[2] *Cf.* p. xxx.   [4] See pp. 94, 116, 120, etc.

[3] Examples on pp. 139, 156, etc.   [5] See p. 82.

trate such a position to a class, which you may be teaching?" "Let me," I say to them, "hear your statements, or witness your modes of illustrating and explaining." In this connection, I frequently call them to the black-board for visible representation. They make the attempt; I remark upon their manner of doing it, and endeavor to show them in what respect it may be improved. Sometimes, instead of reciting the lesson directly to me, I ask them to imagine themselves, for the time, acting in the *capacity* of *teachers*, to a class of young pupils, and to adopt a style suitable for such a purpose. At many of our recitations, more than half the time is spent with reference to teaching "*the art of teaching.*" Besides delivering to the school a written *Formal Lecture*[1] once a week, in which I speak of the qualifications, motives, and duties of teachers, the discipline, management, and instruction of schools, and the *manner* in which the various branches should be taught, I am every day, in conversations, or a familiar sort of lectures, taking up and discussing more *particularly* and *minutely*, some point or points suggested by the exercises or occurrences, it may be, of the day, relating to the *internal operations* of the schoolroom, or to physical, moral, or intellectual education: — I say much about the views and motives of teachers, and the motives by which they should attempt to stimulate their pupils. And here I would state, that my theory goes to the entire exclusion of the *premium and emulation system*,[2] and of corporal punishment.[3] My confidence in it is sustained and strengthened by a full and fair experiment for more than one year in a public school composed of seventy scholars of both sexes. I am constantly calling-up real or supposed cases, and either asking the pupils what they would do, in such case, or stating to them what I would do myself, or both. As a specimen of such questions, take the following, viz: On going into a school as teacher, what is the first thing you would do? How will you proceed to bring to order, and arrange your school? Will you have many rules, or few? Will you announce beforehand a code of laws, or make special rules as they may be needed? What *motives* do you purpose to

---

[1] See Mary Swift's notes of these lectures, pp. 82, 85, 90, etc.
[2] *Cf.* pp. 121, 128.   [3] *Cf.* pp. 117, 128.

appeal to, and what *means* will you adopt to make your pupils interested in their studies? What method will you adopt to teach spelling, reading, arithmetic? What will you do with the perseveringly idle and troublesome? What will you do if your scholars quarrel? lie? swear? What will you do if a scholar tells you he *won't* do as he is directed? If a question in any ordinary lesson, say arithmetic, comes up, which you cannot solve readily, what will be your resort? Should you be chiefly ambitious to teach *much*, or to teach thoroughly? How would you satisfy yourself that your teaching is thorough, effectual? To what branches shall you attach most importance, and why? Will you aim chiefly to exercise the *faculties*, or communicate instruction? Besides these daily discussions or conversations, we have a *regular debate* every Saturday, in which the principles involved in these and similar questions are discussed.

Reading I teach by oral inculcation of the principles, as contained in Porter's Rhetorical Reader, (which strike me as in the main correct,) and by example, reading myself before the whole class; hearing the pupils read, and then reading the same piece myself, pointing out their faults, and calling upon them to read again and again, and even the third and fourth time. They also read to each other in my presence. This is a most difficult art to teach. Very few good teachers are to be found, either in our schools or elsewhere. Spelling I teach both orally and by *writing* from the reading lesson; for I think each method has its advantages. Orthography has not yet received quite its merited attention in our schools. *Most* persons in business life have to *write;* few, comparatively, are called upon to read publicly; for this reason it is more important to be a correct speller than a fine reader.

I have adopted no text-book in teaching geography. Worcester's is *chiefly* used. My method has been to give out a subject, (a particular country, e.g.,) for examination. The class make search, using what maps and books they have at command, and get all the information of every kind they can, statistical, historical, geographical, of the people, manners, religion, government, business, etc., and at the recitation we have the *results* of their researches. Giving to each a separate subject, I sometimes require the pupils to make an imaginary voyage, or journey, to one, two, three, or more countries, and give an account of every thing on their return. If I were to teach geography to a class of *young beginners*, I should commence with the town in which they live.

In grammar I have adopted no particular text-book. I am teaching a class of beginners in the model school without a book.

In moral instruction we use both Wayland and Combe; and our recitations are conducted as above described. There are no subjects in which scholars manifest more interest than in questions of morals. This I have noticed in all schools. It shows how easy it would be to do what is so much needed, if the teachers are disposed; viz., to cultivate the *moral faculties*. In connection with reading the Scriptures at the opening of the school in the morning, it is my practice to remark on points of practical duty, as far as I can go on common ground.

10. *Annexed school, or model school.* — This school consists of thirty pupils, of both sexes, from the age of six to ten, inclusive, taken promiscuously from families in the various districts of the town. The children pay nothing for tuition; find their own books, and bear the incidental expenses. This school is under the general superintendence and inspection of the Principal of the Normal School. After it was arranged, the general course of instruction and discipline being settled, it was committed to the immediate care of the pupils of the Normal School, one acting as superintendent, and two as assistants, for one month in rotation, for all who are thought *prepared* to take a part in its instruction. In this experimental school, the teachers are expected to apply the principles and methods which they have been taught in the Normal School, with liberty to suggest any improvements, which may occur to them. Twice every day the Principal of the Normal School goes into the model school for general observation and direction, spending from one half to one hour each visit. In these visits I either sit and watch the general operations of the school, or listen attentively to particular teacher and her

class, or take a class myself, and let the teacher be a listener and observer. After the exercises have closed, I comment upon what I have seen and heard before the teachers, telling them what I deem good, and what faulty, either in their doctrine or their practice, their theory or their manner. Once or twice each term, I take the whole Normal School with me into the model schoolroom, and teach the model school myself, in the presence of the pupils of the Normal School, they being listeners and observers. In these several ways, I attempt to combine, as well as I can, theory and practice, precept and example. In regard to the materials of which it is composed, and the studies attended to, the model school is as nearly a fac simile of a *common district school*, as one district school is of another. In regard to the discipline and management, I am aware there may be more dissimilarity. The superintendent is not situated precisely as she will be, when placed alone in a proper *district school*. This could not be effected without having several model schools. But, limited as is the field of operation for the superintendent, it is wide enough, as the teachers find, for the development of considerable tact and talent. From the model school we exclude all appeals to fear, premiums, or emulation; and yet we have had good order, and a fair amount of study.

11. *Rules and regulations prescribed by the teacher.* — They are the following:

1st. The school shall commence at 8 o'clock, A.M., and continue till 12 o'clock, allowing one hour for recess; and at 2 o'clock, P.M., and continue till 5 o'clock.

2d. The pupils shall attend constantly and punctually. All instances of lateness or absence shall be accounted for to the satisfaction of the Principal.

3d. During study hours, the pupils shall abstain from all *communication* with each other, and from *whatever* may interrupt their studies or divert their attention.

4th. Scholars shall supply themselves with all necessary books and apparatus. The practice of borrowing and lending shall not obtain in school.

5th. Pupils wishing to leave town shall make known their desire to the Principal.

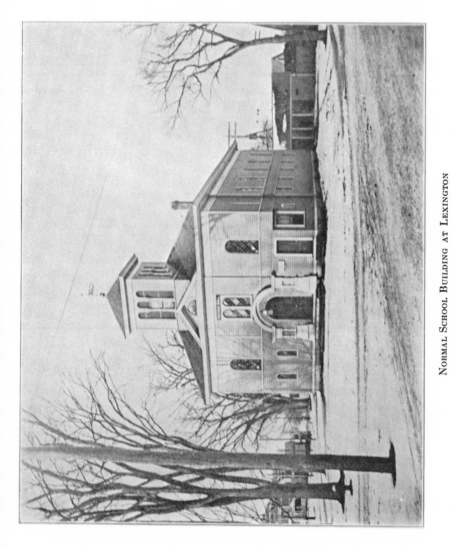

Normal School Building at Lexington

(Photographed about 1890)

6th. The pupils shall attend public worship on the Sabbath.

7th. One hour before breakfast, all the interval between school sessions, and between the afternoon sessions and supper, and two and a half hours after supper, may be spent in physical exercise, suitable recreation, and social intercourse. Other hours, until 9 o'clock, P.M., shall be devoted strictly to reading, study, and the business of the school.

12. *Departure from the Normal School, examinations, etc.* — On these points I refer you to the Common School Journal. Four or five scholars left at the close of the last term, for the purpose of taking schools. No examination by the Visiters was held, no formality was passed through, and no certificate has been given. It must not, however, be inferred from this, that they were thought unworthy or deficient.

13. *Suggestions as to modifications of the course pursued.* — With some slight modifications, which I cannot easily make intelligible in a short statement, I shall pursue, the year to come, the same general course as above described.

In all my instructions, and especially in the *model school,* I depend much upon the black-board and *visible illustration.*

Upon the pupils of the Normal School I inculcate, much and often, the idea that their success depends much upon themselves; upon the *motives* with which they take up the profession and pursue it; upon their correct insight into human nature, and their deep, untiring interest to improve it. They must be moved by a *pure and lofty desire* of doing good. They must be intelligent, discerning. They must be firm, consistent, uniformly patient, and uniformly kind.

It would be easy to be more particular, but this communication is already too long; besides, to go *minutely* into a description of my *manner of teaching* the several branches, both in the Normal and model school, would be to write a book, and not a letter simply.

Allow me to express my high gratification in your late visit to the Normal School. You have had much opportunity to see and compare many schools. For any suggestions in regard to what you saw at Lexington, for the *improvement* of the school, I would be very thankful. I have undiminished confidence in the feasibility of the plan of Normal Schools, if, sustained by the sentiment of the community, it could be allowed to continue in operation long enough to make a fair experiment. But on *this point* I have increasing fears.

Your obedient and humble servant,

CYRUS PEIRCE,
Principal of the Normal School at Lexington.

We were highly gratified with what we saw and heard, at the visit above alluded to. We know of no institution on this side of the Atlantic, at all comparable with this for the training of teachers for Common Schools. If it is permitted to go down, it will be a burning disgrace, not only to the Legislature which shall refuse to sustain it by liberal appropriations, but to the friends of Common School education generally, who should come forward with their sympathy and cooperation to encourage Mr. Peirce in his interesting but exhausting labors.[1] [HENRY BARNARD.]

---

[1] "Connecticut Common School Journal," 1841, p. 164.

THE JOURNAL OF CYRUS PEIRCE

Yours truly,
C. Peirce

CYRUS PEIRCE

THE JOURNAL OF CYRUS PEIRCE

JULY 3, 1839–MARCH 12, 1841

A RECORD OF THE FIRST STATE NORMAL SCHOOL IN AMERICA

CHAPTER I

THE FIRST TERM, JULY 3–OCTOBER 1, 1839

Lexington July 3d 1839

This Day the Normal School, the first in the Country, commenced.

Three Pupils Misses Hawkins, Smith & Damon were examined by the Board of Visitors — viz Messrs. Sparks, Rantoul & Putnam, & admitted —

July 8 Monday School opened this day with 3 pupils Hawkins, Smith & Stowe — one Miss Rolph added during the day Exercises Conversation — Grammar & Arithmetic. Three of the Scholars promise well.

[*July*] *9* This [day] Misses Stodder & Damon came into School as pupils

[*July*] *10* — This Day Mary Swift of Nantucket joined the School — making 7 scholars in all. Our Exercises thus far have been chiefly in Grammar, Reading Geography and Arithmetic. Some of the Pupils not yet provided with Books — Exercises consisting chiefly of conversation and Interrogatories.

July 15 2d Week. This day held a session in the upper room. Hitherto the sessions have been in the sitting room — School visited by Mr Sparks —

July 17 Almira Locke was examined & admitted —

[*July*] *22.* An order of Exercise has been decided upon for the School-Room, and some Rules for the regulation of the House. The Studies for this week, and time indefinite, are to be The Common branches, Algebra, Nat. Philosophy, Physiology, Mental Philosophy, Book-Keeping, Moral Philosophy, & Geometry.

[*July*] *23* Miss Margaret O'Connor entered the School.

[*July*] *26.* Mr Chamberlain brought up the Apparatus — which has been purchased for the use of the School — The Library has been set up — The School-rooms & the Entries have been painted, & the Building now is nearly put in order for the School — The Grounds around the Building are not yet prepared — and the Sleeping apartments still need further accommodations.

July 29 Two Scholars absent this day, Misses O'Connor & Smith — The former had leave of absence to go home last Friday 26th Ins. — The latter is reported sick. The School this day visited by Messrs Rantoul and Woodbury. The Former one of the Board of Visiters — who was pleased to express a decided Satisfaction in the appearance of the School.

[*July*] *30* Miss O'Connor this day returned and took her seat in School.

Aug. 5 The Apparatus and the Principal part of the Library have been received and set up. The Order of Exercises has been adopted, as well as a System of Rules for the Regulation of the House and the government of the School. For a few days past the School has been going on more orderly and systematically and the pupils have made progress, and the Prospect seems more encouraging than at first.

On the 2d Aug. we had a very pleasant visit from Prof. S. H. Newman, who gave some very excellent Advice to the pupils; and which was listened to with great apparent Satisfaction.

Some of the Regulations of the School do not yet receive quite that attention and respect which satisfy me. This point must be attended to.

Aug. This day School visited by Miss Stowe sister of my pupil. Spent the morning in a kind of Moral and religious lecture to the Pupils in connexion with the Reading in the Scriptures. The subject of the Remarks was Herod's Oath & Treatment of John the Baptist; — The Nature of

Mrs. Cyrus Peirce (Harriet Coffin)

Promises and the influence of early and parental Education.
The Scholars seemed attentive, & the Lecture, I think, was
useful.

Aug. 9 Set up the Clock in the Room — Had a visit
from Mr. Wood, former teacher of the Coffin School, Nantucket.

Aug 10. Delivered a Lecture — The Scholars wrote
Composition. School has made some progress this week.

[*Aug.*] *12* Several Scholars absent this day in the afternoon because of the rain. This I was sorry to see. It augurs
ill. It is a poor compliment to their interest and zeal in the
business for which they came hither. Judging from this
example, we may expect to have much absence from bad
weather. But I shall take occasion to remark upon it.

[*Aug.*] *13* After hearing the lessons this morning, I
remarked the absence of yesterday, I hope in such a way as
to do good.

Some of my pupils last sabbath asked the privilege of
walking to W. Cambridge. This I thought an unwise project; but reluctantly consented. One made a visit home;
the others, accompanied her. When the young ladies returned, I believed they in the retrospect, thought much of
the Plan as I did in prospect. I think such a thing will not
be likely to take place again.

[*Aug.*] *15* Many of my pupils absent this day

[*Aug.*] *16* This commenced a new-mode of Recitation by
the scholars giving abstracts of lessons *written* out. I also
this day committed the hearing of the Morning Lesson to
Miss Swift. Both experiments quite as satisfactory as I
expected — Yesterday, I received a visit from Dr. Ware
Jr and Rev. Mr. Putnam — of Roxbury; they did not,
however go into school

[*Aug.*] *19* The Scholars for 2 or 3 days past have been
giving written abstracts of their Physiological Lessons as a
mode of *Reciting*. The Success has been somewhat various.
On the whole, I am inclined to regard it a good variety of
the modes of Recitation.

Aug. 23 During this week the N[ormal] School has been
visited by Miss Stodder of Boston, Miss Starbuck and Mrs
Swain of Nantucket. The Exercises have not been quite

so promptly and well recited as they have been during some of the preceding weeks; but on the whole, I am not certain that they have not made as much progress. The Scholars all continue to seem pleasant; industrious, interested and happy. Miss (*sic*) has been unwell during most of the time; and this morning, in company with her sister, she left for Boston.

[*Aug.*] *27* Very warm weather for several days — and several of the pupils have been so unwell as to be detained from school. — I think the scholars have not been much habituated to hard close and methodical studying. There is great deficiency among them in knowledge of the Common Branches. With two or three exceptions, most that are in school I think will need nearly all of the first year to fit themselves thoroughly to teach in the Primary and Grammar Schools thoroughly. Reading, Spelling, Grammar, Arithmetic Geography all need attention.

[*Aug.*] Tomorrow and next day I shall hold no session purposing in company with some of my Scholars to attend Commencement at Cambridge —

[*Aug.*] *28–29* School suspended — I attended Commencement at Cambridge with some of the pupils; — which as it was new & interesting so I hope it may prove beneficial to them — Miss Parks examined and admitted into School.

Sept 2d Miss Sarah E. Locke examined and admitted into School.

[*Sept.*] *5* This morning I recited the lessons to the Class — or rather I delivered a short familiar Lecture to them instead of the recitation — I think it was a good substitution — and, occasionally, I think, it may be advantageous to a school for Teachers to recite [to] their classes rather than classes to their Teachers. If it has no other effect, it diversifies the modes of operation.

I am having the chambers of the School-house, and the School-rooms better prepared for ventilation. Also a small Wood-shed is building. I am not certain how this last step will meet the views of the Board of Visitors; but I trust they will think of it as I do.

School visited the 3d Inst. by Rev. Mr. Damon of West-Cambridge.

[*Sept.*] *9* The School now consists of twelve Scholars —
They seem industrious & interested; and nearly every one
of *fair* capacity. But many of them are yet backward;
and I apprehend it will require more than one year's Instruction to qualify them to teach. They want language — they
want the power of generalization, and of communication.
But I think in all things they are gaining ground, and I feel
encouraged. Misses Smith, Stodder, Damon, Haskell, Stowe
& Swift give quite as much promise at present as any of
them.

[*Sept.*] *11* This began a Course of Experimental Lectures
— Explained the Barometer and Thermometer — also the
suction and forcing pumps — experimented with each —
experiment in Refraction — all successful. This day commenced a New Exercise; styled 'Conversational Exercise'.
Each scholar relates a story, anecdote or fact — in her own
language. It was quite a hopeful beginning. [Compare this
with the Oral Composition of our own times. — Ed.]

[*Sept.*] *12.* School this day visited by Mr. Mann who
spent the day with us. The School did well — Mr. M. was
pleased to express much gratification in visit — the state of
prospect of the school; and we all felt benefited and cheered
by his presence This Visit will make quite an Epoch in our
history.

[*Sept.*] *13–14* No School — on the 13th the Principal
attended the county Convention at Concord — as the Annual
Address of the Secretary of the Board of Education was
delivered — On the 14 — went to Boston to procure stoves
for the rooms.

[*Sept.*] *15.* School came together rather thin — 2 or 3
absent — Recitations pretty good — some improvement in
reading.

[*Sept.*] *17.* — Much as yesterday —

[*Sept.*] *18* This was our day for conversations. The Exercise pretty successful — I think it will prove beneficial if
[it] is properly attended to — and preparations be well made.
— Many of the Scholars want the power of language — I
[think] this will aid them. Each one is expected to relate a
story, an anecdote, a piece of history, a Biography in good
style. A second familiar Lecture in Nat. Phi. was given —

[*Sept.*] *21.* The week, which now closes has been, on the whole; a quiet, pleasant, and satisfactory [one]. — Most of the pupils need most of their time for the common Branches — There is great deficiency in Reading and Spelling. I mentioned to them it is in contemplation, soon to get up a model School. This will be composed of children of the village and town from the age from 6 to 10 — to be taught by the best Scholars of the N[ormal] School — under the supervision of the principal. — I hope to have it in operation in 2 or three weeks.

I must try to awaken more freedom of *Inquiry* and discussion. I think, the exercise is a valuable one.

23d Sept. A fair and pleasant day — School-Exercises successful. All pupils present except Miss Hawkins.

[*Sept.*] *25.* This day the School-Exercises were a little out of their usual course. A Review in Nat. History, and Moral Philosophy. Besides Physiology, Conversational Exercise and Physiological Discussion.

In Moral Philosophy — the Exercises consisting of partly original thoughts and partly Extracts & Condensations were read. Some of them were very successful.

Yesterday the school was visited by four strangers — In the Evening there was a meeting of sundry citizens, in the Baptist Meeting-House; to consider the subject of a Model School to be connected with the Normal School — Not many present — some progress made. The project seems to meet the views of people well — The meeting stands adjourned at the East Village.

[*Sept.*] *26* — This day's business was somewhat retarded by cold; the room not yet supplied with the means of having a fire — Scholars read abstracts of their Physiological Lessons, which were very good. The Principal delivered a familiar experimental Lecture in Natural Philosophy.

[*Sept.*] *28.* School visited this day by Messrs Dr Webb of Boston and Gen. Wadsworth of Geneseo N.Y. — Put up my stoves in School-room.

[*Sept.*] *30* Had a fire in the School-room.

Oct. 1 School this day visited by Dr. Howe Principal of the Blind Institution S.B. [*i.e.*, South Boston] and one of the female teachers in said Institution.

This day my first quarter closes. (12 Scholars)

In review of the Term I feel encouraged. The numbers have been much fewer than I anticipated; but in regard to most of those who have attended, I believe they have made a good beginning & will make teachers. Few of them think of staying more than one year; all of which with great diligence, will be required to prepare them to teach in the *Common* Branches. — It seems to be a general impression in the minds of those with whom I converse that the next term the school will be filled up. I hope it may be so — I think there will be an addition. The Rooms will accommodate about 90. It is in contemplation to unite a Model School with the Normal School: Some of the incipient steps toward this have already been taken. It will be composed of children selected from those of the vicinity — of the age from 6 to 10 inclusive; to commence next term Oct. 21. This, I think, may awaken some additional interest. There are several mistakes — erroneous opinions prevailing in regard to the school, which I trust (*sic*) have operated and do operate, to its prejudice: These time, and the activity of the friends of the Institution must correct.

Oct. 9 During the Vacation, which commenced on the 2d Inst. Proposals have been made to the Inhabitants of this village and the town to furnish 30 children from 6 to 10 to form a Model School to be connected with the Normal School, to be under the Supervision of the Principal & to be taught by the Pupils of the Normal School. The Proposition meets with a flattering reception from the Inhabitants, and there is encouraging prospect that the School will go into operation at the Commencement of next term — Five children are to be taken from each District — If the more remote districts do not avail themselves of the overture, then a greater number is to be taken from the Centre School District.

CHAPTER II

THE SECOND TERM, OCTOBER 16, 1839–JANUARY 14, 1840

OPENING OF THE MODEL SCHOOL

Oct. 16 This Day, Had a very appropriate and most excellent Address from His Excellency the Chairman of the Board of Education, delivered in The First Church, in which he gave a brief history of the origin, progress and present Condition of Normal Schools — Then what is to be expected from them and accomplished in them. 1 Instruction imparted — especially in the Common Branches 2 The Art of Teaching Taught — 3 The Science of School Government & Theory applied to Practice in the Model School — The whole Discourse was exceedingly plain, intelligible practical and instructive; and evidently made a very deep and wholesome impression on the minds of a large and attentive auditory.

Opened School this morning. A part of the pupils only returned. Mr. Howes visited the School — Short session in the forenoon — In the afternoon no School — The School-Rooms and Premises visited by the Gov. Mr. Dwight & others — With which they were pleased to express themselves well satisfied — Had a Sign-Board put up. Carpenters, & Masons finished their work.

[*Oct.*] *17.* Six new scholars added to the School one from Lexington — 1 from Medford — 2 from Wrentham and 2 from Roxbury — with the prospect of some others. The Prospects of the School seem to brighten a little. — Am not able yet to form any very definite idea of the character of my new pupils.

N. S. Record —

Oct. 19 This day closes the week — New scholars have not yet done much, but I think they promise well. The Term I think has begun rather auspiciously, & I am looking forward with considerable anticipation.

[*Oct.*] *21* Very pleasant day — one Scholar added to the Normal School — Miss Ireson —

This day, the Model-School has been collected and partially organized: about 30 Scholars: ⅓ girls. — All sorts of odd ends. Hope we shall do well; but there is much fixing to be done.

[*Oct.*] The Model School contains 33 Scholars — ages from 6 to 10 — 21 boys, and 12 girls. They have been arranged in 3 classes — The Scholars, I suppose, are a pretty fair sample of those of their age in the Town School. They are not forward — and of the ground that they have gone over, they have explored none of it thoroughly. There is great imperfection. They are in the very undesirable Condition of being familiar with the book[s] without knowing any thing they contain.

Tomorrow I expect they will bring their new books — & take their first Lessons. They are very uneasy — and seem to have no habits of application or order. The Normal Scholars have visited the Model School (some of them) daily, and assisted in arranging it. They will visit daily — and some of them will take the principal part of its instruction and discipline. I feel that it has added greatly to my labours and cares; but I feel also that it is a very important addition to the Establishment, and one on which its success greatly depends. The Prospects of the Normal School, I think are brightening —

[*Oct.*] *23d* The Scholars recently added, are, if I rightly judge, an accession of talent and character as well as of numbers — This Evening a new Candidate, Miss Woodman has applied for admission —

[*Oct.*] *24* This day Miss (*sic*) examined and admitted—been trying experiments — with very partial success — It has [been] a laborious but not very satisfactory day. Have tried some of the Normal Scholars in the work of teaching — They show their inexperience. The scholars in the Model School have slovenly habits both of study, attitude and dress. They need to be brought to *fix their attention.* No. of Normalites 19

[*Oct.*] *26* No additions to the School since my last Entry. The recent additions are of scholars who promise well to the character of the School; all above par in capacity and respectable in point of attainment. All the scholars appear to be orderly and attentive. The Model School every day reminds me how much addition of care and labour it has brought upon me. But I think it is a very valuable acquisition to the Establishment and must, by no means, be allowed to fail. The success of the whole does undoubtedly depend greatly upon the success of this single part. The Model School begins to come to order; and put on something of the appearances of a *School*. It requires much time and patience.

This day delivered a Lecture and heard a lesson in Orthoepy. There is great deficiency in pronunciation, among the scholars. This subject — and Especially Articulation must have a good deal of attention.

Oct. 29 This day I began the Normal School at 8 A.M. remained with the Normalites until 9; then I went down into the Model School, leaving the Normal School to take care of themselves, until 10 o'clock; — at 10 the Normal had a Recess, until 11: at Eleven the Model School was dismissed — and N.S. came together again, & remained in session until 12 — P.M. The Model School came together at 1 O'clock — and continued until 3. The Normal School came to order at 2, & continued in Session until 5. This gives me more time for the Model School, & affords a better opportunity for the Pupils of the Normal School to be in the Model School; it affords, also an opportunity for them to exercise in the forenoon: It leaves the girls one hour by themselves; but this also throws them more upon their own responsibilities. It keeps me engaged in school 8 hours, but I shall notwithstanding try this method for a while until an experiment has been made. I wish to be with the Model School much for the present. Miss Wyman went home sick.

Oct. 30. The School this day visited by Mr. Dodge and Mr. Wood of Washington City. Exercises in Orthography, Physiology, Nat. Philosophy, Mor. Philosophy, & Conversation. Pretty satisfactory. Model School rather still, quiet, and orderly. Things look more encouraging; but we want more numbers.

[*Oct.*] *31* Three Scholars absent on account of sickness —

ROBERT RANTOUL, JR.

Member of First Committee on Normal Schools
Massachusetts Board of Education

Tried some philosophical Experiments this morning — with tolerable success — but my Air-Pump is a very imperfect article; and insufficient for the performance of nice Experiments. I spend, according to the present arrangement, 4 hours per day with the Model School, and 4 with the Normal School.

Nov. 2. Hitherto Mrs. P. — has assisted in the Model School — this day she was not present. Had better order for 2 or 3 days — much [better] than at the Beginning. and there is beginning to be awakened some interest on the part of pupils. I am glad also to learn that the Parents of the pupils are beginning to be interested in the School: Feel the loss of Miss Swift who is sick. I see the girls need practice — experience much — very much. In the Nor. School heard lesson in Nat. Philosophy; attended to the Discussion of The Expediency of Normal Schools. Not a very interesting Exercise this day — none of the Pupils having much to say. I enjoin the Importance of Preparation. Omitted my Lecture for want of time. The School at present is much interrupted by reason of sickness — four pupils being sick — *threatened with fever* as we say. To-day those at school — seem better. Two have gone home. Misses Smith & Wyman — other two Misses Pennell & Swift remain.

Nov. 4. Mr Mann here yesterday — Mrs. Pennell & Miss Mann here To-day in consequence of Miss Pennell's sickness. Sickness rather abated to-day. It has been, and continues to be the cause of much interruption. It is a great Calamity. The lessons have not been this term, what they ought to be and what they were last Term. Many more entire failures and much more Imperfection. The Model School does not yet satisfy me — There is too much Stir & bustle — too much talk and reproof required. They must behave well & go on quietly with very little ado. I must look to this matter, & endeavor to correct it.

[*Nov.*] *5.* In the Normal School the Recitations have been better to-day than for several days past — In the Model School they have also done better —

[*Nov.*] *6* Rainy day — few scholars present both in the Normal and in the Model School — Performances pretty good. The sick better — Several seats vacant — a very discouraging fact. The Subject of Mechanics new to the Scholars and somewhat difficult. They begin to get hold of it. In teaching the Model School, the girls show their Inexperience. It shows that the Model School is just [the] thing we need. I trust that by it we shall effect fully the purpose we have in view.

[*Nov.*] 7 Pretty successful in my Experiments in Nat. Philosophy — Recitations today quite good — The Sick recovering — Several absent this afternoon in the Model School — A certificate to be exacted of all who are absent or tardy. They are becoming somewhat more still and orderly, but there is yet too much noise; and they require too much looking after and speaking to.

[*Nov.*] *8.* Two or three of my pupils Normalites seldom make any answers to questions — Misses X. and Y. especially I have little hope of ever making either of these qualified and efficient teachers. There has been more of laughing in the room today than at any previous time. Of this I must say something, — usually & generally, there is great attention to Order; and in the whole aspect of the school room, I have much satisfaction. The young ladies, who have taken a part in Model-School Instruction, are making a hopeful practical Beginning.

[*Nov.*] *9 Saturday* — This day we attended to our Exercise in reading the Scriptures — Orthoepy in Respect Enunciation, and Discussion of the Question, "Should the Educator offer premiums and appeal to the principle of Emulation in carrying forward his work". The Discussion was of a higher character than any preceding one. I felt a good deal pleased with it, — think the time was well spent. A great majority of the pupils were on the Negative. — A pretty fair day for the Model School — I am desirous that Miss Swift should recover and resume her station in the Model School as superintendent — subordinate.

[*Nov.*] *11* Recitations, today, were in Nat. Philosophy, Physiology, Algebra, Arithmetic, Grammar, & Moral Philosophy: — All pretty well recited by the class in general: — I think there must be more attention still to Grammar and the Common Branches generally. There are two or three young ladies, who need particular attention in these things. The sick are improving.

[*Nov.*] *12* A pleasant day within doors and without.
Lessons and Conduct fair. I have talked much this day to
my scholars and with them. Sometimes I am apprehensive
I talk too much for their Good; and then again that I talk
too little. May I find the happy Medium. The Scholars
seem interested. I think they learn.

The Schools this day (Normal & Model) visited by Miss
Mann. Gave out Questions in Physiology — Discussed the
subject of Gravity & attraction also in Grammar, the nature
of the Adjective. The Fire burns *bright;* the Rose smells
sweet; the Bell sounds *clear;* He feels *well;* the sky looks
beautiful. What are the words underscored? Adjectives or
adverbs? This question has been considered.

[*Nov.*] *13* Went to Boston to get my Air-pump examined
— to purchase some small articles of Apparatus for the School
(Model) & for other purposes. Both Schools suspended for
the day. —

Nov. 14. A warm rainy day — thin school. Miss Mann,
who had been with her sick niece, left — which caused much
sadness, of heart. — The Girls have commenced Scientific
Class-Book — Mechanics a new subject to them, and somewhat difficult. I find some difficulty in making it clear to
all of them. This day resumed the Music Exercise which
has been suspended for a few weeks. There is, however, so
much need of attention to the Common School Branches
particularly Grammar, Reading and Arithmetic, that I think
we shall have but little time for Music.

[*Nov.*] *15* This day tried an Experiment with my Air-
pump — to freeze water by evaporation; did not succeed,
I think the [air-pump] is not in perfect order. For two
mornings in succession I have recited the lesson in Natural
Philosophy — I think it well sometimes for *teachers* to recite
to pupils, instead of pupils reciting to teachers. I think
lessons have not been quite so satisfactory since the establishment of the Model School as before. I begin to be apprehensive that the pupils do not confine themselves so closely
to their studies when I am absent as when I am with them.
I am sorry to have such an impression — I have no other
reason for it than the want of success in their lessons. Some
failure in the Model School discipline on the part of the

young ladies — To these things I must advert in my remarks
tomorrow.

[*Nov.*] *16 Saturday* Not a very successful week. We
have have had many poor lessons. I know not the cause, but
the *Fact* is *certain:* and I think it has been particularly the
case since the commencement of the Model-School. I have
asked the Scholars this day to search for the cause. It must
be that the lessons are longer or intrinsically more difficult
— or more in number — or Pupils study less — or are subject to more interruption, or are less adapted to study —
or I know not what Cause — The Fact is certain. Delivered my eleventh lecture this day.

[*Nov.*] *18* The lessons this day were better than they
have been of late, except the Geography lesson in the afternoon. — Spoke to day to the pupils on the subject of order
and strict attention to study and business during *study-
hours.* — The Importance of appropriating every moment to
its legitimate purpose and object. Misses Z. Q. X. and Y.
are yet deficient in Grammar — particularly the two latter.
It will be a long time before they will be able to teach it. —

Visited this day by Mrs. Cotton and Mrs. Haskell; — and
Messrs. Dodge and Keely. For a few days past, I have felt
as though the School is not making much progress. the
numbers continue small — and the prospect rather dark.

[*Nov.*] *19* This day had a note from Mr. Damon sayin[g]
his daughter Hannah M. (member of the Nor. School) is
quite indisposed — being afflicted with Edematose Swelling
(Dropsy) in the feet; occasioned, as the Physician thought
by too much sitting and too little walking and active exercise. — Prompted by the foregoing fact, I used up the morning in speaking to my Pupils on the subject of Regular,
systematic, vigorous Exercise. I have given them from 10
to 11 A.M. for this purpose. Having given my views on
this subject often and fully, I now for a season take leave of
it; and shall wash my hands clean of this matter, let come
what consequences may. Recitations today — good. - - -

[*Nov.*] *21* Spent the whole Recess from 10 to 11 with the
school — hearing the lesson in Algebra. (inadvertently) —
obliged to omit the Conversation Exercise — Received a
complaint from the Steward about the Girls making a noise

— especially by Dancing   Met a Committee of Conference from the Young Ladies — talked over the matter.   Gave them this Rule of Conduct; viz. "Whatsoever would be proper for you to do in a WELL REGULATED FAMILY, that you may do in this Establishment — and in any Boardin[g] House; unless there is some especial Rule from rightful Authority against it".   Wrote a letter to the Steward on the subject.

[*Nov.*] *22d.*   Cold Day. — Steward much disturbed and angry at my letter; — threatens to go away — thinks the young ladies unreasonable — and that he can give no satisfaction: all this, because I reminded him of some defects about his Establishment, and delinquencies in his Course. What will be the Result I know not; and it gives me little concern.   He should know, that the Dining and Keeping room should be supplied with a good *fire;* and his Table should be furnished with GOOD Bread. — School visited by Mrs. Ford, (aunt of Miss Stowe) — Poor Reading Lesson —

[*Nov.*] *23d*   This day learnt authentically that one of the pupils of the Normal School is under Matrimonial engagement.   The [School] will not suffer a great loss — Her Promise in the profession of Teaching not very encouraging. – – – Recitations, this day, very good — The question Is the Reading of the works of Fiction injurious? was discussed. Quite interesting.   Read half a Lecture on Teaching the Art of Reading.

[*Nov.*] *25*   Rainy Day.   One or two pupils absent.   Altogether an unsuccessful day in both departments — Normal and Experimental — I am apprehensive the young ladies either do not study enough or do not study in a Judicious manner.   They are perhaps confined time enough with their lessons — but do not *sufficiently fix the attention* while studying — Some are not making much progress in Algebra or indeed in *anything else.*   My heart is heavy, and my hands hang down.   I feel sometimes almost disheartened.   Some of the young ladies seem very sensitive, and easily disturbed at *trifles.*   I can hardly express an opinion or rather give free utterance to my sentiments, but some one seems stricken.   I am friendly to a free expression of views, — and cannot yet consent to relinquish the practice.   Perhaps I should be more regardful of the feelings of others. Let me look to this matter. Model School not much advanced within 3 or 4 days. I must [put] forth a hand to this, that it may not *sink* but *advance*.

[*Nov.*] *26* This day Susan E. Burdick from Nant. and Miss Drew from South Boston (Teacher in the Blind Institution) were added to the School. Nor. & Mod. School visited by Mr. Wm. Tidd — who came in the Forenoon & spent the day. Lessons generally pretty fair; — a partial failure in Nat. Philosophy on Gravity. Scarcely any of the Scholars had clear definite conceptions on this point. — Several questions were put to the scholars who board in commons in regard to their manner of spending the Evening. It appears from their answers, that [it] is [not] strictly devoted to the study of School-Lessons [free] from conversation and interruption. They study, but they talk amidst their study. This must be seen to, after Thanksgiving: Dismissed each School until *Monday next*.

Dec. 2 After Thanksgiving we come together; — 5 of our number being absent. This fact is a greater damper upon our feelings and hindrance to our exertions. Lessons pretty fair. School visited by Mrs. Trask and Mrs Fiske.

[*Dec.*] *3* A dull unpleasant day; — Scholars still absent — The influence of which is still felt to our detriment and great regret. I am apprehensive our number may never all get together again. — School visited by Mr. Felch, phrenological Lecturer, and Mr. Hobbs, former teacher in this town. Scholars did not appear to much advantage.

[*Dec.*] *4* Lessons Physiology, Nat Philosophy & Conversation. All of them very fair. This Evening The School listened to a lecture on Phrenology from Mr. Felch.

[*Dec.*] *5* Morning Lessons in consequence of the Phrenological Lecture last evening, not recited. Lessons today "*indifferently good*". Rather a dull uninteresting day. Scholars did not seem elastic and wide-awake. — Feel a little to-day as though I should never succeed in "*filling up and building up*" the school. What can I do? What am I doing? I am stating to my Pupils in a Series of *Conversations* and *lectures* The duties and qualifications of Teachers — the Principles of Governing and Teaching a School — I am showing them daily by my own Method of Teaching them, and teaching the scholars of the Model School, *HOW* they should teach their Pupils. I am giving them an opportunity of *experimenting* themselves in the way of teaching — while I, as much as I am able, observe their manner, and at proper time, remark upon it. What more can be done or rather what different, I *know not.*

Dec. 6 This day I took the Normal Scholars down into the model School. The whole day was spent in their witnessing my manner of teaching. I called out the classes one after another and heard them in the various branches — disciplining and governing the School at the same time. After the Model School dismissed I delivered a Lecture to the Normal Pupils on the subject of teaching and governing School. The Model appeared quite well. Some points of improvement, which I pointed out to the Nor. Scholars.

The Model is now put mainly under the care of Miss Swift as superintendent, and will be taught by the Normalites.

Dec. 7 This day we had a discussion on the question — "Are Capital Punishments ever Justifiable". It went off with considerable interest and Spirit. School visited by Mr Wellington — who made remarks on the question. Finished my Lecture on *Reading.* The week closes with mixed character — though rather favorable.

[*Dec.*] *9* This day all the scholars present except two — hope soon to see the whole. Unpleasant weather — rainy — The scholars did not this day generally walk. It seems very difficult to prevail with them practically to take regular systematic Exercise — Lessons pretty good — not much progress in Algebra —

[*Dec.*] *10* After the School had opened and I had made my Remarks upon various topics, I called the class in *Algebra* and gave them some instruction, omitting the lesson in Nat. Philosophy; and none having been given in Physiology. Recitations, this day, Algebra, Mental Philosophy, Book-Keeping, Arithmetic, Geography & Moral Philosophy; generally good. But there are two or three scholars, who do little or nothing in Arithmetic or Grammar: and I am apprehensive they never will accomplish much in these, or

in *any other* Branches. The prospect of their becoming
teachers is small. I do not feel perfectly satisfied with the
recitation on the Globes; — should like to see a little more
interest in it among the pupils. — Again I am disappointed
in regard to my air-pump; sadly disappointed — having
taken it twice to Boston to be repaired or improved — and
yet it will not exhaust well; failed entirely in my attempt to
freeze water by Evaporation. This day, sent my Bill against
the Nor. School to Mr. Sparks.

Dec. 11. Reviewed Arithmetic, Nat. Philosophy and
Physiology; two last, well performed — Pleasant day; —
School-room, pleasant. Went into the model school, as is
my custom every half day: liked appearances pretty well.
— Miss Damon returned, having been absent several weeks,
from indisposition. School visited by Rev. Mr. Damon of
West-Cambridge.

[*Dec.*] *12* A dull rainy day; — both in doors and without
doors *unpleasant.* Morning Lesson in Physiology indifferently recited. Reading, middling; Punctuation & Orthoepy
pretty well. The principle of *Mechanical* Powers not very
well understood by the scholars. Some easy questions I
have put for the application of principles, that, to my disappointment, were not answered readily or correctly. Model
School, not perfect.

[*Dec.*] *13–14* Call from Mrs Trask and Miss — Exercises
generally quite good — Physiology — Nat. Philosophy —
Reading, particularly interesting and satisfactory. Sat. 14
— Philosophical questions answered — Lecture — Reading
and discussion omitted for want of time —

Spent considerable time in conversation with Steward and
wife — also with his Boarders in reference to this domestic affair — there having been some little difficulty in the
premises —

[*Dec.*] *15* A severe snow-storm, yet all the pupils of the
N.S. were present except two who [live] at considerable distance. The Exercises during both Sessions quite good except
in Algebra. In this but little progress is made by a portion
of the pupils.

The Model School was very thin; about 15 were present
in all.

JARED SPARKS

Member of the First Committee on Normal Schools
Massachusetts Board of Education

[*Dec.*] *17* A very pleasant day. Exercises fair for promptness and accuracy. Physiology, Nat. Philosophy, Arithmetic, Algebra, Ment. Philosophy Grammar, Orthography, and Geography were all recited. School visited by Mr. & Mrs. Smith of Lincoln. – – Model School reported as more uneasy and less orderly than usual. — The storm makes considerable interruption in the school.

[*Dec.*] *18* Lessons good. Nothing uncommon occurred.

[*Dec.*] *19* A pleasant cold day. Twenty out of twenty-one of the scholars present. This is a very pleasing fact; after so much absence and interruption. Lessons, prompt, ready and correct. School visited by Messrs Follen, Dodge, Mulliken and Davis: all of whom expressed satisfaction in the visit.

[*Dec.*] *20* Let this day be blotted out of the Nor. Calendar – – – – School visited by Mrs. Davis & Misses Howe and Goodwin.

[*Dec.*] *21* A pleasant Day — The Exercises were Review in Nat. Philosophy — Reading in Abbot's Teacher & Testament — Lecture and Discussion. All very interesting and good. Proposed to the School to attend the County Convention at Waltham on Thursday next which met generally with a very favorable reception.

Dec. 23d A cold North-east snow Storm. — Thin school. Made some change in the order of studies, that there might be opportunity for more attention to the common branches, for those who need it and that the others might attend to a higher course of study. I trust the change will prove advantageous. Most of the lessons have been well recited. Several of the Scholars went home last Saturday, and have not returned: this is the Evil of leaving School: it is always a great inconvenience and interruption.

[*Dec.*] *24* Pleasant day and good lessons.

[*Dec.*] *25* Pleasant and agreeable day. Remarks were made to the N. School on Christmas. Exercises in Arithmetic, Nat. Philosophy Combe's Constitution of Man, and Conversation — also Algebra; all well performed with the exception, perhaps of Arithmetic. School visited by Messrs. Dodge & brother, Stetson and Robinson teacher in Boston, formerly of Nantucket. The scholars seem pleased; I hope, they are improving.

[*Dec.*] *26* With the whole Normal School I went to Waltham to attend a *County School Association:* — A very interesting occasion. A safe return and pleasant ride.

[*Dec.*] *27* A pleasant School — but not good lessons. This I ascribe partly to the intellectual and physical influence of yesterday. It was a natural and legitimate Cause — When the Faculties have been strained by excitement, there must be a subsequent Relaxation. Formerly I used to punish and reprove scholars after a holyday for bad lessons; but now I think, feel and act, quite differently.

[*Dec.*] *28* A rain-Storm — and very bad walking. Thin School. Model School very few. Exercises — Nat. Philosophy — Music — Lecture — Discussion. — Also remarks upon the Meeting at Waltham. Quite a good and profitable day.

Dec. 30 This day the Superintendence of the Model School has been transferred from Miss Swift to Miss Stodder, and almost a new set of assistant Teachers has been appointed. I feel a good deal of interest in this School. Under Miss Swift it has done well — and care is necessary lest in the change of Teachers from time to time it sink, and decline and fail. Its failure would be a sad disaster to the whole Concern. The Exercises today imperfectly prepared. The girls not unfrequently speak of the want of time — I have urged the propriety of having no more studies than they can prepare *well* and *in season.*

[*Dec.*] *31.* A cold day — lessons well and seasonably prepared. Miss Wyman, a promising scholar, who has been absent several weeks on account of sickness, this day returned, and from teacher and pupils met a hearty welcome.

1840 Jan. 1. New-year's day. — Very cold — Read a few thoughts to them on the day — season. Remarked to them on Nat. Philosophy Lesson, and explained the figures and principles; — heard a recitation in Combe's Constitution also in Arithmetic and Algebra — Conversation — Exercise — School visited by Dr. Haskell of Ashby. Session opened by singing — All quite good.

[*Jan.*] *2* This day I took the Normal School into the Model School — and taught the Model School through the whole day; to give the Normalites a practical Illustration of my Manner; as well as to satisfy myself of the progression which the M — School is making. The result, quite satisfactory.

[*Jan.*] *3d* This day of ordinary character. All the members of the Normal School were present: 21 —

[*Jan.*] *4* Pleasant day — cold — Remarks to the School Exercises in Music, Nat. Philosophy — Combe's Constitution of Man — Algebra — Discussion & Lecture — The Discussion rather dull — and the Algebra — almost a failure. The School visited by Mr Bradbury, a teacher in this town from Framingham — closed ¼ past 12 —

[*Jan.*] *6* General Attendance of Scholars — very good of late. Attention and apparent interest for the most part very good. The whole Course of Exercises gone through with; and with very tolerable success. The Normalites seem engaged — are quite orderly — and I think will be successful. Difficulty is brewing in the Steward's Department: He has felt uneasy from the beginning that he was making nothing. Want of harmony between him and the Boarders — He proposes leaving — and in my opinion, it is not much matter, how soon. I am doubtful whether such a Department is essential or even important, to the Institution, unless it be to keep down the price of Board. If the general price of Board here much exceeds two dollars, I am persuaded it will operate as a serious obstacle to the success of the School. It will show that the Board misjudged in regard to the matter of Location of the School.

[*Jan.*] *7* Quite unwell all day. School matters went on pretty well. Two new scholars entered; Misses Rogers from Billerica. No Session in the Model School, on account of a sleigh-ride.

[*Jan.*] *8* The pupils recited in Combe — Algebra Nat. Philosophy and Con. Exercise.

[*Jan.*] *9* Unwell all day; closed school early. Lessons few in numbers; and to *me*, they seemed not more than ordinarily good.

[*Jan.*] *10* Spent the day in review. I am surprised and mortified greatly at finding how *little* my pupils retain of the Principles which I endeavored to instil into them, & explain

[*Jan.*] *11* Snow all day — Scholars all present except

one. Exercises, after opening the school, were Reading in the Scriptures, Rev. of Nat. History, Men. Philosophy, Lecture & Discussion. The forenoon seemed pleasant and profitable. Announced to the School my intention to spend Monday next in a Kind of General Review — and gave them Liberty to invite any of their friends. Tuesday and Wednesday next, will be a *recess*.

[*Jan.*] *13* This day both the Model and the Normal School were visited by a few people in the Vicinity; and we had a sort of Review of Some of the Studies and Exercises. The whole went off in both school rooms, in pretty shabby style. It is not strange, that Examinations in Common Schools should do badly, when these grown up girls — young ladies — teachers aspirant can fail right *"down flat";* and that, too on points and subjects on which we have spent more time than on any thing else; and about which I have questioned them hardly three *days before! !* This is too bad — too bad ! — —

CHAPTER III

THE THIRD TERM, JANUARY 16–APRIL 14, 1840

[*Jan.*] *16* Two days vacation. A new scholar added this day to the School, from Dracut name — — Kimball. Lessons this day pretty good. Term opens with fair prospects, bright hopes. Our hearts are much saddened by the intelligence of the burning and destruction of the Lexington Steamer, in coming from N.Y. to Stonington — on board of which was Dr. Follen and probably his only son Charles, who was a member of the Model School. "Thou destroyest the hope of man."

[*Jan.*] *17* Nothing uncommon or particularly worthy of remark, occurred during the sessions of this day. School visited by Mr. Parks of Lincoln.

[*Jan.*] *18.* After opening the school, Brigham's Mental Excitement, Arithmetic, Algebra Reading in the Scriptures, Discussion & Lecture were attended to. — The School was visited by Mr. Sherman of Wayland, now teaching in Lincoln — with two young ladies —

Jan. 20 All went pretty fair in school today. Not all the scholars prepared with all the lessons; but they were generally and quite well prepared.

[*Jan.*] *21* In Nat. Philosophy, the Class are on Specific Gravity. I apprehend the subject is not well understood. I must endeavor to make it plain. The lessons this day were generally well recited. All things went orderly and well with one exception: — a striking, glaring instance of departure from school-order. Such things do not tend to promote peace, or good will, or progress.

[*Jan.*] *22d* Pretty good school. Nat. Phi. Orthoepy, Mor. Philosophy, were the Exercises. Met a few scholars in the afternoon for a Reading Exercise. Miss Y. and Miss X. I think, or rather I am apprehensive, will not soon make teachers.

[*Jan.*] *23d* A stormy day and thin School. Lesson pretty well recited; but some failures and not a few tears. I wish

Scholars to know principles so surely, and precisely and familiarly, that they can explain and apply them amidst all the trying confusion which may beset them at the Black-Board. The Model School very thin.

[*Jan.*] *24* Exercises and movements of the School in the ordinary kind and style. Nothing remarkable to-day.

[*Jan.*] *25* Read, and remarked upon Abbot's chapter on *Scheming;* quite a Valuable Recitation or Exercise. The following Question was discussed — "Is it best to notice every transgression, or transgressions singly in school, or to advert to them in the gross — or in general. Majority in the Negative.

Communicated to the School the intelligence, that the Secretary of the Board of Education with other gentlemen would visit them on Tuesday next and spend the day. This Communication was received with some *emotion.*

Jan. 27 Lessons this day of ordinary Excellence. With many of the School, there is still a good deal of deficiency in the Common Branches; in Grammar, reading, orthoepy, arithmetic and Geography; and I see not but it is *likely* to continue. Indeed, neither in its literary nor moral character, do I think, the School has made much progress for the last *three* weeks: and of late, for several reasons; my confidence in the continued progress and ultimate success of the Nor. School, while under my care, (if it may succeed under the administration of *any* one,) has been greatly shaken. IM-PATIENCE, my besetting sin, assails me, and carries me captive at will. May the School come back to its former *unity* of Feeling and *Cooperation*, and hopeful progress. I will leave no measure untried — no pains spared. May the Breath of Heaven '*Flatus Divinus*', swell the sail.

[*Jan.*] *28* This day the School in both Departments was visited by Messrs Mann & Emerson and Dr Howe. The School went through their ordinary Recitations and Exercises. The[y] appeared to good advantage, and the gentlemen expressed satisfaction. At the close, Mr. Emerson made some very good remarks to the young ladies.

With the Model School they expressed especial satisfaction.

[*Jan.*] *29* No session — Cleaning stove-funnel.

[*Jan.*] *30* Some of the Lessons very good: — others quite indifferent. I was disappointed in the character of the day. It seems to me that the Scholars have less interest in their studies & that the Principal has less of their confidence, esteem, and affection than ever. I do not feel so much pleased with the condition and aspect of the school, as I did a month or six weeks ago.

[*Jan.*] *31* The *Complexion* of this day much like that of yesterday; — perhaps a shade or two lighter. There are several of the branches studied in which many [of] the young ladies manifest very *little interest*. There is not, there cannot be in this way much Proficiency.

Feb. 1 Review in Nat. Philosophy, pretty good. Reading in Scripture and Abbot Teacher, quite good; Discussion of the following question — "In Geography Recitations, is it best that Scholars should have the Map open before them;" very fair. Lecture.

[*Feb.*] *3* A quiet fair School: — Recitations middling: Teachers of the Model School, this day changed.

The Steward advertises his Furniture this day for sale; thus purposing to break up his Establishment and turn his Boarders into the Street. This is an outrageous movement.

Feb. 4 Exercises of the usual kind and quality — Nothing remarkable — School visited by Mr. Tillinghast of Taunton.

[*Feb.*] *5* Exercises fair — Model School deteriorated somewhat — in conduct and lessons — This day the young ladies of the Normal House were virtually turn[ed] out of doors very abruptly, and obliged to seek temporary accommodations in the Village. A *Barbarous Procedure*.

[*Feb.*] *6* Session this day quite pleasant and satisfactory. Most of the Exercises recited generally with promptness and accuracy. Mr. Tillinghast kindly pointed one or two errors in the Algebraic Performances. The Scholars have felt somewhat embarrassed by his presence.

[*Feb.*] *7* Rainy day: — Thin School — Three of the pupils boarding at Mr. Muzzey's being absent. Lessons pretty well recited through the day. Steward's Auction has interrupted us in some degree. Mr. Tillinghast left us this afternoon: — He has the seeming of a good Mathematical Scholar.

[*Feb.*] *8* Lessons this day, performed with promptitude and accuracy. The School visited by Dr Swift of Nantucket and Mr. Tidd of Lexington. The Question discussed was, "Should pupils be allowed the use of "*keys*" in Arithmetic and Algebra"? Decided in the Negative.

[*Feb.*] *10* Four Scholars absent A.M. Three P.M. Lessons, except Moral and Mental Philosophy, well recited: Algebra, better than usual. Order of the School fair. Model School better than it has been under Miss Sparrell: — but still quite far from perfection. Her manner is too quick and abrupt. Such a manner will ever *seem* to be devoid of Dignity and personal weight.

[*Feb.*] *11* This day rather strongly marked for good and successful lessons and orderly conduct. Matters went better in the Model School than they have done of late.

[*Feb.*] *12* Reviewed in Nat. Philosophy. Recited Algebra; — and read. Exercises generally well performed. Model School quite thin by reason of a prevailing *Cold* among the children.

[*Feb.*] *13* A quiet pleasant and nearly orderly school: — Misses A. have been visited by their parents from B—, and have gone home with them. This is a foolish movement. They have been here just about five weeks! Such movements interrupt the school, and are a serious inconvenience.

[*Feb.*] *14* The ordinary Routine of Exercises: Several Figures explained in Nat. Philosophy for the morning-lesson. The Scholars went to the Black-board, and explained as though they were teaching a class of young pupils. S. E. Burdick explained the air-pump. The Scholars did quite well: Their style, however, wanted familiarity: It was too much as though they were *reciting* to a *Teacher*, rather than explaining to young inquirers. I think it was a *useful* exercise.

Dr Swift visited the school in the P.M. made some remarks at the close of the session, on the importance of Physical exercise —

[*Feb.*] *15* A very west-wind. A few days since, I proposed to the young ladies the subject of keeping a Meteorological Account or Journal at the Normal House; that the suggestion was made to me by the late Governor who also furnished

me with some Blank Forms, and that if any of the young
ladies was willing to volunteer her services for this purpose
she might report to the Principal within twenty-hours, to
that effect. No Report to that point having been received,
I proposed the subject to Mrs P — who purposes to keep
the Journal commencing next month. Finished my remarks
this day on Grammar — Discussion omitted for want of
Time. Yesterday at the close of the Reading lesson, being
called upon by one of the young ladies to define "*Supersti-
tions*" or "*Superstition*", I gave views somewhat at length
on *Apparitions, Ghosts*, and *remarkable appearances;* and the
state of the *departed* — The *design* of the remarks was to
allay fears and correct errors on these points: I hope such
was their *effect*. I feel it my duty to speak when I can throw
light on any subject — consistently with the great principles
of my connexion with this Institution. I wish much to
steer clear of all sectarian and party views, ways and measures: but on great *principles* to *speak freely*.

[*Feb.*] *17* Finished the subject of Grammar in my Lecture
on Saturday. This day — a very dull day — poor lessons,
and ill recited. Seldom have I closed a day with less satisfaction. It seems as though my scholars were doing little
and that to little purpose. Lesson after lesson unprepared; and scarcely one performed by all the class in decent
style.

[*Feb.*] *18* This has proved a better day than yesterday
far. Lessons generally prepared and performed in satisfactory style. The Model School is somewhat confused and
disorderly. Visited by Rev. Mr. Sullivan. Examined and
returned the Journals; — not quite so good as the Entries
of last week, yet pretty fair. The young ladies return to the
Normal House.

[*Feb.*] *19* This day Exercises went quite well. Yesterday,
for the first time I succeeded in freezing water by Evaporation by the Air Pump.

[*Feb.*] *20* The Exercises A.M. very good. P.M. *middling*.
Geography 2d Class poor. Geometry, Do. I think it would
do no great honor to an ordinary District School to exhibit
such performances as we had this afternoon in the 2d Class
in Geography. I gave the young ladies to understand that

I thought we ought to do better or give up the study and attend to something else, and not waste our time.

In connexion with the Reading Lesson this afternoon, the Moral influence of Balls and Theatres came up for discussion: I think there was a general agreement with the Spirit of the Piece read, that the influence of these modes of Amusement, was bad. Dea. James in company with two or three young folks visited the School.

[*Feb.*] *21* Lessons generally prompt and good. Some in each class in Algebra, failed. Recitations in Geography better than ordinary: but I think this Branch not thriving much in School: neither *Grammar.* These Branches call for Reform.

[*Feb.*] *22d* Washington's Birth-day.

Exercises in Moral Philosophy — Algebra, Arithmetic Reading in the Scriptures, & Discussion — Recitations good: The discussion dull, or indifferent.

[*Feb.*] *24* A fair day *within* doors and without The Recitation in Nat. History led to a discussion in regard to the comparative merits of a Meat and a vegetable diet. Most of the young ladies apparently coinciding with the Author Smellie in the matter. – – School visited by Mrs. Munroe of this town; and Misses Whitcomb, Munroe, and Robbins; in number 5. Who were pleased to express themselves much gratified.

[*Feb.*] *25* This day the School was visited by Miss Reed a teacher from East-Cambridge. The Exercises in the forenoon fair; the afternoon, rather dull.

[*Feb.*] *26* Our purpose was this forenoon to do much by way of Review in Algebra; but so great was the difficulty which the young ladies found in regard to the Nat. Philosophy-Lesson, (it being on the Theory of Music) that I spent almost the whole forenoon in explaining it. This subject, I think, has intrinsic difficulty, and I was not surprised to learn that the lesson was not prepared. The Class-Book, moreover, prepared by Mr. Johnson of Philadelphia on Nat. Philosophy, is in some of its portions, obscure in its phraseology, and incorrect in its Statements. I have never yet found the subject of Music in its Theory, explained in a clear lucid manner. Dobson's Encyclopedia is the most full on the subject of any of the works I have seen.

[*Feb.*] *27* Spent more time than usual this day in conversing with my Pupils, remarking upon the portion read from the Scriptures, and in answering queries. I hope the time was not unprofitably spent, but sometimes I am apprehensive I spend too much of the time in this way. Recitations were generally full and prompt.

[*Feb.*] *28* The Ordinary Exercises and about the usual Style. Schools visited by Mrs. Spaulding and daughter, and by Mrs Reed.

[*Feb.*] *29* Nat. Philosophy, Reading the Scriptures, and Lecture on Arithmetic. The Scholars are in the practice of laying Propositions and queres on the Table for the Principal to answer. The quere came up this day whether it was consistent to read letters or papers in the schoolroom in study-hours! The Principal decided at once that it was not. In this decision, it is believed, most of the young ladies concurred. And that all did not, is, I think, a striking illustration how much the judgment may be influenced by the Inclinations, feelings, sentiments.

It has been mainly my aim to make my school a *practical* exhibition of my Theory; and to have the young ladies, Normalites, *be & do* as they would require of *their* Pupils, when they become *Teachers* I have sometimes thought, that others might doubt whether there should not be some relaxation from this Principle. But it seems to me that a Normal School should be a Pattern in *all* Things.

March 2d This day very pleasant. Lessons generally well recited. School visited by Mr. Forbes teacher of the Public High School in Medford. Misses Stetson and Wellington of Medford, and by Messrs. D. Wellington, J. Smith, and Lathrop in Lexington.

[*March*] *3d* This day the Exercises performed in middling style, except Reading and Algebra of the first Class. —

For one thing, the day is remarkable. It is the *first time*, that the Teacher has had the unhappiness to receive a short abrupt answer from any of the Pupils of the Normal School, or to witness any unhandsome manifestations from them.

To day, I have to record the first exception to this uniform propriety, in the *manner* and *intonation* of one of the Young Ladies. In review of it (*sic*) seems to me, that no provocation was given to justify or palliate any such demeanor.

[*March*] *4* Purposed this day P.M. (Wednesday) to meet the Reading Class, but did [not] in consequence of being called upon to go to Weston. Lessons hardly up to *Mediocrity*. Heard that the young ladies of the Normal House had again been disorderly — in regard to hours and noise. This greatly discour[a]ges me.

[*March*] *5* Teachers changed in the Model School. This comes in the regular Course of things; for they change every month. Nothing remarkable in school.

[*March*] All things went pretty well this day in matters of Order, as also in lessons with the exception of Moral Philosophy: — I have discovered, that the 2d and 3d Class[es] in the Model have done very little in Arithmetic and Geography.

[*March*] *7* On this day of the week (Saturday) we usually have a discussion. To-day the question was "Is it expedient to continue these Discussions". The question elicited free Remarks: Two of the young ladies wrote out their thoughts and read them. This and the other exercise of Reading, Nat. Philosophy & Physiology, went off pretty well. The Discussion resulted in an *almost* unanimous vote to continue them. I have thought favorably of them, and am decidedly in favor of continuing them yet a while longer. The Questions generally relate to their Future Calling, Teaching: The Exercise will lead the Pupils to think, to *arrange* their thoughts, to express their ideas with propriety; and it breaks up the monotony of the School-room, and adds interest and variety to its scenes and duties.

[*March*] *9* Lessons (except Nat. Philosophy) pretty fair. Heard that the Committee on Education had reported to the Legislature in favor of abolishing the Board of Education and the Normal School! I see not how this can be done until the Grant already made by the Legislature and the Donation by Mr. D. have been expended. Contracts have already been entered into, for one two and three years.

[*March*] *10* — The School keep[s] on the "*even tenor of its way*".

to see more, that existing —
the character of my inquiry.
I am glad to see them know more
plainly their individual
peculiar characteristics. A little
observation would show the children
that we have no block in —
mould by which all are cast)

1840
March 11   So that there may be insufficiency of
character in the "preserved teachers"
provide here a way & a single, a single
time; but state trouble just have it
so unyielding and restrictive as to the
child ruthful them will in individual
developments.

— 11,12
report to-day rather heavy and dull:
School visited by Misses Merriam &
a young lady & those name was not
imperfecthod, I who by Esq; Shelton and
his Brother.

— " 13   This day entire I spent — in the
Model School. I took the whole in
direction and management thereof —
into my own hands, and through —
the flexibility in the presque of the
Normalite, that the teste might
have the benefit of my & their
life in teaching. The Boys prepare
to my satisfaction; and flocked to the
Benefit of pictures.

— " 14   Acted Pro tempore this day — went —
to Boston. Returned — to which in
inquiries in regard to matters affer-
ting the character of the Normal
School. Found and saw things both
favourable and unfavourable to the
same. I know not what, it is en-
curies in their ignorance, as in their
wickedness, interesting attempts.

[*March*] *11* Recitations in "Combe's Constitution of Man", Nat. Philosophy, Arithmetic, Algebra, Mental Philosophy & Nat. History. I see more, the distinctive character of my pupils. I am glad to see them and show plainly their individual & peculiar characteristics. A little observation would show the visiter that we have no Block or mould by which all are cast, so that there may be uniformity of character in the "Prepared Teachers". I would have a way, a mode, a system; but still I would not have it so unyielding and restrictive as to *preclude* rather than aid individual developments.

[*March*] *12* Lessons today rather heavy and dull. School visited by Mrs. Merriam & a young lady whose name was not understood; also by Esq. Stetson and his Brother.

[*March*] *13* This day entire I spent in the Model School. I took the whole instruction and management thereof into my own hands, and taught the Modelites in the presence of the Normalites; that the latter might have the benefit of my Example in teaching. The Day passed to my satisfaction and I hope to the Benefit of Parties.

[*March*] *14* Had no session this day: — went to Boston; in part, to make inquiries in regard to matters affecting the character of the Normal School. Heard and saw things both favorable and *un*favorable to the same. I know not what, its enemies in their ignorance, or in their wickedness, may attempt.

[*March*] *16* This day a poor lesson in Nat. Philosophy: other lessons about mediocrity. Afternoon lessons demand more attention; of this I have frequently reminded the Pupils. They are not sufficiently particular to make themselves correct in small matters. School visited by Mr. Smith (Josiah) of this town. Miss Smith his daughter entered School. Tomorrow I am expecting a Visit from Mr. Barnard Secretary of the Board of Education in Connecticut.

March 17 A Fall of *snow* through the day. School well attended and lessons recited; at least in respect to some of the Scholars. There are one or two, who seldom, if ever, recite well; and of one or two, whom I have placed among my best pupils, it must be said, if they have not fallen off, they have certainly made no improvement in their style of

Reciting. It is expected the School will soon lose some of its members. I hope it may not lose any of its character, but that it may be continually advancing to higher and higher degrees of Excellence.

[*March*] *18* This day very fair lessons and conduct Nat. Philosophy, Combe Con. Arithmetic, Algebra, Nat. His. Met the Class this afternoon for Reading. I think this Exercise promises to be useful.

[*March*] *19* This day forms an Epoch in the history of the School. We have been visited [by] seven gentlemen; viz, Messrs Wheeler (two) Adams, Hartwell, Foster from Lincoln; Mr. Crowell from Boston (Ed. of the Watchman) Coleman of Andover (Teacher) and Mr. Barnard of Hartford Conn. (Secretary of the B. E. [i.e., Board of Education] for Conn. Schools. The School sustained itself pretty fairly; and, on the whole, I should think the Impression made upon visitors, was favorable. The School was addressed by Messrs Barnard & Wheeler. In the Remarks of both Gentlemen, the School seemed much interested.

This evening we have heard the favorable result of the discussion in our own Legislature; in which a Movement has been made to abolish the B. of Ed. [*i.e.*, Massachusetts State Board of Education] & the Nor. Schools

[*March*] *20.* Had a tug this day with my Class in Algebra in attempting to explain to them Colburn's Analysis of the Method of extracting the square root. This [is] always a severe Trial to Scholars, and sometimes discouraging. Lessons generally well done. I made several Remarks to the School on visit to the School yesterday.

Had a very pleasant Visit from Mr. Stetson of Medford; who addressed the School in a very serious, instructive and interesting manner. — I think these visits do us good; especially such as that of Mr. Stetson.

[*March*] *21* This has been a very pleasant, and, I hope not an unprofitable day. Exercises, Reading in Abbots Teacher, discussion of the Question. Is it well for young persons connected with a literary seminary to mingle freely with the social amusements of the Place?" and an Experimental Lecture. These discussions consume a good deal of time but I think are attended with good; and I am [not] certain, but that they are the very best way in which a portion of our time could be spent. They set the pupils thinking, draw out sentiments and give the Principal a better opportunity to become acquainted with the real character and purposes and feelings of his pupils — Miss Julia A. Smith took her seat in school to-day.

March 23d School opened as [usual] with Reading the Scriptures, Prayer and singing. Some remarks were made by the Principal. Exercises generally good throughout the day. In the afternoon, the Reading was from Abbot's Teacher, attended with (I hope) some profitable discussion. I cannot agree with all Abbot's views. How can a Teacher, (as Mr. A. recommends) on turning the Key of the School-Room door, dismiss all anxieties, thought and labors in regard to the School.

[*March*] *24* Began to snow early in the day: a severe storm. I suppose the Equinoctial as those say who believe in the matter. Gave out the Journals and made remarks. Recitations went well. Held no session in the P.M. giving the Principal and the pupils an opportunity to attend the Examination of the centre District School. School visited by Mrs. Green of N. Bedford.

[*March*] *25* This day we pursued the even Tenor of our way. Nothing remarkable. I called out the classes in Algebra and Arithmetic giving them questions from other books than their Text-Books for application. I think I shall do more at this mode of testing their Knowledge. My pupils do not pay attention enough to the Didactic Art. They learn the Principle & the Mode of operating, but do not so well succeed in clearly stating them. I must press this matter more upon them

[*March*] *26* The lessons pretty good. Very good Geometry-lesson. Moral Philosophy Omitted. School visited by Mr. Norwood Damon of West-Cambridge.

March 27 This day finished reading Abbot's Teacher. This [is] one of the best Manuals on School-Instruction in print. The Moral Spirit it breathes is excellent. In the Course of Reading we discussed its rules, directions and principles with great freedom and I think the Exercises have been profitable.

[*March*] *28* Exercises this forenoon (Saturday) have been (after opening the School with reading the Scriptures, singing, and prayer as usual) Questions in Arithmetic and Algebra, reading in the Scriptures, singing or rather short music lesson, and discussion of the Question, Can a person be truly polite in the common acceptation of the term, and yet perfect[ly] conscientious and sincere?" – – Then followed and (*sic*) experimental Lecture, and the Session closed. The week, on the whole, has been good.

[*March*] *30* — After the School was opened, the Principal read some Regulations for the Model School; — heard the lesson in Nat. Philosophy — Arithmetic, Algebra and Mental Philosophy; Recitation in Combe omitted.

P.M. Reading Spelling and Grammar. Mor. Philosophy and Nat. History, omitted. The scholars do not seem to me to take interest enough in the Exercises of the afternoon. — I have long felt this to be true — and for this reason they make slow progress —

March 31 The Movements of the School smooth and equable. Lessons fair.

April 1. Wednesday. Yesterday I gave out questions in Arithmetic and Algebra for morning lessons. The scholars generally had pretty good success. After taking their answers, I left the school pretty much to take care of themselves, whilst I attended to, philosophical experiments with Mr. Chamberlain, who had come out for that purpose.

A short session. Mr. Chamberlain came up from Boston to examine & repair Apparatus, and experiment in Philosophy. Left the School to themselves a while. I believe things went on pretty fair.

[*April*] *2 Thursday* Fast-day. No school.

[*April*] *3* Spent the day in experimenting in Nat. Philosophy — before both Schools in the Lower Room. Experiments generally successful; & I trust the day was profitably spent. Both Schools attended though it was a matter entirely optional — Mr. Forbes and Miss Wetherbee from Medford visited the School.

[*April*] *4 Saturday.* After a short Morning session, hearing the Arithmetical lesson and Combe's Constitution. The rest of the Forenoon was spent in experimenting in Nat Philosophy. This day Miss Swift left the school on account of ill-health, with much honor and to the great regret of her teacher & school-mates.

April 6 Experiments in Nat. Philosophy all day; quite successful — Model School Suspended.

[*April*] *7* This forenoon held school from 8 to 12. Afternoon, session continued until half-past 3 — recess half an hour; after which I went into the Room below to set in order my apparatus, leaving the young ladies to hold a session of one hour by themselves.

[*April*] *8* Recitations in Arithmetic Algebra & Combe's Constitution — The Exercises in Arithmetic and Algebra consisted of questions given out yesterday for solution. The classes, generally, were quite successful. Held no Session in the Afternoon, being Wednesday.

[*April*] *9* The Lessons today about middling. Geography poor. It has been a dull and unsatisfactory day to me. It may be, that the fault is my own. That things go wrong in School, I verily believe is often the fault of teachers. I did not succeed in securing the attention of the class in Arithmetic this Morning. When Teachers do not succeed in securing attention, they are apt to blame the scholars, when the fault is their *own dull manner*. Two girls visited the School, this day, whose names I did not learn. Misses Phinney in the Model School.

[*April*] *10* This day — nothing distinctive remembered —

[*April*] *11* *Saturday*. Attended to Reading — Arithmetic, and discussion of the question, 'Is the Model School answering its object? A pretty interesting discussion; in which the different views of the young ladies in regard to the [subject] were developed. There was more diversity of opinion than I expected; & some declarations at which I was surprised. Those, who are most interested in the school, I believe, were generally of the affirmative; of which there was a large Majority. Some had mistaken the object of the Model School and, of course, misjudged. The object of the School is to aid the young teacher in practice. To give her an opportunity to apply her theoretic principles, — to try her skill and strength. It is not supposed to be any thing more than a *near approximation* to what a school, a *district school is*, or should be.

We are approaching the end of our 3d Term and 1st Year. Several of the Pupils are to leave: as many as five or six. I know not of more than 2 or 3 that will be added. I have no applications from abroad, or at a distance. Those, that are to leave, are among the best scholars. The prospect looks dark and discouraging. I cannot think of remaining connected with the school much longer without the prospect of an increase of scholars —

[*April*] *13* Took up the Report of the Secretary of the Board of Education on School-houses; and talked a while upon the same; went into the Model School — after which, took up Arithmetic and Algebra. P.M. Algebra, Arithmetic and Nat. Philosophy. Rather a dull day. All feel saddened and subdued at the thought of parting — some to return no more.

[*April*] *14* Last day of the Term. Tried some Experiments in Galvanism, Magnetism & Pneumatics — Examined a little in Brigham on mental Excitement, & in Moral Philosophy — returned the Journals & Themes. The young [ladies] read — some, pieces selected; others, original pieces. School Visited by Messrs. Putnam, Muzzey and Newhall — The former of Roxbury, two last from Cambridge. Afternoon Spent in *Examination* of the Model School. School did fairly. Present twenty, to twenty-five visiters besides the Normalites.

Chapter IV

The Fourth Term, May 1–August 11, 1840

1840 May 1 This day commences the first Term of the 2d year. Eight new scholars admitted; six having left at the close of last term. The number, at present, connected with the School, is twenty-six. — Made some Remarks assigned lessons to old classes and to new; — examined the applicants for admission. They all passed. Heard a Class in Algebra and in Arithmetic — Gave out subjects for themes and for discussion. Candidates appeared fair — greatest deficiency in Grammar and Geography; particularly in the latter. — Prospects for numbers not very flattering; and for scholarship, not equal to last term. Present twenty-two scholars.

[May] 2 Saturday — after school was opened — The Recitations were in Algebra, Arithmetic Reading in the Scriptures — and a Discussion of the Question — Is it expedient to employ the *older* scholars in school to teach the *younger?* decided in the *negative*. Some remarks from the Principal followed, and then the school closed —

[May] 4 After opening the School; — made remarks upon lessons, classification & exercise; — then adjourned to the Model school in which spent the forenoon. P.M. Heard Reading, Spelling, Enunciation, Arithmetic, Nat. History, and Mor. Philosophy. Remarks — School closed

May 5 Pupils all present, — 24. Exercises as yesterday. Style of Reciting among the new comers is quite imperfect — It shows that they [have] indeed much to learn. They are evidently quite unused to giving abstracts and connected statements of what they have read and studied. They tell me very few definitions of words: — and very little of any thing that they have read. But I think there is a fair share of Intellect among them, and that will improve by training and exercise, and do well by and by.

[May] 6 This day the Lessons all fair and good — Mr.

Locke called at the door. Visited the Model School. Miss Sparrell entered from Salem.

[*May*] 7 School making some progress; Visited by Rev Mr Folsome — Mrs Muzzey daughter, and Mrs. — friend of Mrs. Muzzey. Scholars regular and attentive.

[*May*] 8 *Saturday*. Reading in the Scriptures and diss (*sic*) Geography, and lecture on Botany by Mrs. P. Present 25 Pupils.

[*May*] 11 *Monday* —

[*May*] 12 *Tuesday* Returned the Journals to the Scholars — Made remarks upon their Themes & Journals. Gave directions, how they should manage in order to have something new and various every day.

The pupils, who have recently entered, in their Style and Manner of Reciting are greatly inferior to those who have been long connected with it. This exemplifies the effect of perseverance & Training. They have talent enough, but are deficient in Knowledge, & suffer from the *neglect*, or rather *want*, of early discipline.

May 13 Exercises—Reading of Select Pieces by the First Class — Arithmetic, Geography — Abbot's Teacher, Mental Philosophy & Botany. The Botanic recite in the Model-School-room We make some progress — but there is much to do for those, who have recently entered. I am favorably impressed with their apparent [interest] in their Studies, and trust they will succeed.

[*May*] 14 A very pleasant day — most of the lessons well prepared in the first Class — But few of the Second Class seem yet to understand *how* to study, or recite lessons. Patience and perseverance, I trust, will accomplish the work.

[*May*] 15 *Friday* — Warm and pleasant — P.M. Rain Exercises Geography Anc. & Mod. Arithmetic, Grammar, Ment. Philosophy, Cons. of Man. Ment. Excitement — Reading, Spelling, Orthoepy, & Rhetoric. Performance Fair — School visited by Mr. Oakes and Family of East-Cambridge.

[*May*] 16 *Saturday* — School opened as usual with devotional Exercises — Then followed a Lecture from the Principal on Composition; to which succeeded an Exercise in

Abbot's Teacher, Geography Combe's Constitution of Man — Written Remarks from Members of the Class in Mor. Philosophy, and Recitation in Botany. School closed soon after 12 —

[*May*] *18* Monday very warm. School visited by Jos. E. Worcester; also, by N. Barney & wife & son and M. G. Swain. The School this term is divided into two general classes — viz one composed chiefly of those who entered School this term — and 2d of those who had been connected with the School before. The Former are attending chiefly to the Common Branches; — the latter, to Astronomy, Geometry, Algebra, Arithmetic, Nat. History & Mor. Philosophy one week; and Mental Philosophy, Combe's Constitution, Brigham Ment Excitement. Anc. Geography — Rhetoric, and Pol. Economy, the next week: reciting three exercises in the forenoon and three in the afternoon. On Wednesday & Saturday A.M. We have Botany & lecture & some extra Exercises —

Tuesday [*May*] *19* School visited by Miss E. Rogers pupil now teaching in Billerica and Mr. —. School Exercises as usual. One new scholar added. Miss Mary E. Fiske —

[*May*] *20* It is a great detriment to the School that the Pupils come so ill prepared in the Common Branches. Some of them seem to have been out of school until they have grown rusty; and it requires much time and labour to scour them up and make them bright. We need to spend more time on Exercises relating to the appropriate duties and qualifications of a teacher. My feelings and opinions about the Normal School are variable. We want more pupils and we want them more advanced; and the *public* must say they are needed. Schools are all running into Sectarian Institutions, and what stands on common ground no body cares about.

[*May*] *21* School Exercises rather dull. Not so good Order and Attention as have generally been maintained in School, of this I must speak tomorrow, — or rather advert to it.

May 22d

[*May*] *23d* *Saturday* — Reading, Lecture, Botany — Some signs of Disorder. —

[May] 25 Monday —

[May] 26 Tuesday — A.M. The School visited by Mr. Shaw accompanied by another gentleman, from Bridgewater. At noon I dismissed School until Thursday —

[May] 27 No School —

[May] 28 A warm day; and one of the least successful for studies & lessons which we have had this term. Many deficient — imperfect Performances in every part of the School-room. I *never knew* a *good* School next day after a holiday. But I have something that weighs more upon [my] heart than imperfect Lessons — ; it is indications of slight inattention or disregard, to school-order — This is worse than *any thing*, or *all* things else.

Miss Payson from the West, visited the School.

[May] 29 A cool and pleasant day: Lessons and conduct good.

Last night died Rev. O. A. Dodge, the best friend of the Normal School in all this Vicinity.

[May] 30 Saturday — pleasant day — good lessons —

After opening the school — Remarks by the Principal — chiefly on points of School-order — Mental Arithmetic — Recitation in Combe's Constitution by reading Abstracts — Reading Composition — and Botany —

June 1 Monday — School opened auspiciously; and proceeded well — Model-School under the superintendence of Miss Wyman — with the assistance of others.

[June] 2 Returned the Journals with Remarks — heard the various lessons: but the classes and lessons, and duties are becoming so numerous, that I find it quite difficult to attend to all as they should be attended to. I can do little more than give hints and suggestions. School visited, this day, Mr. Wellington, teacher of this town; through whose instrumentality and advice, several young ladies have been induced to join the School.

[June] 3 Wednesday — Remarks — The Lesson in Abbot occupied one hour & a half — a very profitable Lesson — Mental Arithmetic — Botany and Reading —

More absences than usual in consequence of several of the pupils having leave to go to Boston.

[June] 4 Scholars all present but one; — lessons quite

prompt and good; — School orderly and all things agreeable.

[*June*] 5 ⎰ *Friday*
[*June*] 6 ⎱ *Saturday*   School very pleasant and lessons good.

Saturday was chiefly occupied in reading a piece in the School Journal on the Subject of Managing Schools for Small children; particularly recommending the use of the slate in teaching the pupils to read, spell and write, as well as cipher. — I thought I could [not] do the School a greater Service than to read the whole of said article making my comments as I went along. I think it was heard with interest and profit.

June 8   Monday — This would have been a very pleasant school day — had it not been for the sickness and absence of one of the pupils, and the very ill Reports which I have heard from the Model School. The Teachers, Normalites, ask me what they shall do to keep order. I answer, the Secret of Keeping good Order lies in your own breast — and you must bring it out. The Power lieth within you and you must bring it out ". It will appear in your *looks* and *gestures* and every *movement* as well as in your *words*. If it cannot be found here it can be found *no-where*.

[*June*] 9   *Tuesday* — One of the most nearly perfect days I ever knew. It is June, the Glory of the year   Vegetation is culminating to *perfection*.

Within Doors — Lessons and Conduct good.   School visited by Messrs. Quimby from Pennsylvania; one a teacher.

[*June*] ⎰ 10   *Wednesday*   Short session in the morning.
[*June*] ⎱ 11   Many of the Young Ladies went to the Dedication of the U.M.H. [Universalist Meeting House] in East Village.

Thursday all things went quite fairly — remarked at length in the opening of the school to the young ladies on various Topics —

[*June*] *12   Friday* — Lessons generally good except the Eng. Grammar Lesson. Miss N. though a sensible girl, never has been and I think, never will be a good performer!

[*June*] *13   Saturday* — Remarks — Lecture — Abbot's Teacher Discussion — Mental Arithmetic — Botany.

The Question Discussed is — "Is it expedient to have

Compositions read in School". Affirmative 5 — Negative; 14.

June 15 — A pleasant and, I trust, profitable day. Lessons generally well prepared — and promptly recited.

A young lady Miss B. from Boston examined and admitted into the School. She has attended good schools in Boston; Andrew's and Robinson's: but her examination was far from being splendid — More than ⅔ of the Candidates seem very deficient in Geography and Arithmetic.

[*June*] *16* Exercises generally fair — excepted Nat. History and Mor. Philosophy. I have not done enough of late about teaching *Teachers how to teach.* I must call them more to the Board, & let them practise. They want language They must recite more in the way and manner of "explaining to others. — The scholars, who have recently entered the school, have yet much to do in regard to learning the Common Branches to say nothing about the Art of *teaching.* Patience & Perseverance must effect the business.

[*June*] *17 Wednesday* — An interesting lesson in Abbot's Teacher — Mental Arithmetic Rhetoric — Botany — Algebra —

Must do more about teaching Teachers how to teach. This is the object of the Institution; and this, we must not lose sight of.

[*June*] *18* Ordinary occurrences and events — ordinary trials, labours, joys & success. – – I must go into Model School next week & teach them all day. I think next week to put in only a Superintendent and *one* assistant This will put the school more under the care of the Normals; They will feel more responsibility and endure more labour. — This is experimental; but I trust it will be found an improvement. — It is only by trying various ways that I can find out what is best – – –

[*June*] *19 Friday.* Ordinary Events & occurrences – –

[*June*] *20 Saturday* — Remarks — Made an epistolary Communication to the School on a great variety of matters — read a lecture on Composition — a lesson in Abbot's Teacher Mental Arithmetic and Botany. Discussion and Reading omitted. Met a Class for Reading in the Afternoon — The Tact at Teaching is very much a personal affair — A person may have much Knowledge and be a very good scholar — and have age and experience, & yet be a very indifferent *teacher* —

[*June*] *22d Monday* — Mondays are generally poor days for lessons in schools. So I have found it at least, in all the schools, which I have kept. So it has proved to-day. We have only rubbed and worried through. I hope it will be better tomorrow. —

The Class of Scholars are generally very backward. There are some, who seemed possessed of pretty good natural abilities, but they have had but little cultivation; and their attainments are small. It seems to me it will take all of the three years should they stay so long to give them a decent preparation for the Common Branches. They have come to learn the Common Branches rather than to learn to *Teach* them.

23d June. 29 Scholars in School. All very pleasant — but most of them quite backward; and though pupil and teacher be never so diligent, it will be a very difficult matter to make them good teachers within the Compass of one year.

[*June*] *24 Wednesday* — I have suggested to my scholars the idea of one session from 8 A.M. to 2 P.M. each day in the week; on the ground that it may be favorable to scholars living at a distance. The suggestion strikes them favorably. I am inclined to try it, though I am apprehensive it may prove unfavorable to *lessons*. The Model School, also, may suffer in consequence. Should it prove unfavorable, we must return to the old Plan.

[*June*] *25* Cool and pleasant day. Lessons fair School visited by Mrs Davis of Bangor, and her little daughter.

[*June*] *26* Spent all the day in the Model School — which I taught myself, in presence of the Normal pupils. This I occasionally do with a view to exemplify and carry into practice my own Principles; as well as the better to ascertain what is the state of the School and how the young ladies are getting along as teachers.

The [school] was quite orderly; but did not exhibit so much evidence of improvement as I was hoping for, especially in Reading. I shall next month commit [it to] the care and instruction of a superintendent and one assistant.

This will give them more to do while in the school, and bring round their turns severally less frequently. I trust this will be an Improvement; but time will show

June 27 — Saturday. Mental Arithmetic — Grammar — Discussion — Lecture — Botany. — The question discussed was, Is it expedient so to altar (*sic*) the School as to have but *one* session a day from 8 A.M. to 2 P.M., every day in the week except Sunday. A great Majority in favor of the change, although the vote was not unanimous. The Experiment will be made beginning next Monday. I am very doubtful of its success — Very unexpectedly to me, one of my pupils expressed an unwillingness to go into the Model School. This was wholly unexpected to me. I think she should have merged her own preferences in the interest and usages of the school. I know not whether I shall press the matter; but such movements will not tend to make state and relations of the [school] in any degree more pleasant. I much regret it.

[*June*] *29 Monday* — Commenced on the plan of having but one session a day. It has operated pretty well; the lessons seemed somewhat crowded.

The weather has been exceedingly warm. Lessons pretty fair.

Spent an hour in the Model School — The School quite orderly. It is now going on under the care of Miss A. Locke with one assistant Miss Burdick.

[*June*] *30* A very warm day; Not able to get through my Exercises; This is an objection to the new plan. Whether it will do, remains to be proved.

1840 July 1 Wednesday — Astronomy, Arithmetic (Mental and written) Abbot's Teacher, Moral Philosophy, Algebra, & Botany. —

Astronomy, poorly performed, — other Lessons middling. I must press the matter of learning the Art of Teaching: particularly on the Second Class.

[*July*] *2 Thursday* — Jogging on in the even tenor of our way: Are not yet able to get through all the lessons on the new Plan. But I think we may do it — if lessons are very promptly prepared. Some of the new scholars seem indolent and heavy: They give but little promise as Teachers.

[*July*] *3* It is just one year today since the Normal commenced with *three pupils*. We now have 29. The increase has been very slow. I hope the progress has been certain. But I am suffering grievous disappointment, and I fear the school will suffer, in the not very successful experiment which two Normalites are making in school keeping in this village.

Messrs. Chs Tidd and Simonds visited the School.

[*July*] *4* *Saturday* — Anniversary of American Independence. No School.

[*July*] *6* *Monday*. Experienced the usual effects of Holidays — Bad Lessons. School visited by Mr. Thurston, the gentleman who is preaching here to the Unitarian Society.

[*July*] *7* *Tuesday*. Lessons better than yesterday, particularly in Physiology. I trust they will all learn the art of studying and reciting — I enjoin patience and perseverance.

School visited by Messrs. Pray and Bumstead of the Boston School Committee. They came up to visit chiefly the Model School.

July 8 Wednesday — Exercises in Arithmetic Geography, Combe's Constitution, Abercrombie's Philosophy, Mental Arithmetic, Abbot's Teacher, Simpson & Botany and Reading. Lessons fair. Remarks in the morning — School visited by Misses Damon, Stodder & Estabrook

[*July*] *9*. *Thursday* — Large number of poor lessons — and some absences. The *day*-lessons will be poor unless the young ladies — pupils are willing thoroughly to prepare their morning-lessons before they come into school. On this subject I have plainly and Kindly commented; and I hope it will do good.

[*July*] *10* *Friday* — A fair and pleasant day. Lessons generally prompt and correct. Conduct and order — with the exception in one or two instances of undue activity of mirthfulness.

[*July*] *11* *Saturday* — A very pleasant day.

Exercises — Lecture, Reading Composition — Reading Scriptures, Abbot's Teacher — Grammar — Mental Arithmetic, Physiology & Discussion.

[*July*] *13* *Monday* — No Entry — Mr. May of South Scituate — called at the Normal House, but did not go into school —

[*July*] *14 Tuesday* — Gave back the Themes and Journals — made remarks upon them and also upon various points of school order to the amount of about one hour. I took occasion to express at great length my deep regret and settled disapprobation at the palpable & long continued departure from order in the School Room and elsewhere. Some of the young ladies are guilty of such departures from good order and honest, upright conduct, as are truly *painful*. Such as offering up Themes for Composition which another person wrote — reciting lessons from books, Slate, or paper which they have not learned; and leaving their seats and talking when they have no leave. — I hope for better times; but I am greatly disappointed and tried in this matter. – – The First Class have finished Brigham, Smellie's Nat. History, nearly finished Wayland's Philosophy — and Colburn's Arithmetic: — The Second have commenced Algebra, & Combe's Physiology: Of this last they make a a good deal of complaint; say, it is hard and uninteresting. But this I am persuaded arises from their not being accustomed to study: — of course, it can not long endure.

[*July*] *15 Wednesday* — Remarked upon the manner of opening the school —

Adopted for the first time, the practice of having the scriptures read by the young ladies — one at time. I think this may serve to keep up their interest better in it. Miss O'Connor read this morning. – – The forenoon was spent chiefly in reviewing studies — The Exercises have been pretty successful. After recess the first Class read — The School was reviewed in Arithmetic, Algebra and Astronomy. I hope my next Entry will look a little fairer than this —

July 16 Thursday — Very warm — Lessons have gone quite well, but I have been impatient — I have more fault to find with myself than with my pupils – – We are reviewing Nat. History. In Astronomy I much regret that we must pass over some of the abstruse mathematical parts, in which some of the most important principles are demonstrated, because the Class are not sufficiently acquainted with Geometry and Trigonometry to make them intelligible.

[*July*] *17* A very warm day; but every thing went off in good style. School [visited by] Dr. Jewett, Temp. Agent & Mr. Davis —

[*July*] *18 Saturday* — Exercises were Reading, Lecture, Abbot's Teacher, Discussion, Mental Arithmetic and Botany. Session closed at Noon.

[*July*] *20* Cool day — Lessons well recited —

[*July*] *21 Tuesday* — Lessons well recited. & *all* recited, which has not often been done since the school has been on the plan of *one* session a day. The Lesson of the 2d Class in Physiology was uncommonly brisk and correct.

[*July*] *22 Wednesday* — Review in "Combe's Con. of man" Abercrombie's Mental Philosophy, — Geography, Arithmetic, Brigham's Mental Excitement, & Physiology.

The Lessons middling. Session held only until 12. Botany Class recited at ½ past 12. Went to Billerica to visit Miss Rogers's school, but unfortunate found it was vacation with her.

[*July*] *23d* This day the school visited by Rev. Mr. Putnam of Middlebury & his two daughters and Miss Locke of West-Cambridge — Lessons quite well recited — Three postponed until tomorrow.

Friday & Saturday — [*July*] *24 & 25* No Entries —

Monday & Tuesday July 27 & 28 — School visited by Messrs May, Stetson and Alcott. Conversations from these gentlemen on Peace, Non-Resistance and Transcendentalism; quite interesting and instructive. School visited by Mrs. Lathrop & Lady, whose name I cannot recall. Our sessions have been long — and somewhat exhausting. I am a little apprehensive it may prove too much for the physical strength of the Pupils — These are days and seasons to be remembered. We may not in the Normal School *soon*, if *ever*, see their like again.

July 29 Wednesday — This day, in consequence of the interruptions of the two past days, was not devoted to Reviewing, but to the regular lessons chiefly. The lessons were quite well performed, and the School orderly. I am querying whether it would not be best to say to certain pupils, what I think about the prospect of their becoming teachers. They certainly give very little hope of it to others at least to me. Miss A. Locke left School.

July 30 Thursday I am certain that some of my pupils must have more industry, pay better attention — or learn easier and faster, else in *three* years they will **not be prepared** to teach. There are three or four very doubtful Cases. But I must persevere, & do what I can.

Mr. & Mrs. Brown from Boston, visited the School. Lesson in Moral Philosophy, miserably done.

*Friday	July 31* Very unwell all day, and have much reason to fear that I have not manifested the proper temper under all my trials. A teacher teaches as much by his *manner* of doing and speaking as in any way. Indeed a man may nullify all his precepts and Counsels by an unhappy manner. Impatience is nowhere a very amiable or desirable attribute — it is especially repulsive in a teacher. Mr — Alcott gently rebuked the Principal for impatience. This may not have been very agreeable; nevertheless it may have been strictly Just. It is not often, I suppose, that a teacher receives a rebuke from a visiter in the presence of his own school.

*Saturday	Aug. 1* — Health much improved. A very rainy day. Thin school — Few lessons quite well recited. We have had today a striking exemplification of the fact, how paralizing to the interests of a school the *absence* of members is. Several lessons of yesterday deferred were recited. Subject for discussion deferred until next week.

Monday — Aug. 3d Matters and things wagged pretty much in the old Way. School visited by Miss Phinney.

Tuesday Aug. 4 Held much Conversation with my pupils on various Topics — especially Physiology and Matrimony. I gave them to understand that I thought there were but very few of them, who did not violate the Laws of Physiology in the matter of tight-lacing. I hope, it may do good.

Aug. 5 Wednesday. A dull dog-day morning. Warm. Lessons not very promptly recited. And School order not well observed. On the whole, the day has not been satisfactory to me. My pupils, or rather some of them, are very backward, and we have to spend too much time on the elementary branches. But were they ever so much advanced, we could not have happy schools — without good behavior & good order.

[Aug.] 6 Thursday. — A very pleasant day and a very pleasant school. One of my dear pupils, who thought she did wrong yesterday, came to me this morning and bursting

into tears asked [me] to forgive her; I did most readily; and as a token [of] my sincerity, I presented her three pears. She is a dear pupil and good Scholar, and, I think, will make a good teacher. I think this is the right spirit to cherish; and where this spirit reigns in school, all things will go well. There are others, who were equally in fault, I think, but none came to make apology or ask forgiveness, save this one. – – The above is one of the most interesting [events] that have occurred since the opening of the Normal School.

[*Aug.*] 7 The day spent chiefly in listening to a Lecture or Conversation from Mr. Stetson on Transcendentalism. I thought him happy and clear in his exposition, especially in pointing out the distinction between the *subjective* & *objective;* and in clearing Transcendentalism from the Charge of involving the extravagances of the German Philosophy — & Atheism —.

Saturday   Aug. 8 Quite a pleasant day: and quite a pleasant school session. I gave quite a long lecture on the general Qualifications of Teacher and order of the School-room. The Contributions to the Discussion rather more full and intellectual than they have been heretofore. A very pleasant [visit] from two of my former pupils — Misses Swift & Drew.

Monday   Aug — 10 — A sort of general Review — not very successful.

Tuesday   Aug. 11 This day School visited by Esq. Stetson and Rev. Mr. Rice —

Heard the classes in a sort of general Review in several Branches —

In the afternoon took my school on an Excursion to Horn Pond — myself and 25 pupils, Charles Muzzey and the driver — Mr Brown — 28 in all —

Closed my summer Term — a day to be remembered.

CHAPTER V

THE FIFTH TERM, SEPTEMBER 9–DECEMBER 22, 1840

Wednesday   Sept. 9.   Fall Term opened with 15 Pupils! Not a very hopefully ominous Beginning.   But I will neither relax my exertions, nor despair of success.

We have some further applications, and may yet, before the close of the Term, have quite an increase of numbers.

At any rate, as I have never been sanguine, so I am prepared either for success or defeat.   And whatever may be the Result I am determined so to acquit myself, that no blame or shame, shall attach itself to me.

Thursday.   Sept. 10   1840   After a Vacation of 4 weeks I have only 16 Scholars!   It looks a little discouraging. But this aspect of the Normality has become very familiar. I suppose, however, the peculiar and very exciting exercises of the week may have detained some of the pupils. — But things go heavily; and I cannot, or do not, feel myself interested in the school-movements as I did before the Vacation.   I cannot account for this feeling of Sluggishness & indifference.   I hope I shall work myself out of it soon. — It looks to me more dark and discouraging in regard to the Normal School than it has ever yet done.

Friday   Sept. 11 — School drags very heavily.   The Head is sick; and the heart faint.   I feel almost discouraged; Cannot get my own feelings interested in the matters and business of the School: The scholars seem dull & lifeless! How long, in all probability, will it be, before some of these Normalites become good Teachers!!   The Community do seem to say that they do not want Normal Schools, and we will not patronize them.   Well, then, The Lord send them something better, which they do need.

Saturday   Sept. 12 — The Clouds still hang about the horizon of the Normality.   A part only of the old scholars returned; and but one new one added!   This is dismal and discouraging enough.   The Community are not interested in Normal Schools and I doubt whether they will be.   I

GEORGE PUTNAM

Member of First Committee on Normal Schools
Massachusetts Board of Education

have exhorted, and proclaimed and prayed and labored; and what more can I do? I am still as one beating the Air.

Wednesday, Sept. 16 — Entries of Monday & Tuesday omitted at the proper time and events of these days not particularly remembered. — Exercises pretty fair, except in Arithmetic. School this day visited by Four full grown younkers from the city of Boston. No great honor or advantage to the School. Without letters of Introduction or the usual formalities of presentation — & without any particular professed object. I begin to think it may be well to have some restriction about admitting visiters.

Sept. 17, 18, 19, Thursday, Friday, Saturday I have nothing very good or interesting to record about the school.

To speak candidly, I think I drive or rather *guide*, poorly a dull heavy team; few in number and weak in intellectual strength. It will probably, soon stop of itself, if it is not stopped, and then, and then, what? Why I shall go home, and all things will be in *statu quo*.

Sept. 21. Nothing remarkable in the Session of this day, except that the school was visited by Mr. Bradburn of Nantucket, and Mrs. Peirce spent the afternoon in Reading; in respect to which there is great need of improvement.

Sept. 22. Tuesday — Held no Session in consequence of the school Convention. Attended School Convention. Heard an eloquent and interesting Address from Mr. Mann: discussed the subject, whether a "Scholar should ever be compelled to study or recite his lesson." Scholars generally present.

Wednesday Sept. 23d — The seats are nearly filled. The room begins to have the appearance of some life, animation. I hope the Term may be a pleasant and prosperous one, notwithstanding so ominous a Beginning. I will leave no means untried to make it so. The character of every school depends much upon the character and disposition of the Teacher.

This day of the week we generally review; but the *usual* course has been pursued; and with pretty good success. Miss Davenport called to see whether any pupils are desirous of taking lessons in Drawing.

Thursday & Friday [Sept.] 24 & 25th — I think it is a

great desideratum in school to make scholars free in their inquiries; to bring them out, to express what they know, and make inquiry about what they do not know. In this I fail. Scholars will not inquire. They are evidently in the dark in regard to many things. They choose to remain in the dark. I am doubtful, whether they understand enough of some subjects even to ask questions about them. It will be a long time before some of them will make *good* teachers

Saturday [*Sept.*] *26* After Devotional Exercises read in the Scriptures — then, in Abbot's Teacher with remarks from Principal and Pupils; then followed Discussion of the Question — "Should a scholar under any circumstances be compelled to get his lessons? Discussion was carried on in writing: This Mode has its advantages, but on the whole I think it inferior to *Oral* Discussion — This day, about fair, for character.

Monday Sept. 28 Some of the girls of the First Class made objection to beginning Combe's Mor. Philosophy that they should come but a short time, and, therefore, it would be best to begin no new study. But I advised rather to their going on, even, though it should be for a short time only!

Nothing is worse than this "leaving off studies," because scholars are not coming to school much longer. It has a tendency to make idlers, and destroy all interest in school and school studies, and makes time hang heavy on pupils. The way to keep all things orderly, is to give every one a plenty to do. Nothing breeds mischief like idleness.

Tuesday Sept. 29 — Three weeks of this term is gone!! And yet how little has been accomplished! The Scholars have come in very slowly and irregularly, which has been a great hindrance to our progress. I hope to do much more in three weeks which are to come than in the three which have passed. I hope to be kept from committing any more errors in word or manner. I have done enough in this way.

Wednesday Sept. 30 — Some of the first Class have not quite so much to do as they might accomplish — The young ladies yet do not see fit to arrange themselves in the school as I could wish — There is not manifested quite so much of the Spirit of Accommodation as has sometimes been — Hope things will grow better — This afternoon went in & taught the Model School — They did pretty well. There are among them some who possess the elements of good scholars.

Oct. 1. 1840 — Thursday. The School is much less productive of good, than it would be, if the pupils were better prepared in the Common Branches — As the case now is, we are obliged to spend much of the time upon matters and things, which may be learnt quite as well at any other as here — I must be more particular in the examination of pupils. To-day a candidate presented herself, whose qualifications would not compare with those of many in the Model School — of course she cannot be admitted. - - Miss M. had another *fit of not speaking;* and L. of crying — because she supposed, [I] intended indirectly to rebuke her.

Friday Oct. 2d The School has gone with rather more than ordinary speed regularity, and success. — This day, I had the trying case of examining a young lady of this town for admission, who is not qualified to enter. It is very unpleasant to reject applicants; but the Normal School is not designed for teaching mainly the Common Branches; but to teach the *Art of Teaching.* Too many have got into it already, who are but poorly qualified for their place. The School must not lose sight of his own character and business.

Saturday Oct. 3d Made remarks at the opening of the School — familiar Lecture on Compelling Scholars to Study Lessons — Abbot's ' Teacher — Discussion — Reading in Scriptures — & Mental Arithmetic. I read a *beautiful* little piece on Flowers to the School — It was indeed *very beautiful;* Some of the Young Ladies borrowed them to copy in their Journals — of which honor they are well worthy. — On the whole, this has been a very pleasant day to me —

Monday Oct 5 Fair and pleasant day. All things went quite smoothly; though the recitations were not very brisk — and of consequence, we were obliged to hurry off some of the lessons in the latter part of the afternoon. I feel very desirous that the Morning should be prepared entirely before coming into school; and that all the remaining time, during the session, should be devoted to recitations and the other lessons.

Tuesday [*Oct.*] *6* A very pleasant day. Exercises in Nat. Philosophy, Grammar and Algebra imperfectly recited by the second Class; and this has become a very Common Matter of Fact: — and with a portion of the Class, it is the case in regard to almost all their studies. They neither recite Grammar, Philosophy or Physiology, nor read, nor spell well. They give very little hope of becoming teachers, or rather good teachers.

I made remarks on the Order of the Room. Communication &c. It seems truly surprising, that young ladies, intending soon to be teachers, cannot be willing to control themselves, and preserve order! But so it is: some of them are managing, just like little flirts of girls; and think it no harm to be a little out of the way. They can't be governed by Conscience. This fact is a great Draft upon the happiness of the School-room.

Wednesday. Oct. 7 — This forenoon spent chiefly in review — unpleasant occurrence with M — Z — I am rather sorry that this young [lady] has returned to the School — I think she'll get no Good. – – Disappointed that the Botany Class had not all prepared their lesson.

Thursday Oct. 8 The school visited by a gentleman, Mr. Robinson, from Freetown.

The scholars made some gross blunders — There is a great want of language among them — They have no Power at Communication; can explain nothing. What will they do in the day they are called for? Stand *"mum"*. Several have no great desire to make teachers and a few have not the power — There is a prospect of many leaving at the end of this Term — No expectation of Additions — What shall be done? I know not.

Friday Oct. 9 Some of the pupils are very dull particularly in Mathematical Branches — and never, I fear, will they make Teachers In Grammar also and Reading there is great Deficiency. Some have been hammering away with me almost a year, and it does seem as though they remained almost in the same place as at the Beginning. Purposing to be teachers, why do they give themselves any *rest* until they have for instance, the inflection of the English verb at their entire control?

Tomorrow, we are to discuss the proper interest of woman in Politics? I hope the Discussion will be a sensible & spirited one. But to these Exercises a Portion of the Pupils contribute very little. Indeed, Misses B., C., D. — E. — F. G., contribute very little to any thing. It will take them as long to make good & efficient Teachers, as for vegetables to come into the coal Formation.

Saturday   Oct. 10 Three girls in the Model School & two sick; the seats looked rather naked. But the session was quite good.

Monday   Oct. 11 Omitted one Lesson — That in Mental Philosophy. Sometimes find it impossible to do all the talking I wish, and also hear all the Lessons. The fault is partly my own, and partly my pupils! I am slow and they are not always prepared, some of them in the 2d Class rarely. All the Solomons in the land, I fear, would not be competent to make them successful teachers. They lack interest and they lack ability; and with such *"lacking"*, what can we expect to realize? Some of the young ladies have not recited a lesson in Physiology since they commenced the work; & if one might judge from *appearances* there is not much to be hoped for in time to come. I hope I shall do them all justice, so that, if they fail, the fault shall not be mine. Some of the pupils are making very little progress; and I have half a mind to advise them to leave. They may as well do it, for they will never make teachers. In looking over their Journals, I find entries at which I am equally *surprised* and *grieved*. They make my heart bleed. They reveal to me the sad truth, that there is alienation creeping in among my pupils; and they misconstrue and misunderstand the motives & measures of their teacher. They do not know nor appreciate his motives! I fear (*sic*) They do not observe the order of the room; and especially in the hour of prayer. If so what a piece of Mockery and Abomination are they committing (*sic*) is here, and from those who expect to become teachers too. What shall I say that I have not already said to induce them to do right? I know not — I have appealed, remonstrated, and intreated. God of Mercy and love open their eyes to see the truth — touch their hearts that they may feel. May our School-room be

delivered from the wrath due to such abomination. Oh
Lord wilt thou not deliver unto thy unworthy servant a word
of Reproof & Exhortation, which shall dissuade them from
such folly & sin.

Tuesday Oct. 13 I made many remarks upon the manner
of Devotional Exercises & the general order of the room. I
believed I have now said all that I have to say on this subject. I have remonstrated, entreated, explained, and held
up every motive and inducement. I hope we shall be orderly
and happy — — — —

Let us strive to be uniformly kind, just, obliging, conde-
scending. Let us be consistent. Let us be mild — Let us
all be self denying. — And will not things go well?

Wednesday — Oct. 14 — One of the Pupils is sick —
threatened with a fever — another is absent — unwell —
hope they will both soon be well. Miss Stodder has asked
to go home — had rather a pleasant school today — was
pretty well pleased with the Reading of the First Class.
The 2d Class make some progress — but slow in Reading.

Thursday Oct. 15 — Nothing to say —

Friday [Oct.] 16 — There are certain Girls from B — —n
and one or two from L — that, I think, might as well leave
school. They manifest very little interest in school matters,
and withal bring very poor lessons in almost all branches;
& at almost all times. And what ground of hope is there
concerning them? I do not see that they make any improvement. — They are a terribly lumpish set for scholars, as
ever I took in training. Oh may I have patience and every
needed grace and quality: And may my instruction and
labors be guided by a better wisdom than my own; and may
light be shed in their path & my own.

Saturday Oct. 17 Two scholars absent on account of
sickness — and two have gone home (to Boston) for other
reasons. If Pupils do not feel a deep, commanding, *absorbing*
interest in Education and in preparing to be Teachers, they
will not be likely in time to be qualified for Teaching. Some
of them seem to me. to be more interested in *home*, (in going
home and hearing from home) than in anything else. It
will be as much as some of them can possibly do, with all
diligence and application, to make Teachers — even *mid-*

dling Teachers. Miss Clarke and Souther recently added to the School —

Monday & Tuesday Oct. 19 & 20 No Entries —

Wednesday — General Review — Pretty good — School visited by a man who professed to be Deaf & Dumb — said he had been at School in N.Y. — bought some charts of him: descriptive of the mode of talking by signs — with the fingers. — Upon reflection, I am not satisfied that he was not an impostor. He made a very unattractive appearance.

Thursday Oct. 22d Clearing up of a pretty long rain — Windy; and wet walking. Scholars from remote distances attend quite constantly and seasonably. The new scholars seem girlish, and do not take hold like many of the old ones. I feel as though the school would be stripped ⅞ths of its interest & glory when the older & more advanced pupils withdraw, as I suppose they will do at the end this Term. The scholars which have recently entered, do not seem equal either in talents or attainments to the first pupils.

Friday Oct. 23d — I find it very difficult to interest scholars in the Exercises of Orthoepy — viz reading in the Dictionary & Rupel's Enunciation. This I deeply regret, for there is great deficiency in *reading*, and much need of the *benefit* of these practical Lessons. The *Common faults* in Reading, I think, are very happily pointed out in the work named; and I am persuaded, that a portion of the time of the Normal Scholars could not be better appropriated than in Drilling in these Exercises. But perhaps it is not wise to continue them beyond the period of interest; although, I hardly know what I can substitute of equal importance: — one [of] my Pupils, after school, desired leave of absence to go to Framingham. I do not like this interruption in school matters; & mean to grant less and less favors of this sort. If young ladies enter the school and mean to *make* teachers, *efficient* Teachers, they must give their minds, hearts, and time to the Business — They must make school the great object of their attention and of their affection. It must be uppermost in their souls. If they are not willing to do this, they have not yet counted the cost. I did not approve the scheme, — though I did not refuse — she *left* in TEARS.

Saturday Oct 24 — Remarks from Principal — Lecture

Recitations, and Discussion — The question discussed — 'Is the oral or written mode best?' Most in favor of the latter. But the object of the Exercise is to improve in language and the power of Communication; attainments very important to the teacher. Undoubtedly then the oral mode has decidedly and by a great difference the advantage.

Monday   Oct. 26   This is the first day that the Class in Physiology have recited in somewhat the style and manner I desire; Giving abstracts rather than answering individual questions. This mode of Reciting should prevail in all our schools: It should especially in our Normal Schools; for it aids very much in the acquisition of Language: a matter very important to the Teacher. We do not have so much discussion as I could wish; I think not so much as we formerly had. Some of the pupils appear to me much as though they felt no interest or concern in preparing to teach — or felt that they should, as a matter of course, be qualified for the business after staying here awhile.

Tuesday   Oct. 27 — If the girls, who are at school professedly with the intention of becoming Teachers, have not enough interest in the subject to learn the inflections of their verbs in Grammar, I think they may very properly give up the whole thing. We have been day after day and week after week hammering upon this matter, and I think it is provokingly ridiculous and absurd —. Why do they not set about the business — learn it, and [have] done with the matter? — !

Wednesday   Oct. 28   By no means a pleasant or satisfactory day to me. Poor, poor, poor Lessons. From some of the young ladies I get little or nothing. They seem dull and uninterested. I do not know how they think to make themselves teachers! What progress are they making towards the attainment of the requisite qualifications! They are not moving even a Snail's pace.

Thursday   Oct. 30   I think, we have had a more than usually quiet and satisfactory school. We do not do enough in the way of Learning the Art of Teaching. From some of the scholars, especially from some of the New Ones. They neither ask nor answer questions. It would be well, if the scholars would note questions, queries and difficulties for considering, proposing and answering. Of this very little we have. It would seem as though some had come here to enjoy themselves rather than to labor and get an Education and learn the Art of Teaching. I do not mean to watch my Pupils; nor to hear them recite for the purpose of satisfying myself, that they have studied: This, I think, I should take for granted. I should believe they have done what they can. My principal object in hearing recitations is to explain Principles & illustrate; and give the young Ladies an opportunity of acquiring by practice in reciting to me and before the class, the Art of Teaching.

Friday   Oct. 30 Of this day not much to say: There was a more general Failure than usual in Physiology. I am much disappointed in this Lesson. Scholars recite it poorly: and some of them complain of not being able to understand it. This Last must arise from a want of interest in the subject; for there is nothing difficult in the nature of the subject, & the language with the exception of a sprinkling of *Technical Terms* is plain and simple almost to homeliness. With regard to some of my pupils it would be difficult to say what they are interested in; unless it is in times and opportunities, ways and means of going home.

Saturday   Oct. 31 — Last day of Oct. Not a Day that will leave Joys for memory. The School has not been a (*sic*) very pleasant and satisfactory. I am not certain that I am not in the wrong myself; but I think, to-day, surely I am entirely clear of manifesting any angry or unkind feeling; but I have felt greatly disappointed in the success of the Lessons & Exercises of this Forenoon. Some of the scholars seem to feel about every lesson or almost every lesson that is given out, that it is either beneath their notice, or of no value to them in the present stage of Education. And it makes me feel chagrined and mortified, and as though, I would blush and hide my head for them — when they come out and make such a flat and stupid appearance. Yes, I almost wish that the Floor would open and let me into the room below, that I may be spared such mortification. They don't feel as I do about it; if they did they would, I am sure (if they could) prevent such confounding and mortifying results.

Monday   Nov. 2d Nothing in particular to say.

Tuesday Nov. 3d — This day I attempted to get up a little more briskness of manner in recitation. It succeeded quite well. It seemed a little like old times. The Steam was fairly up; and the whole Machine moved with no tardy Speed — & much business was accomplished. The day is on the whole to be remembered with pleasure —

Wednesday Nov. 4 — I pity the man or woman whose scholars are of that fitful temperament that they must either smirk, laugh and show their teeth, or look sullen and cry. Such or very nearly such are some of mine. This is a source of much annoyance to me; giving me more dissatisfaction than any thing else or all things else in the School-line — J. is of this class. —

Kept the Model School this afternoon — Did not feel so much pleased with them as last week — They are very restive & have many bad Habits — which I shall make it my Business to enjoin on the next set of teachers who come in next week to correct.

Thursday Nov. 5 I think it is very [little] use to hear my Class in Grammar & Reading in the style and manner they are going on. It is a dull profitless Business. And I am pretty much determined not to pursue it long; unless it awaken more interest and do more good. Some do not know where the place is — some appear to know little of the meaning of words, & others, of the Sentiments. They may continue to read in this way until Dooms-day without accomplishing the purpose. I see but little studying either of Spelling Reading, or Grammar; and any impartial Judge would regard I fear, our efforts in this Department, as a mere Farce — I think; some of the young ladies may well be ashamed of their performances in this Department.

Nov. 6 — Friday — This day the School has had 4 visitors from Roxbury — Mr. Wyman and wife, daughter and niece. I think it well to have visitors in school — if they do not stay too long or come too often —

Several of the scholars absent in the Model School: This is well if they do not do too much of it. I think it well for them to go in and see each other do. The Model School is one of the best Means we have of carrying on our Scheme of making Teachers. It is now in pretty good condition;

and I think is exciting considerable interest — which I hope will be sustained and continued.

Saturday   Nov. 7 I have made so full an Entry in regard to this day in my other Journal that I shall [write] nothing here; being much hurried by other matters.

Monday   Nov. 9. Rainy day. Held a Session only in fornoon; (*sic*) it being the day of our general Election. School visited by Mr. Pennell of Waterville College — brother of R.M. & E.A. Pennell.

Tuesday   Nov — 10 I have heard this day one dozen Lessons, besides performing much other labor and duty; and I had actually rather perform them all over again than to endure the trial and mortification which I underwent this P.M. from the disorderly conduct of even *one irregular* scholar. This afternoon, there was a visitor present, and during the Recitation of the First Class in Moral Philosophy there was a good deal of smirking and laughing among them; which somewhat interrupted the Exercise, and made them appear greatly to disadvantage. I should think that a moment's Reflection — on their duty, their relation, & the unfavorable light in which such movements show them, would be sufficient to put a stop to them at once and for-ever. — What shows up a pupil in a more disadvantageous light, than to be turning her head first over one shoulder and then over the other to look at her classmates, and then turning away and laughing; and so repeating this process again & again ½ dozen times. And can this possibly be true of my Normal Scholars? It is to my astonishment and grief. — Alas! Alas! on the principle, that one must first learn to be a good scholar in order to become a good teacher, what sort of Teachers will such pupils make?

Wednesday   Nov. 11 Being much pressed with business (and for want of time) I shall make no entry.

Thursday & Friday   [Nov.] 13 & 14 — For these days — see the general Entries —

Saturday   Nov. 14 — A very pleasant Session — The only Drawback upon its satisfaction, is that we did not accom-plish so much as we had assigned for the day. — This, how-ever, not unfrequently happens. — A very interesting and profitable exercise in Abbott's Teacher — after which, the

School listened to a Lecture on Phrenology from the Rev. Mr. Burton of Waltham. He gave us the a priori argument in favor of the Truth of the System, drawn from the *harmonious grouping* of the *organs*. A view of the subject to me quite new and interesting. The Lecture was listened to with great attention; and, I trust — with profit —

Nov — 16, 17, 18 — Monday Tuesday & Wednesday. Since I have been in the practice of making more full entries in my other Journal, there is less need of being particular here and I have less time — I have felt more satisfied with the school this week than last, or, indeed, for several weeks past —

Thursday Nov. 19 I hardly know how I came to make such an Entry as the above: I feel now as though it were not more than half true, or at least not true of more than half the School. The truth is a portion of the School do well in Lessons and conduct; but there are several who seem to me hardly to have found out what they have come for, or to be sensible of the obligations they are under either as pupils, or as learners. It is pitiful and lamentable to see them offering up their eye-service as a substitute for genuine hearty — obedience. They need to be regenerated spiritually and intellectually; before they can present any fair claims, or give any reasonable [hope] of making Teachers, that would be called for a second time in the same place; & what they are here for, I know not; unless it is to plague others. What will Misses E., B., C., K. D., G, do towards raising the the standard of Teaching?

Friday Nov. 20 Sometimes I am not far from believing, that it needs nothing to have an opinion or a measure rejected by some of my pupils, than to know that it came from me. Only let it be known that a doctrine, or way, or method or plan, is *Normal*, and nothing more is wanting to render it odious; reprehensible, absurd. Shall I continue to teach under such circumstances —

Saturday Nov. 21 — The only Exercises were Abbott's Teacher and the Discussion. Some of the Scholars have neither recited in the Teacher nor said any thing on the Question discussed. They recite nothing — and manifest interest in nothing: and how under heaven they are going to become Teachers I know not; unless it is by sitting in

the school-room, and yawning like a sluggard or looking
gravely like an owl, or turning about and grinning & showing the Teeth 5 or 6 hours in the day. They say nothing,
know nothing and do nothing. This is their recipe for making
a Normal Teacher.

Monday   Nov. 23d — A dark, dismal depressing Day.
Many vacant seats — & some poor lessons: — I think the
Moral Atmosphere of the school is not so good as it once
was. There is less unity of spirit — kind sympathetic feeling: less of the feeling of Responsibility, less of a spirit of
Accommodation — less disposition to fall in with and carry
out the views of the Principal. The School to me in this
feature of it is less interesting than it once was. It is obvious
that something besides numbers is necessary to render the
school pleasant and flourishing. Some of the additions
within the last six months, have done nothing to elevate the
character of the Institution.

Tuesday   Nov. 24 — This day like a thousand others came
and went —

Wednesday   Nov. 25 — The School wore a grave and som-
bre aspect; just like the day before an expected Recess.

Monday   Nov. 30 'I have been looking over some of the
Journals this Evening. It makes me feel sad and almost
discouraged, that after all that has been said & done in
regard to order, study hours &c — so little success has been
secured. The Fact is not only diverse from my wishes but
from my expectations. I did hope better things. But both
in the School-room and *out* of it I am greatly disappointed;
but, I believe, I must give it up as hopeless. I must manage
to control the matter as well as possible during the little
time that School may remain under my care. I have said
much, and believed much about governing Schools by persuasion &c. But I have met with a greater poser in the
Normal School, where I expected no difficulty, than I ever
met with any where else.

Tuesday   Dec. 1 — School visited by Mr. Charles Tidd
a teacher in this place, and a gentleman much interested in
Education. — Notice a great difference in different persons
who come into the School. Some are all attention — manifest the deepest interest: These do a school good: Others

look only with a general superficial glance, or vacant stare. Mr. T — — is of the former class of visitors.

Wednesday   Dec. 2d — Nearly all — quite all, the Pupils have returned from Thanksgiving. Two pupils, who have been absent teaching, have returned. One has left from ill-health; and another, for I know not for (*sic*) what reason; — but so far as making a teacher is concerned, it is of little consequence, whether she comes or stays away. There is no prospect that she would ever secure the object of the School —

Thursday   Dec. 3d 1840 Quite a pleasant School. The Return of Miss E.A. R.... s to the School may be regarded as a felicitous occurrence: She is of the Nervous bilious temperament — good developments, full language, and possesses more than ordinary interest in school lessons. Her manner imparts a life and exhilaration to Exercises — of wholesome influence. To one such scholar School is greatly indebted. What would not be the influence of many?

Friday   Dec. 4 This was one of our ordinary Days; when things go pretty fair and even —

One of the young ladies, who has been a short time at school but has never manifested much interest in its operations, has withdrawn from school i.e — declined to attend our Sessions waiting for permission from her friends to leave the school entirely and go home. — If she feels no interest in the school, or is disappointed in its character, or in the character of its Teacher, she would do well to leave; — but while she is a member of the school I am sorry to have her conduct so disorderly.

Saturday   Dec. 5 Exercises Arithmetic, Reading, the Journal — Remarks from the Principal, Abbott's Teacher — Discussion of the Question for debate, and Lecture from Rev. Mr. Burton.

In the Afternoon Mr. B — — — examined heads in the Sitting-Room. — I attended Examination of North-School The Day has been a pleasant & interesting and I hope a profitable one.

Monday   Dec 7 — On account of the Snow-Storm yesterday, we have a thin school today

Spent one hour in reading in the Scriptures — then

Teacher's Manual — PM — Reading, Grammar, Rhetoric and Mor. Philosophy — Pleasant, quiet school

Tuesday — Dec. 8 The seats were generally filled — School orderly; Lessons successful. Misses Burdick and Kimball in the Model School — Appearance thereof quite satisfactory. Miss Smith asked leave of absence on account of sickness — Miss K. still continues to absent herself from school —

Wednesday — Spent most of the Session with the class in Arithmetic — Not very pleasant, because I manifested some impatience — Tears shed &c. Some Teachers get along without any tears. They are always calm — have only kind and smooth words; and probably seldom press their pupils with hard questions. This is the pleasantest way if not the best —

Thursday Dec. 10 A pretty smooth quiet uniform day. Such a day as when we do some good, and avoid generally evil. not strongly marked, nor long remembered.

Friday Dec. 11 — Lessons quite good and room orderly. When I say lessons *good* I mean *generally;* There are some who never give *good* lessons — never: I might almost say, never give lessons of any kind. You might as well attempt to get an answer from a stick of wood. What their calculations & Expectations are I know not. If schools depend on them: — Oh Lord deliver us.

Sat. Dec. 12 — I think this may be made one of our most interesting Session-days — I am sorry that there is any appearance among the pupils of a tendency to think lightly of it.

Met the second class for Reading in the afternoon —

Monday Dec. 14 — A day which were it lawful, one would gladly blot from the school-calendar.

Heard one [of] my pupils, this day talking about Combe's Physiology being *"dry" "so dry".* Dry! Combe's Physiology *dry'!* If it were as dry as the seared leaf I am sure there is *sap* enough in her soft head to moisten it.

Tuesday Dec. 15 — All the scholars at Mrs. Muzzey this afternoon — I understand it was for *"Social Reasons".* Does this show a commendable interest in Normal Schools, and preparation for Teaching?

Wednesday Dec. 16 — I frequently am made to believe there is a very moderate amount of Talent in the Normal School. I am sure there is much less than there was in the High School at Nantucket. What miserable clumsy work some of these girls make in Arithmetic, Grammar, Philosophy and Algebra! And they manifest very little Curiosity. Even in the first Class, it seems that some are satisfied with skimming over the surface. There is not enough Curiosity — enough perseverance, enough searching into principles and deep things [of] science. Why, I should think those who mean to be teachers would be wide awake — all inquiry — all agog.

Thursday & Friday Dec 17 & 18 — Good deal of absence these days and lessons many of them only of moderate degree of Excellence. It seems to me Study Hours are coming to be less and less regarded; and I am securing and enjoying less and less interest and respect and love on the part of my Pupils. The Relation, which I sustain is becoming every day less and less pleasant. And I feel indeed that the day of my usefulness and happiness was here drawing to a close I know in the impetus of my feelings, I have uttered hasty and even harsh words; but I cannot accuse myself of settled unkindness or neglect towards any of my pupils; on the contrary, I do feel conscious, that towards every one, without exception, I have felt a spirit of kindness and good will, a strong desire for her happiness and improvement; and that I have given myself entirely to my school and the advancement of my Pupils, not sparing health, strength or comfort. I am sensible my labors have been poor — that I have effected little enough; and that very imperfectly, — but still it all has cost me much labor, time & expenditure of energies. The School has not prospered as I anticipated or have I succeeded in my favorite plan of governing by purely mild means as I hoped — and sad enough is my heart made by it. I am sensible that every day the school continues longer in my hands, it is moving retrograde; and it is high time, that it passed into other, abler and better hands. I have sent in my Resignation, and shall soon see Mr. Mann and urge its acceptance. My wish and hope are, that the

School may go on, and prosper and increase, but of this, I have many doubts & fears —

Saturday   Dec. 19   Messrs Burton & Rice visited the School — The former delivered a sensible lecture on Health: it [was] chiefly a condensed statement of some of the Chs. in Combe's Physiology — The Pupils did not seem so much interested as in the lecture on Phrenology; though I thought it a more useful one

Monday   Dec. 21 — In the entry above, is a Mistake — Mr. Burton delivered his lecture this day.   P.M.   Went into the Model School and attended Examination — The School did fairly.

Tuesday   Dec. 22   School Visited by Messrs — Tidd & Hobbs.   Heard a lesson in Physiology — Discussed some questions on School Matters — read the Journal made remarks and closed at one.

CHAPTER VI

THE SIXTH TERM, JANUARY 6–MARCH 12, 1841

Jan. 6 1841 — Wednesday At ½ past 1 P.M. School opened with 20 Pupils — five new ones: — greeted them all with a hearty welcome — made remarks and gave out lessons — School closed at an early hour.

Thursday Jany 7 — School opened with Reading the Scriptures, singing and prayer — Heard Recitations, which were quite good — The new pupils seem to take hold as though they were in earnest. — Our hearts are made sad by the sudden departure from us of our much loved and highly esteemed Pupil S.E. Burdick — "Sweet is the odor of her name." — The best of Earth, and all of Heaven be her Portion.

Friday and Saturday Jan'y 8 & 9 If we have not had more scholars, we certainly have had more quiet, orderly and satisfactory Sessions than we had last *term.* — May this state be perpetual.

Monday Jany 11 — To be remembered as a good day for lessons and conduct. Model School began under Misses Locke and E. Johnson. Success to them now and hereafter —

Tuesday [Jan.] 12 — I went to Groton to attend School Convention — The Girls kept themselves at School — I am inclined to think pretty well. Am glad I attended Convention — had an opportunity of explaining the object and character of Normal Schools — and of removing from not a few minds unfavorable and wrong impressions —

Wednesday [Jan.] 13 — Session in the Forenoon — Business was Remarks, Lecture, Discussion & Reading Composition. A quiet, pleasant and I trust, profitable Meeting.
P.M. No Session —

Thursday Jan y 14 Very hard prospect with duties and labors this day. — obliged to curtail some of the Exercises this day. — Some doubts whether I have not undertaken to carry on too many studies and branches. It is quite possible

Lexington, 1926 — Building used by the Normal School, 1839–1844

to multiply them too much, — as well as to have too few — a happy [medium] is desired so as to keep both teacher and pupils in wholesome Activity all the time.

Friday Jan'y 15 1841 This is the first day there has been any thing in Recitations to notice as deficiency. In three or four of the Branches today there was a single instance of Failure. — When Scholars attend parties or Soirees, I think they ought not to neglect lessons or School. —

Miss L. has a low voice; and an unpleasant habit of not answering to questions readily and audibly, even when there is no difficulty in the nature of the question. Neither does it arise from obstinacy. It is very important to overcome and do it away.

Saturday Jan'y 16 — Some little smirking today — between two pupils, commencing with Miss J.; the first I have seen this Term. Would to heaven it may be the last.

Monday Jan'y 18 Some Hinderance in Recitations for want of the proper Books — This is a perplexity and plague. The School should be supplied with sets of Text — & Class Books; and moreover, it would be if we could touch the hearts and loosen the purse strings of a few rich Hunks. The Lord made (*sic*) them uneasy until they see and acknowledge their duty; and move in this work of Charity. By giving a few hundred dollars, thousands of dollars worth of Good might be secured. I have applied to Messrs — C and B & A — but what has been obtained more than *kind decided Negatives*

Tuesday Jan'y 19 Another new scholar added, Miss James, who promises well. I believe the room will be full of scholars. My greatest anxiety now is to do them good — To make them teachers.

Wednesday Jan'y 20 I examined three candidates last night and admitted them all; but they were not very well prepared. If they are devoted to their business and strictly industrious, they may get along and do very well. All depends upon that. Heard that Miss Harris had taken a school. Much success attend her efforts.

Thursday Jan'y 21 — We have had a good deal of Delay in procuring Books, and even now all the Pupils are not supplied. This has been the cause of much hinderance:

— Would that some kind benefactor would relieve our wants! —

Friday Jan'y 22d Two of my Pupils recently entered, came to me this morning with the Serious Proposal whether they had not better quit and go home. I regard it as truly a strange proposition for those who have just put their hand to the plough to become Teachers!

Saturday Jan'y 23d Have had no Visitors this Term. Last winter ere this time we had several. I wish that we might be noticed in this way a little more; but I have asked, and wished and hoped until the heart begins to grow sick — A visit now and then from the Board would serve to give us consequence in the eyes of the Community, and break up the monotony of the every day-business (*sic*) of the school-room. The School has now been in operation over 18 months; and we have scarcely had a visit once a six months from any member of the Board —

Monday Jan'y 25 Warm and pleasant day. — Several Pupils absent. Lessons rather indifferently prepared in some of the Branches. Shorter session in the afternoon than usual; giving the scholars time to take a walk —

Tuesday Jan'y 26 A very pleasant day. Full seats; — successful lessons — pleasant Sessions I have very considerable doubts whether Misses B., C., E., K. & G. will ever do much at Teaching or make teachers. I should say the same of Miss M., had she not been a Teacher for several years — In these cases, I should hardly know what advice to give. — Some of the late additions, promise well.

Wednesday — Rather a dull Discussion; but as some compensation for this several very good Pieces of Composition were read by sundry Pupils. The session a good and profitable one. Some of the Scholars recently added are, it is reported, sadly homesick: — They must have resolution to withstand the Trial: — A deep interest in Education and an ardent desire to become good Teachers will carry them through.

Thursday Jan'y 28 — Rather a heavy day — Lessons not very brisk or correct: — I have not felt so disagreeable on leaving school one day since the school began.

Jan'y 29 Friday Snow — Two or three vacant seats, —

which are usually occupied with pupils, who, I fear, are not so much interested in studies as they must be, if they would become good Teachers. This sort of *"dilly-dallying"* way of coming must be put to an end. We have had already too much of it.

Saturday Jan'y 30 Recitations in Geology, BookKeeping, Abbot's Teacher and Reading in the Scriptures. Felt much more interested today, (for what reason I know not) in the opening Exercises than usual. — read a piece — gave a sentiment; and made Remarks to some considerable length on the proper observance of the Sabbath. — The Session, on the whole, I think was a profitable one.

Monday Feb'y 1 — All the Pupils (33) present. Commenced Snowing, during the afternoon session. — Our Room is full. — Must alter the location of the seats and add to their number. This is rather an unpleasant job, but I see not how it can be well avoided. Like to have Scholars added; and the more, if they are well qualified.

Tuesday Feb. 2d A.M. All present but one: — P.M several absent — know not from what Cause: — It is pretty certain, whatever the cause may be, that these interruptions will never advance the work of Preparation for Teaching.

Wednesday Feb. 3d A.M. One Session this day.

Gave my views on the Mode of using the Bible — Speaking of God and attempting to teach children the idea of God at a very early period — The Discussion, though not general, was interesting, and instructive; — and the session truly a profitable one. I felt it my Duty to rebuke those who do habitually decline taking any part in the discussion. They cannot be doing their best to make themselves teachers —

Thursday Feb. 4th — Nothing remarkable occurred either in the forenoon or afternoon, except that all the pupils were at school, 34 in No — As I have only 32 seats, I have called in the carpenter to consult and take measures about altering the room and adding to the number of seats. — I know not how the Board will like this, but as they do not come to see, advise and direct, I hope they will not complain.

Friday — Feb. 5 — Scholars punctual — Seats full and lessons well recited — P.M. Session closed $\frac{1}{4}$ past 3 — that scholars might have time to take Exercise; but all did not seem anxious to improve it.

Feb. 6 Saturday This day 2 men Davis & Sumner came into the room in the midst of our session and took down part of the Funnel to reverse its direction with a view of preventing its leaking: very much troubled with stove pipe: never will put it up so again It is better to have more stoves and less pipe. But these rooms should be heated by a Furnace.

Monday Feb. 8 A.M. Met my Pupils at 55 minutes after 8 — All present except one who has left for sickness — After Devotional Exercises, several sentiments were [given] by the Principal and the pupils — The Journal was then read — having been omitted on Saturday — Made remarks — heard reading in the Scriptures — Held a Conversation A.M. Conversation and Reading — School visited by Miss Stodder & Mr Rice —

Tuesday Feb. 9 School this day studious — visited in the afternoon by Dea. James & wife —

Wednesday Feb. 10 One of the Normalites this day wished to be excused from writing composition because she had a little swelling upon her wrist!!! Were it not winter, we might fear next time, a Mosquito Bite!!

Another Pupil staid away for want of India Rubbers! Verily they give encouraging promise of becoming efficient Teachers soon!

Thursday Feb-y 11 Gave out the Journals — commended them — Remarked on study hours — The neglect of their observance, has in time past, been the cause of much dissatisfaction. The like to which, I hope we have not to go through again. May Heaven avert it —

Friday Feb. 12 This day nearly all the pupils present; Pretty good Lessons. — All recited. — A note placed on my desk by one [of] the scholars — saying that the Conduct of the Modelites is complained of out of school — that their language is vulgar and conduct rude and unhandsome: — Difficult subject to control — If Parents will be coarse and vulgar and profane, — what can we expect of the children?

Saturday, Monday, Tuesday Feb. 13, 15, 16 For these days, I strangely forgot to make any Entries in this Book at the proper time.

Wednesday [*Feb.*] *17* — Had a very strange and improper and unreasonable request from my pupil Miss J., that I would excuse her from a Lesson without cause: No faithful conscientious Teacher can do such a thing. In such a case, a pupil must be regarded as derelict to duty.

Thursday [*Feb.*] *18* This has been a pretty fair & successful day; only one thing has happiness [happened] to mar its features — oh yes, there are two. When I corrected one of the young ladies in Reading Miss James — She was so overcome that she could not read; and 2d — The Young Ladies did not readily come to order at the Commencement of the afternoon session — I think I must be very infelicitous in my manner towards the young ladies — especially in correcting their faults —

Friday   Feb 19 A still uniform day — oh no — no — Had a visit from Messrs Mann & Howe — quite a thrilling time.

Saturday   Feb 20 A good day — Lessons above par — so was discussion, or rather conversation —

Feb. 22d   Monday A very orderly pleasant quiet day. A better pattern for order than for lessons; although the latter were not *bad* —

Tuesday   Feb'y 23d — This has been a poor day for the Normal School — Not very successful Lessons for the afternoon Lessons; — and no laudable attention to order; yesterday, I thought we were making some progress in good, but to-day we are all aback again.

Wednesday   Feb. 24 I have been tried today: and I hope have learned a profitable lesson — May I profit by it. Count it all joy says the apostle when ye fall into divers temptations". In looking over the Journals of my Pupils into which they put whatsoever they please, I find my motives and purposes often quite misunderstood and misinterpreted. To have any of my pupils feel toward me after all that I have done for them & am doing for them as some do, is truly trying. I have one girl for whom I have done everything in my power that conscience would allow, to make her happy — to advance her improvement, and secure her success, who seems only to retain her connection with the school for the sake of showing her gratitude by finding fault with the measures of the school and misinterpreting on every possible opportunity the motives of her Teacher. She ought not indeed to retain her connection with the school. I devoutly hope she will not long – – Saw trespasses on the order of the Room – – Scholars make much ado about reading Composition. This seems to me childish and unreasonable.

Thursday Feb'y 25 I cannot say this has been a quiet day, for all has been bustle and hurry in Recitation; but it has been a pleasant day. Operations have been brisk and quite successful. Scholars have seemed industrious and orderly; and I think good has been obtained —

Friday Feb'y 26 Held a session only this forenoon which was a pretty satisfactory one.

In the afternoon, having called the school together and made a few remarks on the subject of trade winds — and appointed the lessons for tomorrow I dismissed to attend the Examination of School in North district. The Examination proved better than I anticipated; though I am disappointed in Mr. H. He did not throw himself into his School. His manner is dull monotonous and heavy.

Saturday [*Feb.*] *27* — Bad walking — and rain until near night. — Many both of the Normal and Model School absent. In this I was a good deal disappointed. The thought came over me strongly that they who have not zeal and interest enough in the Cause to attend school through such weather, being well, have not enough to make teachers and keep a good school. Mrs Pierce walked from Mr. Bridges to school — and some of the young ladies who came to school walked much farther than some of those who staid at home would have had to do. There are three or four girls boarding at Mr. Muzzey's, who do not manifest an encouraging interest in the school, and whose connexion with the Institution, I fear, is exercising an unfavorable influence upon it. It is hoped that they will come to a better mind and different practice.

Monday March 1 This has been a *review* day out of the usual course, chiefly Mathematics pretty successful; full school industrious orderly. Disappointed of late in Miss E. Johnson; particularly in Algebra and Arithmetic. I think

she cannot be well indeed I know she is not — a devoted and
I think will become a successful Teacher.

Tuesday   March 2d   A pleasant quiet day — many absences and not very good lessons especially in Combe's Constitution and Philosophy.   Some of the pupils evidently take
very little interest in what they are doing and others perhaps have not the ability to accomplish much, of both of
these I think they had better be away.   Among the former
is — and the latter Miss B.   They are pleasant girls enough
but they do nothing for themselves, or the school.

Wednesday   March 3d.   A.M.   Lecture, Discussion, Geology, Globes, and Rhetoric.   Pupils did well except in Discussion — This goes heavily, heavily.

Thursday   March 4 — The lessons in the early part of the
day went so heavily that I was obliged to omit 3 lessons in
the afternoon session.   There is hardly anything that so
lightens the Burden of the School-room as correct and
prompt lessons — Spoke to two or three pupils concerning
their lessons and interest in them.   Some of them seemed
affected to tears — I moved in the case, a matter of duty;
to ascertain a fact and its cause, and not to administer reproof.   The Pupils were Misses Johnson, Viles & Ireson.

Friday   March 5 — A cold Bleak March day; but quite
pleasant within doors; and the internal state is far more
important than the External.

Saturday   March 6   Pretty fair day — except that I was
obliged to put off my Conversation —

Monday   March 8   Spent the day in teaching the Model
School —

Tuesday [March] 9 — Spent as yesterday yet with more
success and satisfaction.   I think well of the Model School
and think it may be made an instrument of much good to
the Normalites —

Wednesday [March] 10   The principal part of the forenoon
was spent in conversation as a substitute for discussion.   The
subject was — The Model-School —

Some statements made which I was not prepared to hear;
particularly by Miss Ireson, — that the school is governed
by fear and not by love — the story of a little girl who was
afraid of Mr. Pierce —

Thursday   March 11. School visited by Miss [Dorothea] Dix — Much mortified and displeased at the behavior of Misses B., C. & K.: — It is time they were withdrawn from the Institution. It is not right for those to continue in the institution who feel no interest in its object.

Friday March 12. Not a pleasant day; lessons not good, generally; and not perfect attention to order. — Two young ladies who have never manifested much attention to the order of the room, or deep interest in the studies, had leave to withdraw from the Institution, — Misses B. and C.

[NOTE. — The journal ends abruptly at this point. Did Peirce discontinue it, or were further entries lost or destroyed? Diligent search has yielded no answer to this question; no trace of a later private journal has been found, either for the remainder of Peirce's stay at Lexington (to August, 1842), or for his service at West Newton (1844–1849).

Peirce's increasing ill health is evident from the tone of the entries after Jan. 1st, 1841. His request for release from his position at the end of 1840, Mann's appeal to him to remain, as a public duty and as a service to the public schools, and Peirce's reluctant assent to continue in spite of his exhaustion, are noted above (page xix). A month after the decisive battle for the continuance of the normal schools had been won in the legislature (March 2, 1842) Peirce again resigned. His moving appeals, and the appeal of his wife, that he be allowed to "depart in peace" show the cost at which he had carried on the work:

"DEAR SIR [he wrote to Mann]: You know something of circumstances under which I came to Lexington, — the sacrifices, personal, domestic, and social, of me and *mine*, which it cost. I thought at that time that my long experience in school teaching might be of some service to the "*New Experiment.*" I came, and if I have done one-half of what you say I have, be satisfied, be satisfied. We have fought and conquered, the battle's won; the Rubicon is passed. An Opportunity to make a fair Experiment (all we asked) is *secured.* I consider it certain now that the Normal School (a Branch of your Scheme of Education) cannot fail unless there is something radically defective in it; and if so, let it be abandoned. And now, dear Sir, kind Sir, let me go, — and have no hard thoughts. . . . Should I stay much longer I must lay my bones here." [1]]

[1] Horace Mann Papers, Massachusetts Historical Society.

THE JOURNAL OF MARY SWIFT

AUGUST 1, 1839–APRIL 4, 1840

MARY SWIFT (MRS. EDWIN G. LAMSON) ABOUT 1849
(From a daguerreotype)

Journal

COMMENCING AUGUST 1st, 1839

LEXINGTON ACADEMY

CHAPTER I

THE FIRST TERM, AUGUST 1–OCTOBER 1, 1839

Agreeably to the wishes of our teacher, Mr Peirce, I have purchased this book, which is to contain an account of the business of the school, & of the studies In which we are engaged. –

This morn we were favored with a visit from Professor Newman, who is going to teach the Normal School, at Barre in Worcester County. — At the close of the school, he addressed the scholars. Some of his ideas upon the subject, were the following; he said that when the students in medicine were attending a course of lectures, they took notes & were enabled in doubtful cases, to recur to these & derive instruction from them in practise. Many acquired great facility in this; so that they could take the great part of every lecture. As we were studying a profession, we could adopt that plan, & we should find that we should be able to recall past events much more easily, by having written notes. By writing abstracts we should acquire a better use of language & make the ideas contained in the works our own, so that, when we were required to write Composition, we need not be obliged to say that we had no ideas. He commended the spirit of inquiry which seemed to pervade the school, & said that it created a much greater interest in our studies. — The business of teaching, he said, was regarded as very laborious, but if the teacher attended to the normal and intellectual education of his pupil, he would find the drudgery greatly lessened. Instead of doing

this, many thought the business of teaching consisted only
in instructing the pupils in Reading, Writing, & Calculation,
& this is the cause of the low standing of our Common
Schools at the present time. — He had several children &
there was a public school near his house, but he had never
sent them.   He feared that they would be injured by the
company of the scholars.   It is the business of the teacher
to remove this impression concerning public schools, by
elevating their moral standards; and to do this the teacher
must think seriously upon the subject, and influence the
pupils both by example and precept. – –

[A long, detailed abstract of the second chapter of Combe's
Physiology is omitted.]

.   .   .   .

After writing the above abstract the remaining time on
Saturday morning was occupied by Mr P— in delivering a
lecture to the pupils. — The subject of which was Normal
Schools, their origin & the expectations of the Board of
Education & of the Friends of Education in general.   When
our forefathers first came to this country, (he said) they
saw the necessity of schools, and established those which
we call Grammar Schools.   As the population became more
numerous, the demand for public schools increased, and
various kinds have been instituted, from the High Schools
down to the Infant Schools.   A better idea of the number of
these schools, can be formed, by considering that nineteen-
twentieths of the children of the United States, receive
their Education from them. — As our commerce increased,
and the tide of emigration flowed more rapidly, the people
found it necessary to do something for the support of the
government, and knowing that it must devolve upon the
rising generations, they turned their attention to the subject
of Education.   It was discussed freely, and Periodical
Journals were established devoted to the subject. — Finally,
the Board of Education was formed.   While we were thus
rousing to activity on this side of the Atlantic, our intercourse with the inhabitants of the other world became more
frequent, and we learned that the people of Prussia under
their despotic government, had advanced farther than we,

notwithstanding the celebrity which we had acquired. They had established Normal Schools; and it was expected that teachers should be prepared for their work, as much as those of any other profession. The legislature of Massachusetts were awakened, and by the assistance of private munificence, the school, whose advantages we now enjoy, was established. To us, therefore, all the friends of Education turn, anxious for the success of the first effort to establish such schools. For this success, we shall depend, chiefly, on three particulars: 1st on interesting you in the studies to which you attend & in the daily remarks; 2nd on the course of lectures to be given & 3d on the Model School. —

Monday 5th Aug. This morn the Natural Philosophy lesson was unprepared, owing to a misunderstanding among the pupils. Accordingly, the time was occupied in a review of the part which we had gone over. The lesson in Physiology was well recited, & was very interesting. — That in Intellectual Philosophy was not quite prepared. — In the afternoon, our first lesson was in Arithmetic. The subjects were the proof of Multiplication, by casting out the nines and Division. Both were satisfactorily explained, and the processes made perfectly intelligible. — We recited our first lesson in Wayland's Moral Philosophy. It was a new study and the class found it difficult to remember. Mr P. seemed pretty well satisfied, & foretold the same improvement in this, as in other recitations. — The Lesson in Geography was omitted for want of time. —

Tuesday 6th This day passes very much like its predecessor, & a particular description of it will be superfluous. The lessons were, generally, well recited in the morning. In the afternoon the lesson in Grammar was upon the subject of Tenses. Mr P. read over the portion in Peirce's Grammar on the subject of the verb, which part of speech he calls *asserters*. His names of the tenses seemed to [be] more appropriate than those employed by many grammarians. The lessons in Wayland's Science was omitted & after copying some problems on the globe school was dismissed. —

Wednesday 7th — Mr Peirce read the story of the daughter of Herodias, and the parable of the five loaves and two fishes.

After reading, he remarked that it was not his intention to make any observations, which should affect, at all, the sentiments which individuals might hold with regard to religious subjects. But that the portion which he had read, was so fruitful of instructive matter, that he did not feel that he could pass it by silently. — He then commented upon the influence which old people exerted over young, as instanced in the story mentioned, where the daughter of Her — was told by her mother to demand the head of John the Baptist. He said that the person who had wicked parents was much to be pitied, on account of this influence, and the person having wise parents, was proportionably blessed. — Few stories in the Bible were so full of interest as this, & it was especially so to the young of the same sex. The question arising from this, would be, ought Herod to have considered himself bound by his oath to perform this? — If for example she had asked him to have sent her to the moon, he would have refused, giving as an excuse his physical inability. For the reason of moral inability, he could have declined her last request. — The manner in which a promise is taken, should depend on the spirit in which it is made. —

The exercises of the forenoon were similar to those of the two past. – –

Thursday. [*8th*] The lessons for this morn were N. Philosophy, Physiology, N. History. The subjects of the first were Light & Refraction. Our teacher explained the rule, that the intensity of light diminished as the square of the distance increased, in such a manner as to make it much more clear than it has been before in my mind. — The lesson in Physiology was very practical, & he made some remarks in connection with it, upon tightness of dress, apparently, thinking that it was the fashion at the present time to dress tightly. He has not probably heard that the wisdom or some other good quality of the age has substituted the reverse fashion for the time present. — The lesson in N. History treated of the divisions of animals into warm & cold blooded & of other minor divisions. — In the P.M., we read in Abbott's Teacher, & copied some more Problems upon the Globe, which occupied nearly all the

LEXINGTON — "THE OLD [HANCOCK] CLARKE HOUSE" IN 1926

time. After that, we punctuated some sentences and school
— closed. —

Friday. [*9th*] The morning passed like the preceding —
Philosophy lesson upon the refraction and reflection of
light, and the reason of the appearance of the rainbow.
Physiology, upon the efficacy of the warm bath, its superior-
ity of this over the cold for most people, and especially
invalids.   Natural History, upon the Classification of
Animals, and their division into Genera, Orders, and Species.
Recited the first lesson in Political Economy, from the work
by Professor Newman. — At noon, received letters from
home, and returning to dinner, found Mr Wood with Mr
P. in the sitting room. He spent the afternoon in school.
The time was devoted to Reading, Orthoëpy, and Music.
Reading exercise was principally an illustration of the
divisions and subdivisions which the teacher should make,
in order to bring the subject down to the comprehension
of the pupils. – – – The example given was the manner of
ascertaining the longitude of a place, by noticing the
eclipses of Jupiter's satellites. — After tea, took a short
walk in company with Mr & Mrs Peirce & Mr Wood. The
former related some anecdotes concerning the former owners
of the house now occupied by their descendant, Miss Clark,
and concerning the old tree in front of it. – –

Saturday. [*10th*] After reading a portion in the Scriptures,
Mr Peirce proceeded to give a Second lecture to the
pupils. — The object of the lecture was, to show what the
teacher is to do. The two grand divisions of the teachers
work, are 1st, the discipline of the faculties, 2nd, the communication of instruction. — These appear to be synonymous, but the difference between them, may be made
apparent by an example. Take the case of the lecturer;
he understands his subject fully, and communicates facts
to his hearers. — He, perhaps, carries most of the hearers
along with him. They hear and understand, but it is without any exercise of the faculties of the mind. It is thus with
the scholar; the teacher may talk upon his studies, and
impart knowledge, but his faculties will remain unimproved.
— The effect of showing a scholar, may be illustrated by
the case of two boys, both eager to see all that they can.

In walking, both come to a hill; the one is enabled to surmount all difficulties by the assistance of his parent, who
carries him to the summit, where he enjoys the scenery.
The second has no one to aid him; but by the use of much
dexterity, he succeeds in reaching it. They come to a
second hill. The one who was carried before, ascends in
the same way again, but he who ascended alone, will find
this much easier. If the parent of the first child be taken
away, he can do nothing; but the second will be able to
help himself. — In like manner, the pupil who is assisted
in one thing, is not prepared by that assistance to understand the next, any better, on the contrary he will like the
boy, find himself utterly unable to take a step alone. Our
faculties gain strength by exercise, just as our bodies do;
as in walking, & in any trade when a particular part of the
system is brought into continual use, we shall find that it
becomes much more powerful. Various teachers have
different ways of instructing; thus one will assist a scholar
in every difficulty; another will teach the scholar to assist
herself. As in the case of two apprentices; one is sent out
skilled in the use of one or two tools; another knows the use
of all. — There would be little difficulty in deciding which
would be the better able to assist himself. — A child's
faculties are his tools: to discipline them, it is necessary
that the teacher should know what they are; hence the use
of the study of Intellectual Philosophy. But it is not only
necessary that the intellectual powers should be cultivated, but that the physical & moral should receive due
attention. Education signifies to draw out. It has been
confined in past time, to the intellect alone, & popular
opinion has seemed to demand it. Still we find that man's
happiness depends upon his moral nature. How can a
teacher feel that his work is done, when this is omitted! It
is a great work, to communicate the manner of improving
the moral character; and to do it the teacher must have the
co-operation of his pupils. — The next subject to be attended to is the trials & pleasures of a teacher's life. The
teacher always has one consolation; that the work in which
he is engaged, is useful; on account of the good he may do.
The advantages of education are too numerous to mention.

School education is at the basis of every profession. The
business of teaching is not only honest but honorable: the
ancients employed only their wisest men as teachers, for
instance Aristotle, Plato, & Socrates. The wise of every
age will honor the teacher. Females are peculiarly adapted
to teaching: they possess more patience & perseverance,
than the other sex, & if the moral cultivation of the school
be attended to, they will find little difficulty in governing.
The teacher must be the servant of the school; he must
devote much of his time to it: slight indisposition, dejec-
tion, or any such thing will not exempt him from attendance.
He will experience much trouble from the ignorance &
obstinacy of his pupils, & from indifference in the parents.
The teacher has his pleasures, as well as trials. He is improving himself, while he is attending to others, and he has
the satisfaction of assisting those around him. The next
lecture will be upon the motives which should influence
teachers, and the qualifications which a teacher should
possess. —

Sunday 11th Left at one quarter before eight in the
morn, to go to West Cambridge, in company with Miss
Damon & Miss Stowe. Reached the place of destination at
nine and one quarter, feeling very little fatigue. We went
into the Sabbath School, & from there, to the Church. The
minister, Mr Damon, was absent & Mr Richardson filled
the pulpit. The text in the morning was "Unto every one
that hath, shall be given & from him that hath not, shall
be taken away, even that which he hath." In the afternoon
"There are some among you who believe not." At half
after six, we left to return; & at half after eight were in the
academy, not feeling averse to taking a seat. The distance
that we had walked was eleven miles. —

Monday [12th] Morning lesson in Philosophy, on the
subject of Reflection. Mr P. related some anecdotes in
connection with the lesson, which illustrated the fact, that
a body can be seen by reflected light, when the incident
rays are intercepted from the eye, and also showed that
the apparent presence of some supernatural power, may
often be resolved into the effects produced by natural
phenomena. The first as near as I recollect was the fol-

lowing: a friend of his was passing a house late one evening, which he knew was unoccupied, when turning towards it he saw a bright light within. He stopped a moment, & walked towards it, when as he had got very near it suddenly disappeared. He walked back, and at about the same distance, it again became visible. He approached; it disappeared. Summoning up all his courage, he went to the door & called loudly to know who was there; he received no answer, & at length returned home, troubled & perplexed, that he could explain the phenomena in no satisfactory way. It was afterwards ascertained that it was the reflection of a light from a house in the neighborhood, which he could not see, & the disappearance of it, was probably owing to a change in the direction in which he walked; this making the line from his eye to the building, separate from that made by the reflected ray. Another anecdote was of his grandfather; he was passing a house which he had just vacated when he saw a brilliant light. Supposing someone had taken possession, he walked nearer, when it disappeared, as if unwilling to be seen there. It was afterwards found, that the light was from the planet Venus, reflected in such a manner as to appear to be a burning lamp. The ordinary lessons of the forenoon were recited; and the afternoon passed as usual, except that a severe storm prevented the attendance of some of the pupils, so that our number was reduced to six.

Tuesday [13th] This day would seem hardly to need a separate account the exercises thereof so nearly coincide with those of Monday — Mr P. instead of hearing our lesson in N. Philosophy explained it to us & deferred our recitation until tomorrow morn. —

Wednesday 14th We recited the lesson which was explained yesterday on the subject of Vision. On opening the school Mr P. made some remarks on the manner in which the words prevent & let were used in the bible, as differing from their present use. The lesson in Physiology was a review of the 3d Chap. upon various subjects but especially recommending the use of the bath & teaching the manner in which it should be used. — After reciting a short lesson in Political Economy the school closed the lesson

in N. History being deferred until the next day – – – In the
P. M. spent an hour in writing home & after mailing the
letter met Mr P. who gave us an invitation to attend the
fair at the East Village. We accepted & had gone as far as
the Monument House, when we met Mr Morse the preceptor of the High School in Nantucket. — He was intending
to return to Boston in a short time & Mr P. stopped to
speak with him, promising to overtake us before we got to
the Village. He did so, and accompanied us up to the
scene of action — Upon the hill called Mt. Independence
was a building which appears to have been erected for an
observatory — It was prepared for the refreshment table,
and hung with evergreens. To contain the articles for sale
large tents were made covered with canvass — adjoining
this was a tent at right angles in which a long table was
set for the entertainment in the eve. – – – – There were many
people from the neighboring villages & all the tents were
crowded — Groups were scattered among the trees and
others were standing at the edge of the hill admiring the
scenery around & below. – – – – After viewing the fancy
articles we entered the observatory & went into the upper
part where Mr P. named many of the hills around & showed
us the state of New Hampshire, & the commencement of
the White Mountains. We also saw the ocean but it was
at so great a distance that it appeared like mist over the
land. — When we had become wearied with standing we
descended to the refreshment room, where Mr P. treated
us to ice-cream & cake — Contrary to the principles of
Blakewell's Philosophy, we felt much cooler after eating
the cream. — We sauntered through the grove & again
through the tents, when it grew dark & we returned home,
very well pleased with our afternoon excursion. — Went to
tea with Mrs Muzzy in company with Miss Stodder's sister
who had just come out from Boston. —

Thursday [*15th*] Our lesson in Philosophy was upon the
subject of vision — Physiology upon the Muscles — Political Economy upon the objects of the work, & Natural
History was deferred. In the P.M. we read from Abbotts
Teacher on the subject of making the lessons which we
attempt to learn familiar. — The lessons in Pronunciation

& Orthography were well recited & the school closed with a short recitation in Music – –

Friday [16th] This morn, Mr Peirce wished to try the experiment of having one of the scholars hear the recitation in N. Philosophy. Accordingly he gave to me the charge of the recitation. The feeling caused by asking the first question tended rather to excite my risibles, but feeling the necessity of sobriety — I was enabled to play the teacher for a short time. I think that he can judge very little about our idea of teaching from the example which we give him in hearing a recitation for the manner in which it is carried on depends very much upon the interest felt by the teacher in the scholars & in their study. — To furnish a variety in conducting a recitation I think it will answer very well. Our lesson in Physiology was conducted on a different principle that of learning the lesson & then writing an abstract which we read instead of recitation — During the exercise Mr Thompson from Nantucket came in & passed the remainder of the forenoon with us. The exercises were Political Economy & Natural History; neither of which were well recited. — The afternoon passed like the preceding & after tea I called to see Miss Starbuck from Nantucket who is here on a visit. —

Saturday [17th] This morn after the recitation in Orthography, & the solution of a few problems on the Globe, Mr P. gave his weekly lecture. — He commenced by giving a brief abstract of the preceding lecture. He then stated the subject of the present: "the motives, qualifications & responsibilities of a teacher". — the motives by which a teacher should be influenced are various, 1st I will give the negatives. We often hear it said that such a person is qualified for nothing else. We should then be led to think that she was qualified for that but poorly — Inadequacy in common trades, is felt only by the person himself, but in the teacher, its consequences are felt by the pupils, & their influence does not only extend to this moment or year, but is felt in succeeding generations. As in the constructions of a watch, of an inconvenient house, of a smoky chimney, these will all admit of remedy or, at least, will last only for a time, while by imparting wrong ideas to a child you not only injure this child but the errors are transmitted to posterity. It is better to make one thousand machines wrong, than to train up a child as he should not go. No person should take up the business because it is less repulsive or because it is more honorable, or easier or more advantageous in a pecuniary view. The question to be asked is, how the best good can be obtained by others & not ourselves.

It should be regarded as a sacred office, to be approached only with a desire to do good. He must have a conviction that it is the way in which he may do the most good. He should feel a deep interest in his scholars, & a love for his business. — Those whose object is to get money, or to pass away time, should be advised to turn their attention to another profession. — There are certain qualities which are very desirable to a teacher — not that he intended to say they were indispensible, but that they were very great additions. The 1st is Health — some leave other occupations as too laborious and teach a school, thinking that the trials of the school room are much less than those of any other station. Health is essential to the teacher, not only on his own account but for the sake of his pupils. To the sick, every trial is doubled. — Some suffering bad health are better teachers, than those enjoying good, but if the same person were possessed with health, he would be probably a much better teacher. — Personal deformity would be an objection not but that a dwarf or cripple *may* keep a better school than one formed with most perfect symmetry, but it would be better that the children should have the beauties of nature presented to them, than the deformities. 2nd a fair reputation and good standing in community. If people speak slightily (*sic*) of you in the town in which you have a school, you will find your scholars will disrespect you. — 4th, a well balanced mind, free from eccentricities & from the infirmities of genius. — A person may have too much, as well as too little genius for a teacher. — 5th a deep interest in children — she must feel an interest in whatever interests them; in their joys & their sorrows. Children readily perceive those who are interested in them, & feel hurt by coldness. 6th Patience, mildness, firmness, & perfect self control, are essential properties to every teacher.

Patience is requisite to meet the various trials which will beset you. You may not make so much impression by mildness in one instance, but in the end, much more will be accomplished. Mildness in manner, measures, language, countenance & in every thing else.

Firmness is especially necessary, be firm to your plans; let your measures be the same each day — A teacher without these virtues, may be compared to a city without walls; which the enemy enters without opposition, & does what he chooses after entering. 7th nice moral discrimination, a high sense of moral responsibility, & accountability — The knowledge that you are accountable to a being superior to man, sustains you. — Teachers should be acquainted with their difficulties, and know how to surmount them. The government should be just, uniform, & impartial. All rules should be made so that the pupils can see they are for their good, & the reasons for making them should be explained. Teachers should be well acquainted with the branches they are to teach. — The next lecture will be upon the responsibilities of a teacher & School order & government. —

Sunday. 18th. Attended church in the morn & heard a very good sermon from the text — "for Demas hath forsaken me having loved this present world and is departed unto Thessalonica", — preached by Mr Buckingham, 2nd Timothy. 4 chap. 10 verse. — In the afternoon, the text was Ephesians. 2 chap. 4, 5, 6, verses. The following are some of the ideas as nearly as I can remember them by the assistance of notes taken at the time — We enjoy in this world much more than the ancients, on account of the hope we have of future existence, The warrior with them, thought only of the present & if he had a hope in the future, it was that he should meet others in another world, & still pursue his favorite occupation. The philosopher expected to meet Lycurgus, Solon, & other wise men. The hero was inspired to deeds of valour, by the hope of celebrity, & no higher wish entered his mind. Their prophets & kings were no more enlightened than their subjects. This was the state of the world until the revelation came, disclosing to man the future, & exciting in him the wish to prepare himself for that existence. — Death to the Christian, is as sleep to other men. Sleep is a rest from worldly cares, to enable us to resume them with renewed activity; death, to prepare us to take up our heavenly labors. — We may suppose that the good of other worlds will join us in heaven; the inhabitants of the stars if any there be will be sharers in its happiness. The hope of heaven will sustain us, and urge us to the performance of our duty; it calms many anxieties & enables us to bear many trials. This hope is very different from any earthly good; the former is enjoyed by all; while only a few participate in the latter. The parent & child, rich & poor, master & servant, all are invited to lay aside sin & enter heaven. —

Every one has hope, but of a very different nature; many exclude the thought of death from their minds entirely. — . Without it life would be embittered — Only a few feel a sincere hope of heaven; but God has inspired no such distrust neither has Christ favored a doubt. — If "hope deferred maketh the heart sick" then hope destroyed blasteth everything. Look around in the world; would there be so much sabbath-breaking if the hope of heaven beamed upon all hearts? Would not religion appear more lovely if you felt that you could obtain the privilege of entering heaven by striving for it? — It is only through consciousness of sin, that we despair of heaven; yet though God is purer than all ·beings he does not regard our sins as the world regards the sins of those who offend it. Whatever the condition of our hearts, if we believe in him we can be forgiven, & enter heaven; and this has no exception. Since God has offered forgiveness, & has sent a messenger into the world to us, let us accept the conditions, and all strive for future happiness. —

Monday [*19th*] The subject of the Philosophy lesson was the Images of Objects. Mr P — saw fit to continue the recitation under my direction for a week, therefore I heard it this morn. In Physiology we wrote an abstract of the lesson and some of the scholars read but there was not time for all. — Book-keeping & Mental Philosophy were the other exercises of the morn. The P.M. was occupied with a variety of studies chiefly the simple branches as Arithmetic Geography &c —

Tuesday [20th] Philosophy treated of Optical Instruments. The subject is one that requires much explanation & therefore I requested Mr P. to take the recitation fearing that the scholars might suffer if they depended upon my explanations. He consented & heard the recitation but as I had anticipated the lesson was badly recited & therefore was to be repeated on the next morning. In the P.M. Mr P. called the class on the Globes & explained subjects connected with it until 4 o'clock when he gave us an intermission and after that we attended to sketching a map of North America, but none of us succeeded very well & it is to be repeated. This closed the afternoon & school was dismissed. —

Wednesday [21st] This morn we recited the lesson in Philosophy & it appeared to be better understood than it was yesterday. This took up an hour & half & after recess we read our abstracts when there was a half hour before school closed. Mr P. gave us the question, Can the proper object of schools be secured without appeal to corporal punishments & rewards or premiums? to discuss & we each in order proceeded to give our opinions upon the subject — Mine is that it is very seldom necessary to appeal to corporal punishment & that rewards should not be given. — One or two agreed with me, & some approved of punishment & others, not. — After conversing a while upon this subject it was nearly 12 o'clock & school closed. —

Thursday [22d] The time generally devoted to recitation was occupied in explanation of the principles in Philosophy, therefore the exercise was deferred till the next morn. — The abstracts in Physiology were generally good as far as they were read. Political Economy, as usual, just passable. Natural History treated of the circulation of the blood and was not recited as well as usual. The subject seemed to be difficult & the distinction between the different parts of the system & the offices of these parts not well understood. — In the P.M. the lessons were all recited except Orthoëpy which was omitted for want of time. —

Friday. [23d] A.M. Absent on account of the headache — P.M. Lessons similar to the day before — all recited in season. —

GLOBES USED AT LEXINGTON, 1839–1842

(Now at Framingham)

Saturday. [*24th*]   After some reviews, Mr P. proceeded to
give a lecture upon the subject of the Responsibility of the
Teacher. — To have some conception of this, remember
that you are to influence the character, the future standing
of the ten, fifty, or an hundred children who are committed
to your care.   Imagine each in his course through the world,
& that your work will shape all their feelings, & the influence which they will exert through life.   This will be imparted to those who are placed under their care, & thus
your influence, instead of being confined to the hundred
under your eye, will extend to thousands. — The situation,
by taking this view of it, assumes a high responsibility —
It is responsible in every stage, but chiefly so at the beginning.   It is like a building; if the foundation is laid
uneven it totters to the base, but if the contrary it will
stand for ages.   It is the same with physical, mental & moral
education.   If you instill false principles into their minds,
your successors will have to root them out, before they can
begin to act.   The wife of Dr. Cornelius, said, that if she
had but ten yrs. to act upon the character of a person, she
would prefer the first ten.   This part of education is generally committed to females.   You may begin the education
so that he will dislike the school-room & cause him to avoid
it.   A little girl enters school for the first time, & being
unaccustomed to restraint was as lively as at home.   Her
teacher passing her, said, if you do not sit still I will cut
your ears off.   The child, of course, was very much alarmed,
and whenever the teacher was near her during the day,
covered her ears with her hands.   The consequence of such
treatment was, that she was unwilling to go to school for a
long time after that, & caused much trouble to her parents.
You may conduct your school in this manner, or you may
make first impressions pleasant, & thus make your successors work easy. — The instruction given in primary schools,
is in many instances all the education, both moral & intellectual, that the children have.   If 1st impressions are
right, others will hardly be wrong, thus if you sow a field
with good seed, the tares will be few and easily uprooted.
All intellectual habits take shape & coloring from the hand
first forming them. — The physical organs are becoming

more & more rigid, and if children are allowed to give indistinct utterance to their words at first, as in lisping, they will carry this habit through life, and it will be almost impossible to correct it. — It is easier to teach a child who has never learned anything, than one who has learned a few things, & has wrong ideas of those. For example, a General in the last war had troops under his command composed of raw soldiers & militia men. In making his report after the war, he advised Congress to enlist the former, as it was easier to make good soldiers of these than of the latter. — The coloring to *all* their actions is derived from light reflected to the pupil from the teacher. There is a great difference in the effect upon the pupil, whether he is driven to his studies, whether you laugh at his blunders, whether you deal with him in such a manner as to cause him to be open & frank, or to use duplicity & cunning. Whether you govern by flattery, hope of reward, or by sense of duty. From the consideration of all these things, we see that the teacher takes upon herself a work of great responsibility. Children governed by the rod at home, & those hired by hope of reward, differ from those in whom the sense of duty has been exercised. In stepping over the threshold of your school-room, you have stepped into a very great responsibility. – –

The next lecture will be on the subject of school order. —

Examined by Mr P — thus far.

Sunday. — *25th Aug.* Went to church all day & heard Mr Buckingham. The sermon in the morn was better than that in the afternoon, but both were very interesting. The text in the morn was Gen. 2.15. "& the Lord God took the man and put him into the garden of Eden to dress it and to keep it". That of the P.M. was from Job — The words have passed out of my mind, evincing the bad effects of *procrastination* as this should all have been written one week ago. — After tea we took a short walk & found it very pleasant, the heat of the atmosphere having abated.

Monday 26th The lesson in N. Philosophy was upon the kite & the subject not being well explained in the book Mr P. occupied the time in giving additional illustrations. —

In the morn the Brigade Band from Boston came out &
with the Lexington artillery marched up in front of this
house and then through the Mall. — The scene was entirely
new to me & I liked the order and regularity with which
they moved. — To proceed with the lessons in the morn.
Physiology was upon the effects of Muscular Exercise on
the principal Functions of the Body, on Shampooing & the
time for taking exercise. — Book-keeping was an oral exercise and not so interesting as when it is making entries in
the Journal.   The afternoon exercises were Arithmetic,
Grammar & drafting the map of North America. — We
succeeded better in this than usual, & therefore were allowed to take the map of South America. — Orthography
with Moral Philosophy closed the session. —

Tuesday [27th] The exercises were similar to those of
the day before. The lesson upon the kite was well recited as
I thought but not quite satisfactory to the teacher. —
Physiology lesson was a continuation of the subject of exercise. — Book-keeping similar to the previous lesson; &
Political Economy upon the subject of the aid to production
rendered by Nature. — The map of South America was
drafted very well, for the first attempt. — Mr. P. gave us
an invitation to go to Commencement, with him on Wednesday as he was intending to have no school either on that
day or Friday. —

Wednesday 28th The morning dawned, but apparently
not very auspiciously upon our projected excursion. The
clouds were rarefied & condensed by turns; at one time
the rain fell in large drops, at another, a fog appeared on the
hills surrounding. — At seven the stage drove up to the
door and Miss Stowe & myself in company with Mr P., his
sister & niece, were soon on the way to our place of destination. — We arrived at a hotel near the church in which the
exercises were to be performed at nine & went from there,
to the church. — Crowds of people were standing on the
pavements waiting the moment that the doors should be
opened. Some wore no bonnets & others only veils thrown
over their heads presenting when grouped together quite
a motley crowd. It seemed to be made by many an occasion
for exhibition of finery & dress. — The exercises commenced

by a prayer by Mr Walker formerly of Charleston & then they proceeded to the orations &c, the president announcing the name & subject in Latin before each one. From the various speakers & subjects I preferred the poem by Thomas Dawes of Cambridge & the Oration upon "the Old Age of the Scholar" by Samuel Elliot of Boston. — The exercises continued until three. P.M. & were closed by another prayer by Mr Walker. We walked to the hotel & waited there for the stage when we returned to Lexington feeling very well satisfied with our day's occupation, but ever ready for whatever is allied to excitement, a proposition was listened to & eagerly accepted that we should go down again on Thursday to attend the meeting of the Φ.B.K. Society. —

Thursday 29th The weather was not more favorable, but we had found that it was more comfortable without the sun & regretted but little to find the sky overcast & the thermometer many degrees lower than on the preceding day. — This day we took seats down stairs & near the speakers which proved to be a more favorable position than that of the preceding day in the gallery. — On seating myself, I was agreeably surprised by seeing an old school acquaintance in the pew before me whom I had not met before for several years. — I had heard that commencement was the place for meetings with old friends but I did not expect that it would be my lot to see any there. — The exercises were commenced by the prize speaking which continued until after eleven when there was an intermission of a half hour, during which the names of those to whom prizes had been awarded were read. — Then the sound of distant music was heard & approached nearer until it stopped in front when a procession was formed and the members walked in headed by the President & Governor & seated themselves on each side of the pulpit. — After a prayer by Mr Sternes, Mr Cushing delivered an oration on the subject of reform. — The most part of it was interesting although I did not agree with him in many things. — Music followed & then Dr Flint delivered a poem which was very interesting & caused much laughter. — The subject was the change or rather the difference between Commencement when he was a pupil & the present day. — After this the

Society marched out & forming a procession walked to the
hall in which a dinner was served. — We returned to the
hotel & Mr P. took a carriage & conveyed us all to Mount
Auburn, about a mile & a quarter from Cambridge. We
occupied all our time which was very short, in rambling
about & returned to the Colleges. We saw Spurhtzeim's
[Spurzheim's] tomb & also one of Appleton's which was
brought from Italy & was in the form of a small house.
— The scenery was much more beautiful than I had anticipated & there were many more tombs there. – – The
College library consists of upwards of 50,000 vols. 35000
of which were contained in the rooms we entered. — We
walked hastily through & returning found the stage waiting
for us — The weather was now decidedly cold, & we found
that it was difficult to keep warm in returning.

Friday. 30th. Were it the 29th of Nov. instead of Aug. the
weather would not seem so much out of season, but now by
enveloping ourselves in shawls & sitting by the fire as much
as possible we can keep ourselves tolerably warm — The
lesson in Nat. Philosophy was upon the subject of Sailing
& was understood with difficulty probably owing to the state˙
of our mental powers as sympathizing with our physical in a
state of semi congelation. — Physiology succeeded better
& the remaining lessons of the day were recited very well.
We spent the most part of eve in preparing for the work of
the succeeding day; *id est* by sitting near the stove & re-
storing action to our benumbed senses. —

Saturday 31st The last day of summer, & we have been
here two months. 'Tis true that time waits for no man &
it would appear that he had left us far behind but on taking
a more favorable view of the subject we find that we have
become initiated into the customs & rules of the school &
thus have laid the foundation for future advancement. —
After reviews in Problems & reading in the Bible, Mr P.
called on us for our opinion with regard to the question —
"whether the pupils in school should change seats", & all
were found to agree in the negative. — There was no time
for the discussion & Mr P. expressed his sentiments. He
said that he objected to it for several reasons. 1st that it
would tend to foster bad passions as pride, emulation. —

2nd it turns the attention from the chief thing & induces a desire to excel others. 3d it lays the foundation for competition & strife & emulation. — By emulation is not meant thirst for knowledge and love of approbation for they may exist without it. — When we are asked what we depend upon in the absence of this inducement; we would answer; let the teacher gratify the natural curiosity of his pupils, present knowledge in an attractive form, rely upon their desire to have the love & good will of their teachers and their friends, present it to them as a means of usefulness — Talk of their duty to society & God & these will be found to be sufficiently powerful motives. — Besides there is harm done by holding up anything as better than knowledge. — After these remarks, he proceeded to deliver his lecture, which was upon the subject of *School Order*. He commenced by calling our attention to the importance of the office of the teacher, with how many & various & invaluable interests it may connect us; if we are faithful how many will be rendered more happy by our instructions. — Follow each into life, notice his effect upon others & all his actions and after doing this we shall be able to answer the question "is not the relation of teacher one of unspeakable responsibility. — A good school must be orderly; whatever its object or title, or whoever its teacher may be. A school may be pleasant & forward, or even more than this, but order is necessary to make it a good one. The work of Education is a work of order. Order was Heaven's first law. The apostle directs that every thing should be done with order & the wise man associates the want of it with confusion. Look where you will, on celestial or terrestrial things; when you will in time past, present, or future & you will find it essential. If a man has failed, we hear, almost invariably, soon after, that his affairs were in a disorderly state. Death is put to all hopes of success without it. Oxygen is not more essential to vitality. — For your encouragement, I will add, that children, much as they like freedom, are fond of order & system. This is the cause of their admiration of regular figures, as the circles, & of their preference of such, when many are offered them. Consequently they are better suited by an orderly school, & if you would wish to please them,

confine them to rules.　This will also be more satisfactory
to yourselves as you will be more successful & will know
that nothing is neglected. — The 1st aid in keeping a school
in order is a good location & well furnished room.　These
are generally given without choice in public schools, but in
private the teacher has the entire regulation.　It will add not
a little to the comfort both of teachers & scholars. — 2nd
Have for your motto "a place for every thing & every thing
in its place"; adhere strictly to this & not have it merely a
rule upon paper but a practical one.　Assign a place to each
scholar & have everything put in its proper place at night.
This may appear of trifling importance but it will very
much influence the character of a school & will create habits
of order in the pupils. — 3d. Have everyone furnished with
proper utensils & books.　In many schools the pupils are
allowed to borrow the articles needed, but this practise is
always attended with confusion.　4th　With order neatness
is connected. — This is very important upon many accounts
but especially upon account of the influence it has upon
health.　Enter one school & you will [find] neither scraper,
mat or broom or if they were supplied lying useless.　In
another the scene is entirely varied.　All the air neatness &
tidiness of a domestic department are found there. — If
you wish to train a child to habits of neatness & order you
must present him with an example of these.　The teacher
must be as particular as he requires his pupils to be.　His
dress must partake of neatness.　If he is faulty, he cannot
expect his pupils will regard his rules.　The above mentioned qualities have many advantages.　Time is wasted by
disorder & comfort is lost by slovenliness.　Many teachers
appear to pride themselves upon their negligence in dress
but we may ask such what right they have to appear in
society to annoy others & to offend their eyes.　We all owe
something to the world & we must either attend to that
obligation, or keep out of sight.　5th　Have a time for everything & everything in its time.　Have a time to begin & a
time to end.　Let a programme of exercises be made embracing both the number, & time for each, & adhere to it
without deviation.　There is great economy in doing this —
Attempt to do only one thing at a time & order will be more

easily preserved.   Have all the time of teachers & scholars
fully occupied for without occupation they will be engaged
in mischief.   Fill up their time with just what they can do
& nothing more.   We must be daily examples of what we
enjoin.   If we would have our pupils punctual we must be
punctual ourselves; if we would have them orderly & neat
be so ourselves.   Do not be satisfied with being pretty
punctual, but have perfection in everything.   6th.   Soft
& gentle movements contribute to order.   Walk lightly;
move gently; speak softly; one touch of the bell is better
than many.   It is said that Caesar by one tap upon the table
silenced the whole Roman Senate. — Let the first thing
done, on entering a school, be to arrange the scholars &
make out a plan of exercises remember that whatever be
the name or quality of a school it cannot be good, without
order.

Next subject — School Government. —

Sunday, Sept. 1st. — Went to Church and heard Mr
Buckingham preach all day. — The text in the morning
was from John, 21st 4th verse.   "But when the morning
was come, Jesus stood on the shore: but the disciples knew
not that it was, Jesus."   It was Communion Sabbath & the
sermon was adapted to it. — I thought it was not quite so
interesting as some I had heard from him. — In the afternoon he preached from Ecclesiastes 7th 29th.   "Lo this
only have I found, that God hath made man upright; but
they have sought out many inventions." — After Miss
O'Connor & sister came out with a cousin from Baltimore.
The evening was passed in Writing Reading & Studying. —

Monday [2d]   Mr P. opened the school by reading a part
of the 23d Chap. of Matthew.   After reading he made a
comment upon the passage "these ought ye to have done,
and not to leave the other undone."   He said that it was
customary for us in our zeal to perform one thing to leave
another undone & that when he saw this the text was brought
forcibly to his mind.   The next verse "Ye blind guides!
which strain at a gnat & swallow a camel" he thought
would be rendered more intelligible according to the present
use of words if it were strain out instead of at. — The lesson
in N. Philosophy was the last section in the book, upon the

subject of Flying. — It was explained upon the same principles as Sailing & I think the Author was more happy in
the illustrations than in several of the preceding chapters.
It seems to me that as the subject grows more difficult he
is less & less particular in his demonstrations or at any rate
his manner of explanation is not nearly so interesting. —
The lessons in Physiology are more interesting than any
others to which we attend. They are so practical that one
can not but feel that they are addressed as much to himself
as others. —

Book-keeping increases in interest & I am surprised to
find it so easy. The difficulties of which I have heard so
much are probably before me. The lessons of the afternoon
were as usual. Owing to indisposition I asked leave to
retire & thus lost an hour. The Moral Philosophy lesson
was omitted for want of time. — School closed at half after
four. The hours for commencement for this & the ensuing
month being $8 + \frac{1}{2}$ & $1 + \frac{1}{2}$. – – – – – – – – – –

Tuesday. [*3d*] The weather this morn appears more like
the season than it has for some time, & the birds are singing
merrily as if to hail the returning warmth. Upon such a
morning one can but feel that their tasks are lightened and
apply themselves more busily. — The lesson in Philosophy
was repeated & to fix more permanently the latter part it
was determined that we should review it. — The Physiology was well recited & the plan of asking questions will be
very successful if everyone take as much interest as I feel.
I think that we shall learn even more than by a recitation
if we express ourselves freely upon every subject. Mental
Philosophy was deferred for want of time. — The lessons in
the afternoon were well recited with the exception of Arithmetic & the pupils do not seem to comprehend Mr P's
ideas upon that. The Moral philosophy lesson is very
tedious, I think, as the commencement of almost every
study is. When we get more acquainted with the author's
style we shall comprehend his work the better. — This
evening the heavens presented the most splendid appearance that I ever witnessed. The Aurora Borealis appeared
from the N.E. & one glare of light round to the S.W. as
brilliant in the S. as in any part of the heavens. The rays

from every point converged & immediately over head a spot of the size of a cart wheel was dark the rays forming the circumference distinctly. — This was the appearance about 9 in the eve. The whole sky was red above but in the northern horizon one continued line of light extended from east to west. —

Wednesday. [*4th*] This morn we recited in N. Philosophy. the principal part of the time was passed in explanations of the Trade winds which was the most difficult part of the lesson. — The Physiology was upon the Bones & was not less interesting than the last. Mr P gave us some sentences in false Syntax to correct & these were done by most of the scholars. — In intermission I asked the cause of Aurora Borealis & in reply he read the following from the 3d vol. of Scientific Tracts.

"Aurora Borealis. — Mr. Fisher, of the Royal Society, who has written very sensibly, and more recently than any one else, to our knowledge, has come to the conclusion that the aurora borealis is an electric phenomenon arising from the positive electricity of the atmosphere, developed by the rapid condensation of the vapor in the act of freezing, and the induced negative electricity of the surrounding portions of the atmosphere; & that it is the immediate consequence of the restoration of the electrical equilibrium by the intervention of frozen particles, which being imperfect conductors, become luminous while transmitting electricity. In tropical & temperate climates, says the author of this truly ingenious theory, this phenomenon does not occur because the electric equilibrium is restored by means of aqueous vapors, a process which often gives rise to thunder & lightning, but never to the Aurora borealis." — After this the class read in the bible & then school was dismissed. — This P.M. walked out to Squire Phinny's in company with Miss Damon & stopped to tea. It is a very pleasant walk only about two miles and a half. Returned about 7 not feeling at all fatigued —

Thursday. [*5th*] This morn Mr P. conversed during the time generally devoted to the recitation in Philosophy upon the subject of Light & read & explained to us the two theories commonly received & the objections to them. — They are the following 1st that light is composed of particles constantly emanating from the Sun. 2nd that [it] is an elastic fluid which prevades the universe & is put in motion, in some unknown manner by luminous bodies. A strong objection to the supposition that light is a fluid, is that its motions are in straight lines, this is an argument in favor of the materiality. When it passes from one medium to another it is acted upon according to the laws which govern matter. — To its materiality, it has been objected that particles moving with such a velocity would have a momentum which would be irresistible, 2ndly that such a number of rays would interfere upon one another & 3dly that the sun & stars would waste & grow dim by such a profuse expenditure of matter. These objections are answered 1st that the quantity of matter is small in proportion as the velocity is great, 2ndly that it is not necessary that the rays should consist of contiguous particles because the retina has the power of retaining the sensation of objects after the object itself has passed, long enough for light to pass 22,000 miles. 3dly the danger from waste is very slight for in 6000 yrs the waste would only be 670 pounds avoirdupois. — The recitation in Physiology was also explanations and a brief analysis of the last lesson with the advance lesson. – – Natural History had only a few moments left to it so after hearing a short account of it we were dismissed. The lessons of the P.M were all recited. — That in Orthoëpy not so well as might have been.

Friday 6th This morn was all devoted to recitation; the 1st, Philosophy, was a review of the theories on the preceding page & some account of the reflection of light & the manner in which the earth appears to the Lunarians if there are any. — Physiology lesson upon the bones, principally relative to their composition, with a review of the last lesson on the same subject. Political Economy — upon the division of labor. This is a very interesting study to me & I like the manner in which the author treats it very well. If he succeed as well in making every subject intelligible he must be an excellent teacher. — Will you, Mr P. tell us about the school at Barre — something about its numbers &c? — It will be pleasant to hear of the success of those

engaged in a similar undertaking. Natural History described
animals under the order Carnivora comprehending various
tribes 1st the Bats, 2ndly the insectivora. 3d the animals
like the tiger & lion bear & badger & dog. 4th Amphibious
Animals as the Seal & Moose. — This subject has all the
charms of *Novelty* which do not seem to diminish as we
advance in the book. —

Saturday 7th   Mr P. opened the school by reading from
the 26th Chap. of Matthew. He commented upon the
parable of the talents & explained the value of thirty pieces
of silver, the sum for which Judas betrayed our Saviour.
Each piece was about fifty cts. making the sum fifteen
dollars. — With regard to the parable he said that he should
speak chiefly of the servant who received the one talent. He
said there were many who made the same excuse in the
world that this servant did. They would not do such &
such things because they had not the power the wealth, the
talents, the knowledge that others had. The same remark
was applicable to the school as to the world generally because one scholar had not power to express herself in a
manner as happy as she would wish she would be discouraged & cease to try at all, forgetting that it is probable that
if the one having the one talent had used that talent well he
would also have been approved as well as he who gained
five having five given him. — The next exercise was
Orthoepy & after that Composition. The latter exercise
consisted in reading aloud the pieces. Some seemed to feel
very badly at being obliged to do it, but I think that it is
about as easy to read one's ideas as to speak them as we do
every day of our lives. It is only the associations connected
with Composition that renders it so difficult to scholars as
it almost invariably is. — After some comments upon the
pieces in which Mr P. expressed himself pleased with the
attempt he proceeded to give his lecture. — The subject of
the remarks was School Government. This is necessary to
every school. Teachers or scholars must govern; it must be
a Monarchy Democracy or Republic. It is the same with a
family as with a school, if the reins of government be put
into the hands of the pupils or children, failure must be the
result. The most which can be done in a school is to admit

the scholars to a qualified participation. Let their opinion be asked & let them assist the teacher in devising means for improving the school as much as possible. But it is best to go no farther than this. After you are convinced that the teacher must be governor decide on what principles the government shall be based. Whether you will govern by fear of punishment, by force of persuasion or by both, Have the question settled at the outset as far as possible. A teacher's views may be changed by various things after her commencement, but she ought not to begin without a fixed determination. Let her not at one time rely upon hope at another upon fear, thus varying continually. — System is valuable in every thing in Agriculture Manufactures & Commerce but especially in school keeping. — A government conducted by caprice is no Government at all: the end of it is only failure & mortification. Decide whether your government shall be by threats & blows or by presenting knowledge in an attractive form & as a means of happiness. — The mode of governing by premiums & rewards, is objectionable in principle, & not easy in application. It is something like attempting to bribe a moral being to do her moral duty. In some families, children are bribed or rather hired to be good & obedient & kind to each other: now this may be very effectual, but it is not making them virtuous; they love the reward, more than truth, duty & obedience. The proper exercise of all one's faculties, carries with it its own reward & on this, the teacher should depend. There is something absurd in hiring children to eat, to exercise & to study: for physical exercise is of itself a reward to the child & therefore he needs no other. Every child is willing to eat when he is hungry. The same is true with the intellectual powers. The scholar has a moral character & filial obedience & love must be obtained by influence over this. If these are secured they should be the fruits of moral training. The child who is good from the promise of a guinea is not better than he who said "I go" & went not. Children should not have in school any expectation of reward. Besides direct appeal it is well to hold up to children all the fruits & rewards of well doing, their peace their usefulness & the approbation of those they love, but not to leave this train &

have something else as the main thing. — If he may not do this he may after the occasion has passed let them know that he is not dissatisfied with them. If the reliance be upon rewards he may no doubt produce immediate effects, he may secure good order & make some good scholars but he is not promiting (*sic*) the object he intended; for his training should be extended to all the faculties & he should look to the end in all. There are particular objections to premiums & also to the recurrence to fear as a principle of government which will be the subject of the next lecture. —

Sunday [8th] Attended church and heard a gentleman who has just taken his degree, preach. The morning sermon was from the text 1st Corinthians, 15th 31st. I protest by your rejoicing which I have in Christ Jesus our Lord, I die daily. — In the afternoon from Timothy 1st 2nd Chap. 8th v. I will therefore that men pray every where, lifting up holy hands, without wrath. He succeeded very well & seemed little embarrassed. —

Monday — 9th This morn Mr P read a short portion from the scriptures & then made some remarks upon death, the manner in which it should be regarded, & the feelings which should attend the bed of sickness. — The exercise in Philosophy was the asking of questions prepared by the scholars for that purpose the lesson given out being deferred until the next day. — The lesson in Physiology also deferred. — The afternoon studies as usual. The problem in the globe was rather too deep for me to fathom but I succeeded "in making land" as Mr P. said. – – The lesson in Moral Philosophy was badly recited. The subject as yet seems to excite but little interest among the pupils. – –

Tuesday 10th This morn Miss Stodder heard the lesson in Philosophy, the subject of which was Refraction. She succeeded very well I think. The lesson in Physiology was upon the subject of the Bones & was a very long lesson, being composed of the one which was omitted on the previous day & another in advance. After the lesson in Book-keeping was recited we had a short recess & then the lesson in Mental Philosophy. After the exercises were completed Mr P. made some remarks upon the subject of school order & we were dismissed. In the P.M. he gave us some problems to perform in Arithmetic & after that taught us about

the Globes which subject I think we were all rather dull
in comprehending. — After this exercise he informed us
that there was to be an examination at the Public School
& therefore he would dismiss school that those who wished
might be able to attend. Many of the pupils attended but
owing to some premonitory symptoms of the head-ache, I
thought it better to take some exercise in the open air.
This I did but it did not have the desired effect & I took my
bed soon after study hours commenced.

Wednesday [11th]   The exercises of the morn were commenced by reading from Matthew, on the subject of Christ's
betrayal & of Peter's denial of him. — After the devotional
exercises we began upon a new style of recitation i.e. reciting stories giving descriptions or whatever kind of recitation we chose provided it was not taken from the ordinary
school exercises. — The 1st by Miss Stodder was an account
of or rather a story of Dionysius the tyrant of Sicily &
Damocles one of his courtiers. The 2nd by M. Swift a
description of a ride to Mt. Auburn, 3d by Miss Stowe an
anecdote Faith & Works — 4th Miss Rolph on the Eman-
cipation in the W.I. islands. 5th Miss Locke, the pride of a
cow. 6th Miss Smith — the knowledge which the Indians
had of the flood — 7th Miss Haskins anecdote of Rev. Mr.
Adams — 8th Miss Haskell, of a child on hearing a sermon
upon the subject of being good. 8th Miss Eliz^th Locke of
a slave, who was told in Eng. that he was free, 9th Miss
O'Connor anecdote of King John of Scotland. — All succeeded in a degree; but some much better than others. —
After this exercise Mr P. gave us a lecture in Philosophy
being the first of a course upon that subject. It included a
description of the Thermometer, Barometer, Forcing Pump,
Common Pump, with the exhibition of these & gave us an
illustration of the Refraction of Light.

[Remarks upon thermometer and barometer omitted.]

·   ·   ·   ·   ·   ·   ·   ·   ·   ·   ·

At the close of the school he made some remarks upon the
necessity of order, & then gave us the heads from a work
upon a subject — 1st Form a plan & carry it out. 2nd
Acquire a habit of industry. 3d Cultivate a habit of per-

severance. 4th Cultivate a habit of punctuality. 5th Be an early riser 6th Be in the habit of learning something from every person you meet. 7th Act from fixed principles. 8th Be simple & neat in personal habits. 9th Whatever you do at all, do well. — After this the school closed.

Thursday 12th Sept.—This morn for the second time three rows of seats were filled, thus making our number twelve. The subject of the verses which Mr P. read on opening the school, was the denial of Christ by Peter. — After reading them he made some remarks upon them. He said that the life of Peter was full of instruction; it showed us how easily we may be lead away by those who are around us, and how little we know of our own weakness until we make a trial of ourselves. — When Peter was told by his Lord that he would deny him ere the cock crew thrice I did not believe he should, but we see him yielding on the first occasion. Had it not been for the company with which he was surrounded he would not probably have yielded so readily. This is a striking example of the sacrifices that many in the world make for popularity. It was this desire which caused Peter to leave everything & deny his Lord. — The life of this apostle exhibits many striking features & a review of his life made by collecting all the facts scattered through the New Testament would be a good Moral as well as Intellectual exercise. — When this exercise, was nearly completed Mr Mann entered the room. — In a few moments the attention of the scholars was called to the morning lesson in Philosophy. It happened to be upon the subject of Colors, one of the most interesting Chapters in the book. An abstract of the lesson was given & then Mr P. took out the prisms & made two spectrums upon the wall. One made by the smaller prism exhibited a phenomenon which could not be produced by the other. It was this; after the spectrum was formed once upon the wall the Red being at the bottom, & the Violet at the top, the intermediate colors between in their orders, we noticed a repetition of the colors Violet & Indigo as distinctly as in the Spectrum. This could not be seen by Mr P. or Mr Mann owing to some defects in vision but was easily distinguished by the scholars as well as by *myself*. — The fact was left without explanation, and if we can find any comments upon it Mr. P. wishes us to let him know. — In connection with this subject Mr. Mann mentioned a rainbow which he saw when standing upon a mountain formed in the mist around, this not being sufficiently condensed to form drops. — It was formed very near him & therefore appeared nearly horizontal instead of assuming the shape of an arch and was several yards wide, though the colors were quite indistinct, on account of the rareness of the mist.   Mr P. said that he had seen a rainbow after the sun had set which of course was formed high in the heavens. — He had also seen a *Lunar* bow. — We recited a lesson in Physiology which was a review of the *"first two"* chapters. — 1st telling of the intentions of the author and the use of the book. 2nd the use of the skin. – – The Natural History lesson was upon the orders Rodentia or Edentata. — The question was asked whether animals are governed by instinct or reason. & Mr Mann said he thought the latter was so. — In illustration of this Mr M. spoke of the Elephant at Exeter Change who was unable to reach a piece of money and therefore acted upon the law of reflection & refraction.   He blew upon the wall and the wind reacting against the money forced it towards him – – In the afternoon Mr Mann again came to the school and during the reading exercise Mr Dodge entered.   The examination of the class in the subject of the Chapter was not so good as usual.   Most of the pupils failed in answering the questions that were put to them the lesson in Orthoëpy was not very fruitful of questions & after punctuating a few sentences, the school closed. – –

Friday [13th]   This day has been spent in writing home, & the latter part of it in taking physical exercise.   A walk was taken by all the Normalites residing in the Academy and by one residing near.   It extended as far as the sign board saying two and a half miles to Lexington and then returned; it was rather bleak but walking rapidly kept us warm. —

Saturday [14th]   This morn we expected to have to go into school and write our pieces in Composition but last eve Mr P. entered to tell us that he would give us one more day as he was going to Boston — We did not much regret this as we had many jobs or chores to do and this would give us a good opportunity to make our accounts balance. — Received two letters from home tonight.

Sunday. 15th Sept. — The preacher of to day was Mr. Crofts the same who filled the pulpit last Sunday. The text this morn was from the 39th Psalm 3d verse. "While I was musing the fire burned." — Some of the ideas expressed were the following — Reflection is necessary that the divine fire may burn within us. — Notice the transactions in the world; we see that a person is daily in the habit of reflecting ere he takes the first steps in life. — Every act in business is studied and thought upon before it is performed. — The sailor on the ocean turns to his guides & reflects & considers upon them. We are voyagers on the sea of life; then it is necessary that we look to the quicksands and examine our chart under whose guidance we may reach the destined port. — The remainder of the sermon is upon the subject of the necessity and advantages of having stated seasons for musing. — The class who say these are not needed are numerous and are rapidly increasing: but if we consider their religious experience we shall find it is from their early habits that they have reached thus far towards perfection. There is, doubtless, too much reverence paid to external appearances. There are many who think attending church on the Sabbath, prayer meetings &c. is religion. — What does experience teach us with regard to stated times? What gives our New England her superiority? Is it not their regard of the Sabbath, which is shown by the number of heaven-directed spires which every where meet the eye? Why do we hear of the derelection of principles among our young men who go to the West? Is it not because there they have no religious ordinances? How many mothers sit lonely upon the banks of the western rivers bathed in tears & wishing that some such blessings could reach them there, as they enjoyed in their younger days?

The advantages are very obvious. The most prominent is that they draw the souls from the things of the world. — To remember a friend we retire and endeavor to recal his voice and features. It is thus with the Christian; he calls up his God and reflects upon his character. — He feels his

Students' Desk used at West Newton, 1844–1853

God to be nearer in affliction; for then he can better realize the messages of his Holy Spirit dispensing consolation, descending like a dove and lighting & relighting upon him until he can say, it is good for me that I have been afflicted. — We are to muse fervently and habitually, ere the divine fire can burn in us. — In the afternoon the text was from the 5th Chap. of Matthew 3d v. "Blessed are the poor in spirit, for theirs is the kingdom of heaven'. The first Beatitude. The sermon was very good. —

Monday Sept. 16 The school assembled again this morn, but two of our seats were vacant. After reading from the Scriptures Mr P. spoke of the erroneous views that were pervading the state with regard to the conditions of entering the Normal School. Some believe that the pupils must bind themselves to instruct a certain number of years; while others carry the story farther, and suppose that they are obliged to bind themselves to keep school for their life time. Some that they must teach a public school and others that the school must be in this commonwealth. — He told us these that we may be able when we meet with any person entertaining such opinions to contradict them & tell them the true conditions. — He also told us of his intentions concerning a Model school; that this would according to the plan marked out be included in the third year, but that as we should probably stay only one year he should interest himself immediately to procure one upon which some of the scholars might operate. — — — — — The lesson in Philosophy was heard by Miss Stodder upon the subject of Reflection. — Physiology was in review the 3d & 4th Chapters but for want of time the latter was deferred — Book-keeping & Mental Philosophy — recited —. — The afternoon was rather less happy than the morn on acc't of misunderstanding with regard to lessons, but all were recited. —

Tuesday Sept. 17th Two seats still vacant. — Miss Stodder heard the lesson in Philosophy, the subject of which was Vision. — After the recitation Mr Peirce gave us an explanation of the phenomenon called "the Mirage". He explained it upon the principle of Refraction & of Reflection. To illustrate it he told us a fact which none had noticed viz; that when you look through two contiguous pains (*sic*) of glass without changing the position of the eye; when looking through the lower you can see the sky above the object; but upon looking through the other you see a part of the object apparently detached and resting upon the air. — The cause of this is the different refracting powers of the window glass. — The recitation in Physiology was deferred until the morrow. — The other forenoon exercises performed. — The P.M. spent a short time upon Arithmetic and then passed to Grammar & Geography. In connection with the latter subject he spoke upon the origin of the word Asia & said that there were various opinions. Some say it is derived from the Phenician Language; some from the Asiones inhabitants of Asia Minor. — There is also a doubt about the division; it was used for Asia Minor lying between the Mediterranean & Black Seas; also for Ephesus, situated in the west of Asia Minor. This last is the signification given in the scriptures. — For the next lesson in Geography different parts are assigned to each scholar & she must learn all she can concerning that. —

Wednesday Sept. 18th The first exercise was Reading a portion of the Scriptures commencing the 50th verse, 27th Chap. Matt. Mr P. made some remarks upon the 52nd verse. And the graves were opened; and many bodies of the saints which slept, arose, — And came out of the graves &c; he said that he had often wished that there had been something more mentioned upon this subject because he believed that it was a real resurrection and not merely a phantom. — Still if it were fully explained, what part of the New Testament referred to Christ there would be a great many other parts that would still remain doubtful. — The 2nd exercise was Physiology & the 3d the Globes & 4th the Conversational Exercise. — This succeeded tolerably well & I think that after this it will be regarded as a pleasant exercise only. The 5th was a Lecture on Optics — This is the most interesting part. The sight as Addison says, is the most perfect sense, and to it we are indebted for our greatest pleasures. — Those only who examine a landscape, can form a correct idea of it for no description of it can convey a correct impression. — How much is a person hearing a speech or oration influenced by the emotion of the

speaker expressed upon his countenance. — The eye is a
natural telescope or microscope. The telescope is an imitation of the eye. — The glasses are arranged to imitate the
humors & lenses of the eye, but notwithstanding our knowledge of this we do not know how it is that the eye sees. We
know that the rays are conveyed and brought to a focus in
passing through the lenses & humors and form an image
on the retina, but how the mind is able to see them we are
unable to tell. When we have gone so far we have arrived
at the ultimatum. By knowing the laws of refraction, and
the composition of the eye, we see how if any of the lenses
or humors are injured, vision will be injured. — In case of
Cataract, when a coat grows over a part of the Chrystalline
Lens, it must be removed by an operation called Couching.
If the aqueous humor is lost it can be restored, but if the
vitreous humor is lost the eye is destroyed. — The reason[s]
that owls see in the dark are two. The first is on account of
the power of expansion & contraction of the iris. — 2nd The
lining of the Choroid is light instead of dark and thus assists
them in seeing. This is the cause of the luminous appearance of the cat's eyes when seen in the dark appearing like
phosphorus. There are some natural faults in the eye —
Some have too much convexity & bring the rays to a focus
too soon Others have too much concavity & do not bring
the rays to a focus soon enough. The eyes of old people are
too flat and sometimes near-sightedness is corrected by age.
The former use convex & the latter concave. — It is called
lense from a supposed resemblance to a sort of bean. —
Thursday. 19th The morning lesson in Philosophy was
upon the subject of vision. It was short and well explained
by Mr. Bakewell. — The lesson in Physiology, a review of
the Fifth Chap. in Combe's Physiology, which treats of the
effects of exercise upon the muscles, and the different times
& kinds of exercise which are best for the health. Political
Economy was upon Economical Arrangements, and principally on Division of Labor. — The subject of N. History
was the order Ruminantia under the class Mammalia.
The Camelopard or Giraffe was mentioned and there was
some doubt between those who had seen the animal whether
it was white spotted with brown or brown with white. I

think it must be a very singular looking animal if there is so much difficulty in deciding upon the color. — In the afternoon we recited all the lessons except that in the Dictionary and in Music, which were omitted for want of time. – – Mrs P. met us again this day after an interval of two weeks. — Mr P. made some comments upon the subject of the Model School: the manner in which he intended it should be conducted &c. – –

Friday. 20th Lesson in Philosophy on Magnyfying Glasses. which as Mr P. said is not made very clear. I think that the latter part is very obscurely expressed. — I omitted to mention the lesson in the Bible in its proper place. — The portion read was from the first Chap. of Mark. The 6th verse was the part which was commented upon — Camels' hair was used by the ancients as a mourning dress as black is now used by us. There have been disputes concerning the locusts which were used by John the Baptist as food; whether they were the insect called by that name or the fruit of the locust tree. — Mr P. said he had little doubt that it was the former for that the insects were eaten in these days by the poorer class of people in a famine. — The morning lessons were the same as yesterday & also the afternoon, the lesson in Music being neglected for want of time. Mr P. remarked upon the subject of straightness of the body in the sitting body and expressed some fears that we should be crooked as the young ladies mentioned by Mr Combe in the boarding schools. —

Saturday 21st This morn Mr P. wished to go to Boston and therefore requested the scholars to come to the School room as early as possible. — The hour of meeting was 7½ o'clock and the first exercise was in Arithmetic. The second on the chapter upon Religious Influence in Abbotts (*sic*) Teacher. — Then the Conversational Exercise. The question to be discussed was, can any method be devised for a system of exercise which shall be consistent with the plan of this institution and not at variance with the rules of Physiology as laid down by Mr Combe? — This was carried on with some spirit by the scholars and it was stopped; because the time was passed. Mr P. requested us to think upon the subject and make out a plan to hand to him. The

next exercise was the delivery of the Seventh Lecture. —
All appeals to the fears of children are very objectionable.
It is true, that some have secured their objects by such
means but the *best* objects are not reached by it. There is
nothing of that kindly feeling between teacher and pupil
which should exist & which does exist between parent &
child. There is a degree of industry and order obtained by
such means, but it is the submission of fear. Take two
schools for example; in the one everything is carried on in
love: the scholars do not comply with the rules for fear of
punishment but because they are unwilling to cause any
trouble to their teacher. In the other they are ruled by fear,
ranklings and discontent are continual. Which of these
will make the best scholars? In which will they be made
the most useful? In which will they be prepared for heaven
and a future life? — Could all the traits of these two schools
be contained in the heads of two individuals, how different
would these two persons be! Who would not prefer to be a
teacher or a scholar in the first? The teachers of these
schools are performing very different services for their
country. — In one we see open dealing and honesty in the
other art, cunning and duplicity. — You may indeed carry
forward at no slow rate, a school, by a system of fear &
punishment, but instead of having feelings of kindness
among your pupils, the lower passions will reign and you
must expect to have to meet them.

You will find that on every opportunity which offers they
will disobey and when the teacher is absent they will take
the time to break the rules, & all mischief will be carefully
concealed. — When fear is removed all restraint is taken
away. The teacher can not govern by appeals to hope,
conscience & virtue after governing by fear. The choice,
then, lies between fear & the rod on one hand and conscientiousness, love, & desire of happiness on the other.
One way opens a field for the exercise of ingenuity & benevolence, the other calls for strength of muscle and force of
nerves. Are we never to appeal to the rod? Can schools be
governed entirely without it? Mr P. is not ready to admit
that it should be banished but everything short of that. —

Very few teachers have done all that pleasant words,

smiles &c can effect. From his own experience he can say
that he has never been into a school as teacher or visiter,
where the law of kindness has done her perfect work. — He,
himself has got along best when he has punished the least.
The Scriptures not only allow but enjoin the use of the rod.
Ferrenburg, Pestalozzi of the ancient school as well as
Abbott, Hall, &c have the same opinion. — It would be
much better if the teacher would be mild firm and unvary-
ing. The chief difficulty is that teachers do not rule their
own spirits. Those who wield the rod, do not always succeed in obtaining obedience, so well as those who do not. —
By the use of it you alienate the child from the school and
yourselves, and cause him to feel hostility to you. One
thing, every one agrees upon which is, put off its use as
long as you can and use it as seldom as possible. There are
certain rules for the use of the rod which will always hold
true. 1st Always be sure you have the good of the pupil in
view. 2nd Punish with a feeling of reluctance: it will have
a subduing and a melting effect 3dly Punish sparingly:
frequency hardens the character. 4th Be not in haste
review the case again & again, delay awhile something
mitigating may appear, 5th do not administer punishment
of any kind in anger, whether corporal or any other. The
offender will think that you punish him merely for your
own gratification. 6th Be sure it is deserved & if it is possible convince the culprit of his guilt. — 7th Never resort
to physical suffering when an appeal to any thing else will
answer as well. 8th Take care it is not too severe. —

Sunday 22nd The texts, this morn was taken from the
17th Chap. Acts 30th Verse. In the P.M. from 16th Chap
of John 1, 2 & following verses. — Both were very good, that
in the afternoon exceeded that in the morn. — The preacher
was Mr. Crofts. —

Monday 23d. — Exercises were opened by reading from
the 1st Chapter of Mark and 32nd verse. After this, Mr P.
remarked that on this day the sun crossed the line & the
days and nights are equal in every part of the earth. — The
usual lessons of the forenoon were recited well by most of
the pupils. The afternoon lessons were Arithmetic, Gram-

mar, Geography, Orthography & Moral Philosophy. The last was recited much better than usual. —

Tuesday. [*24th*] This morn Mr P. explained the manner in which the houses of the eastern nations are built. They are built surrounding a court on three sides, and over the court a roof is some times erected. This is referred to when the lifting up of the roof is spoken of in the Scriptures, as being raised to lower the sick of the palsy. — The lesson in Natural Philosophy was upon the subject of Optical Instruments & as it was rather complicated the explanation of the figures was deferred until the next recitation. — That in Physiology after a slight notice was also deferred until tomorrow. — Book keeping & Mental Philosophy were recited rather better than *usual.* — In the afternoon the lessons were as usual, but the monotony was varied by a call from Wm. Banton Prof. of Profile Taking. A rap at the door announced his approach & when Mr. Peirce opened it, he was met by a *volley* of words, which from their nature led me to think that he was not unacquainted with the business of solicitation, whatever might be his knowledge of his Profession. — The parley at the door was soon stopped by Mr B's asking if "the precious young ladies would like to have their profiles taken?" But if the young ladies had wished to reply he did not give them an opportunity, for his organs of speech were kept in continual use until he left the room. — Mr P. was obliged to inform him, ere this took place how precious our time was, & that we must improve every moment: — at the same time, begged him not to consider him abrupt — "Oh no!" said Mr. Banton, "it is wisdom in your cerebrum & love in your cerebellum," & took his departure promising to call again at four. He has probably forgotten that he was to come again, as he has not been in. — The conclusion arrived at by some of the scholars was that he is what may be called "demented." After he had gone three ladies from Woburn called and staid till the close of the school. —

Wednesday [*25th*] This morn Mr P. told us that the bottles of the ancients were made of skin & that, therefore, it was not customary to put new wine into old bottles.

— After this remark we recited the lesson in Physiology, upon the subject of Hereditary disease. The Conversational Exercise was next & this was principally confined to Anecdotes. After this we had a short discussion upon the subject "Is animal food injurious to the system or not?" There was a large majority upon the negative side. — After reading abstracts of the 1st Chap– 4th Sect. & 2nd Chap. 1st Sect. of Wayland's Moral Science & reciting a review lesson in N. History school was closed. — This forenoon has been one of the most interesting of any since I have been here, & the lessons were all well recited. —

Thursday 26th The next exercise after reading from the Scriptures, was in Natural Philosophy. The exercise this morn was not an ordinary recitation but a lecture from Mr P. upon the subject of Concave & Convex Mirrors. He illustrated the different effects produced by the degrees of divergency & convergency of the rays falling upon them. As I have learned the same several times I think it will not be necessary to put them down here. — After this we had an intermission & then read our abstracts of the Physiology lesson, the subject of which was the necessity of a due supply of air. — When this was completed Mr P remarked that as it was cold in the room he would dismiss school if we would exercise. — This P.M. the exercises were Reading Punctuation & a lesson in the Dictionary. — After these were recited Mr P. said that he would close the session early for the same reason as mentioned above. —

Friday 27th The thermometer this morn, stood at 50°. The lesson in Natural Philosophy was on the subject of Optical Instruments. In Physiology, Ventilation & in Natural History, the Class Mammalia. — Political Economy continues very interesting. — This P.M. the first exercise was Reading from the Teacher, on the subject of Religious Instruction. Mr P. made some remarks upon the necessity of taking our Savior for an example of teaching. — Writing, Orthoëpy & Punctuation closed the school – – A very good day, taking the cold weather into consideration. —

Saturday 28th Mr P. made some comments upon the 3d Chap. of Mark and after that the whole school attended to a reading lesson in the Bible. — We then were reviewed

in Music: & at the close of this exercise Mr P. delivered
the eighth lecture. — The subject was Premiums & Emula-
tions as a means of awaking interest in pupils. The question
of awarding premiums for conduct has been spoken of
already & the subject has been debated. He is no less
opposed to them as a means of rewarding good lessons than
good conduct. It almost invariably occasions bad consequences & that school is most healthy which does best without it. The 1st objection is that they are the occasion of
trouble to teachers, committees, parents and children. —
Committees find difficulty in deciding between candidates
for premiums and it occasions bitter feelings jealousies
envy & bad feelings between parents and bitter disappoint-
ments among children. Imagine a case; the examination
has passed and out of ten candidates four bear off the prize
and six are disappointed. This is an evil and unless there is
some good to balance it, the decision must be against it. Even
if we allow that the effect of premiums is good the manner
in which they are awarded is not good. — They are promised
to those who recite the best and thus only a few of those
most forward try to obtain it & in this way those who do
not need it are induced to exert themselves more, but three
fourths of the class are not at all moved. — The foundation
of many incurable diseases has been laid, in this way, & the
pupils forget that no amount of good lessons will compen-
sate for bad health. In connection with this Mr P. read an
extract from an address of the Mayor in Boston and expressed his approbation of all the sentiments contained. —
Nothing is more unjust than the principles upon which
premiums are awarded. Suppose two boys one having ten
talents the other two. — The latter is industrious and does
all that he can do; the former is idle & Playful, but bears
off the prize, when truth says that he deserves it who has
studied the most. Premiums if awarded at all should be for
good character and not for good lessons. Most every
scholar feels that he can behave well if he chooses. — Suppose a father should offer to his children a new suit of clothes
if they would be obedient, or good; they would likely exert
themselves & do well for the time specified, but he would
be very much mistaken if he thought he had improved the

moral nature of the children. — There is no more reason
for its application in the school-room than at home. Teach
the scholars to look for their reward in the legitimate fruits
of well doing. If premiums must be given let them be
awarded to those who have made the most exertion Their
influence upon the mind and habits is bad. Scholars with
a premium before their eyes study for effect, they are anxious
to appear well. It is not certain that those who carry off
the medals would prove the best scholars if they were examined off of the usual routine of school studies. — Such
scholars are most apt to close their books after they leave
school – – They should not be taught to consider money or
a reward as better than knowledge. Solomon says that
Wisdom is better than pearls or rubies. — He would not
have us beget in our pupils the thought that there is any
thing better than intellectual endowments. Open to them
the beauties of knowledge and teach them to embrace her.
In this way, teach them the value of knowledge and you
can tell the true advancement of your scholar much better
if he have no reward offered to him. You love & respect a
pupil more if you know that he labors only for his advancement. Another objection to premiums & place-taking is
that they excite feelings already too active, and lead to unhappiness: they are based on selfish feelings which are
carried farther than the school-room & are the foundation of
that scrambling after office which we see in life. Education should have for its object the improvement of the
pupil. — The System of rewards appeals to Emulation. —
This quality as defined by one writer is a desire to excel
for the sake of the gratification felt in being superior to
others. It consists in the pleasure of seeing our own superiority & thinking others see it too. It is nearly allied to
pride, & envy & hatred & even malice are only higher degrees of it. — While Mr P. was delivering the above lecture
Dr Webb of Boston & Gen. Wadsworth of Gennessee County
N.Y. came in & after hearing it wished that the school
should be examined in some of the branches. Accordingly
we were reviewed in Natural & Moral Philosophy & in
Arithmetic. — School closed after 12 o'clock & Mr P. announced the probable time of the vacation to us — i.e. it

is to commence Wednesday morn. — This statement has
been since confirmed by a letter from the Secretary of the
Board. —

(Very good journal — writing rather fine.)[1]

Monday 30th   This morn Mr P. was engaged so that he
could not be in the school room the first hour, therefore
after telling us what he wished us to do, he left, & did not
return until just before recess. — As there will only be two
days more, in this term, he proposed that they should be
devoted to review. Accordingly the remainder of the forenoon was spent in a review in Natural Philosophy. In the
afternoon, we attended to Natural History, Grammar &
Arithmetic. — These exercises occupied all the time, &
school closed. —

Tuesday. Oct. 1st   This day will close the term, & tomorrow we shall be scattered in various directions. — Miss
[———] took her books this morn, and is intending to return
to her friends, for the want of means to defray the expenses
of board. The exercises of the forenoon, were N. Philosophy, Exercise in Worcester's Dictionary, & Geometry. A
gentleman & lady called, *she* looks like a *"to be"* scholar. —
P.M. What a poor guesser for a Yankee! The gentleman
was Dr. Howe the superintendent of the blind institution
in South Boston & the lady one of his teachers. — The exercises have been Rules for Spelling & Punctuation, Problems on the Globe & Mental Philosophy & Algebra. —

---

[1] Note in pencil, Mr. Peirce's hand.

CHAPTER II

THE SECOND TERM, OCTOBER 16, 1839–JANUARY 14, 1840

2nd term. - - Wednesday October 16th. This morning, three of the scholars formerly members of the Normal School came together, and ere long were joined by a number more, but we missed some of our old acquaintances. After a few remarks from Mr P. & the assignment of the exercises we were dismissed, and passed the remainder of the forenoon in social converse. After dinner the people living in the vicinity came into town, to attend the oration, to be delivered at the church by Gov. Everett. With the people, came, some new scholars; two from Roxbury, & two from Wrentham; the latter the nieces of Mr Horace Mann.—At three, we all went to church, which was was *about* filled. After a half hour, the Gov. & a No of the Board of Education entered, and the exercises were commenced by a hymn which was read by Mr Dodge, & 2ndly by a prayer, by Dr Follen, which was very appropriate. The address followed, and the following are the topics that I recollect.

Abstract of Gov. Everett's address, delivered in Lexington, Oct. 16th, 1839. The object of this assembly is to celebrate the commencement of the second term of the Normal School, established in this place. — The derivation of the word Normal is from Norma, a Latin word, signifying rule or direction. This school is not literally the standard, but the principles taught in it and the manner of teaching, are the standard or model for others. The first school of this kind was a private one, established by Dr Hecker — and under his direction This was in 1748. Frederick the Great of Prussia, in 1819, established ten schools in the states of Germany; Wirtemberg, Bavaria, Saxony &c. imitating the private school of Hecker. France & Switzerland & Holland soon followed this example, but England was behind the neighboring countries. In this country, *model* schools only were established. Recently petitions

Edward Everett.

Governor of Massachusetts, 1836–1840
Chairman *ex officio* Massachusetts Board of Education

were made to Parliament for an appropriation for this purpose, but were unsuccessful. —

In New York particular attention has been paid in some of the schools, to the instruction of those intending to teach; but none were devoted to that object alone.

In Massachusetts, there has been a school in Andover for some time, especially for the education of teachers. [Established as a department of Andover Academy by Samuel R. Hall in 1830] — None, however, have been established at the public expense. While the legislature of this state were considering the subject, a gentleman (Mr Dwight) offered $10,000 provided they would appropriate as much more. — This proposition was accepted, and it was determined to establish three schools in different parts of the state. The sites chosen, were Lexington, Barre, a town situated in the western part of Worcester County, and it is probable that a third will soon be located in Plymouth county. – – The design of these schools, is to furnish practically educated teachers. — For the sake of clearness the subject was divided into four heads. —

1st. Necessity of thorough teachers in the common branches, best called by the old-fashioned names Reading, Writing & Arithmetic. The statute requires, that teachers shall be thorough in these; yet it is more common to find a distinguished lawyer or physician, than one who is of this description. — It is important for a person to be well acquainted with a *trade* before he practises it, then how much more important is it, that a teacher be acquainted with his profession! A person unaccustomed to driving a nail will seldom succeed without hitting his hand; so in riding on horseback there is a great difference in that of a person unaccustomed to it, and a skilful horseman. — The bad hand-writing which is so common, shows the necessity of attention to that branch. Those people who oppose the establishment, take one of two arguments. To those who assume the first viz: that we have a sufficiency already of thorough teachers, we have nothing to say; to those who say that the salaries given to teachers now, are not sufficient to warrant so great an expenditure in obtaining an education, we say that as the teachers are more thorough, the salaries will be raised. —

2nd Capability of imparting instruction intelligibly.—It is important that truth, be held up to the view of the child, as the diamond to the sun; turning it in every possible light that all its faces may be seen. In ancient times the manner of teaching was very defective. It left the teacher in ignorance of the effect of his instructions. — This is exemplified by the boy studying in decimal fractions. — After he had performed all the sums several times, he one day discovered some thing which he thought probable was as novel to the world as to himself. — On communicating this to his parent, he said to him the world has known for some time, that a decimal fraction was merely a vulgar fraction the numerator of which were the figures expressed, & the denominator, the figure one with the same number of ciphers annexed. — Some have a natural aptness for teaching which enables them to succeed without instruction; thus two persons, one of whom had every advantage of education, but who had never known the want of anything. — He passed through schools & college, & was after all, ignorant. Another obtained his education with difficulty, and after passing through college, was a thorough scholar. — If the circumstances of these had changed the one who had been under the teaching of stern Necessity, would have been prepared for any situation, but the other would be destitute of the means of existence. —

3dly Government, There is a great difference between that of persons governing by fear, and of those governing by mildness, and patient, enlightened, Christian love. — Miss Edgeworth in her remarks upon Practical Education, has treated the subject very well but she has omitted one very important topic viz: Religious Instruction. Mr Abbott's work entitled the Teacher is the best upon the subject. - - In many schools the teachers misunderstand their scholars and do not give them credit for their acquirements; this was the case with the celebrated Bowditch: when he was a boy he performed a difficult sum in Arithmetic, which his master thought impossible; and asked him who assisted him? He replied no one. The teacher thinking that he had deceived him, punished him severely. — This treatment was sufficient to damp the genius of the boy, and to injure him for life. — A scholar may be a Herschel or a Newton, but if treated in this manner he will be worse than nothing. — I would prefer a son, who was an obedient child to one who was the wonder of the world but who nourished in his breast a viper's nest. —

4thly The model school.—This is [a] very important part of a Normal School. — The benefits which will result from such an establishment are very great. — Time would not allow more comments upon this subject. —

He hoped that the legislature would be farther interested, and also some of the richer members of the community, that appropriations might be made, since the present schools were established only for three years, the funds appropriated being only sufficient for that time. — Though other states may excel us in population in extent of territory, and in fertility of soil, let them not surpass us in literary acquirements. — He extended his congratulations to the people of Lexington, on their good fortune in having the Normal School located in this place. He solicited their kindness to the teachers & to the pupils. He said that under such teachers as had been provided for the schools, the pupils must, necessarily, improve. – – – – – – –

After he had concluded, a hymn was read by Dr Follen & a prayer offered by Mr Dodge & a benediction by the same. — The Board of Visiters called, after the meeting & with the Governor walked through the building & stopped a moment in the sitting room. — The evening was passed very pleasantly until the study hours, the young ladies all appearing to do their utmost to make the strangers happy & pleased with their new situation. —

Thursday, 17th This morn, the lessons were deferred until a late hour, on account of the necessity of making some remarks to those just entering the school — In consequence of this only two of the lessons were recited, Natural Philosophy and Physiology. — The former was the first two Chapters in Bakewell's work, which is to be reviewed until the Class can obtain the Scientific Class Book. In the afternoon the usual studies were pursued with the exception of Enunciation. —

Friday 18th After the reading of the Scriptures, Mr P made a few remarks and we proceeded to recitations 1stly in N. Philosophy on the subject of Cold. N. Physiology was upon the necessity of proper exercise for the expansion of the lungs. — The lesson in Natural History was upon the Class of birds & considered the order Accipitres of Birds of Prey. Political Economy on the restrictions laid on trades by the English & of the disadvantages of these. — All the exercises of the P.M. were performed.

Saturday 19th The first exercise for the morning was reading in the Scriptures from the 21st & 23d Chapters of Matthew. Mr P. then said that he had so many remarks to make that we should have no time for any thing more. —

The ninth lecture was upon the subject of Premiums The power of premiums, he acknowledged, was very great sometimes. They have made those who have been idle, industrious and good scholars. They have wrought almost miracles but such cases are the exceptions and not the general rule. — They are not the greatest evils — they are not so great as mischief & disobedience. — The chief objection to them is that they are too exciting. — They have had the countenance of distinguished people, it is true, & Franklin made a bequest in their behalf. But because they were approved by him it does not follow that they were in the right for no one is always wise. There is seldom anything which has not at some time, had the countenance of distinguished persons. You will ask if the rod and appeals to fear are excluded, how you are to rule your schools. The same means will not suit all. What you do for one age will not answer for another and what for one person will not answer for another. — It is the part of the teacher to study the character of the pupils and then decide. The conscientious teacher will appeal to no motives which are not just. As an inducement to study speak of the pleasures & utilities of study. Of the latter, remind them, as a source of wealth, as a means of ascendancy and superiority teach them that "knowledge is power" & illustrate it by examples

from ancient & modern history. Let them see her as she is
represented holding length of days in her right hand and in
her left riches & honor. — All are not to be moved by such
inducements. They will be heard principally by the older
& more advanced scholars but calculate not too confidently
upon the effects of these arguments upon the young. To
others open the pleasures of learning. Children have curiosity: gratify it; direct their inquiries; present truth in its
most attractive view, and let them ascend the hill of science
without knowing that they are doing it. There is a wide
field for the teacher and in nothing do they differ so much
as in the power of presenting knowledge in an attractive
form. Some present as some ministers present religion as
unattractive & repulsive. — If the roots are bitter mingle
the sweet with the bitter by allowing them to taste the
branches & the leaves.[1] It is not best to remove all difficulties for that would be to take away all efforts from the child
but present it as the diamond — spoken of in the preceding
oration in its most attractive points. — Even this will not
reach many, but all the means are not yet exhausted. Speak
of Gratitude to parents & friends as an inducement to them
to be industrious and orderly, remind them of the advantages they are enjoying & represent them as the fruit of
parental love. — If this is not felt by every scholar the
greater part will be found to be affected. — Others who are
not moved by this, are possessed of pride of character or of
a good name. Over such, gain the ascendancy by showing
the connection between the different stages of life, between
childhood & manhood, and that the actions of childhood
determine in a great measure the character of the man.
Many are able to see this & few will be entirely reckless of it.
Take it for granted that all have a sense of right and wrong
and appeal to it: calculate upon it. This appeal may be
often almost in vain, especially in those whose early training was unfortunate. There will be many who will strive
to do right for conscience' sake. Although this may not be
the most powerful motive it is appealing to some thing which
is correct. — Scholars will be much moved by sympathy
and will imitate each other. They will forget everything

[1] Correction in pencil by Mr. Peirce — "See the flowers & taste the fruits." — Ed.

in order to follow another.　Mr Abbott is in the right when he says, gain the sympathy of your pupils.　The best way to accomplish this is to affect those who are the leaders of these companies, but be careful that they do not think they have you under their control.　Scholars, of whose sympathy you have no hopes, will not be likely to be much benefited by your instructions: everything depends upon love.　To secure their sympathy; do good and be good; take interest in those who are entrusted to you; in their amusements, studies trials, and difficulties, in all that makes them joyful and in all that makes them sad.　"If it is in you it will out".　If they discover self in your plans they will think meanly of you and will be likely to transgress.　Grant such requests as you can and if you deny let them them see the reasons for such denial.　Children thus treated will from mere sense of Gratitude, take care not to disobey.　He concluded by reading a Chapter from Mr Wires "How shall I govern my school" which was very àpropos.

(Have you paid your customary attention to Punctuation?[1]　I intended to have done it before handing in my book but forgot it.)

Sunday　Attended church this morn and heard Mr Green of East Cambridge.　The text was from Romans, 12th Chap. 8th v: "And be not conformed to this world".　"He said that we are "not so much conformed to what the Bible teaches, as to the opinion of the world, in regulating our characters.　It is better, to be sure, to act up to the standard of public opinion, than to have no standard whatever, but this standard is affected by the fashionable and great. We are wanting in piety on account of our unthankfulness for the blessings which Providence has lavished upon us. We enjoy all these without once turning our thoughts to our dependant (*sic*) situation.　We enjoy our health without return of thankfulness; our wealth, without, charity.　We are too apt to feel satisfied with ourselves, if we live up to the rest of the world.　That man who follows the golden

---

[1] Question in writing of Mr. Peirce. — Ed.

rule may suffer temporarily, but we believe that he will not fail to receive his reward. — The discourse in the P.M. was upon Poetry & Music. —

Monday Oct 21st (1839) This morn, the Model School was collected, the number being about thirty. The Normal School was opened, as usual, with devotional exercises, and the first morning lesson was recited, the subject of which, was the Expansion of substances, by Heat. – – After this was accomplished, Mr P. took us all down stairs, to observe the manner in which the school was opened. — We found Mr Dodge & Mr Benjamin Muzzy there. Mr P. first addressed the scholars, upon the subject of neatness, keeping their attention fixed, by asking them to look around the room, and notice the walls, floor, &c & then to open their desks, and to observe the manner in which other scholars had used them. — He then asked Miss Stodder & myself to assist him in taking the Names, ages & parents of the children. After this process was gone through with, he commenced to examine them in Reading, hearing each one read a short portion. He heard them spell a few words, in the same manner, & set down a number, corresponding to their advancement. At the close of this exercise, the school was dismissed. — In the afternoon, we recited in Grammar, and at the close of this, Mr P. asked us to go below, and assist Mrs P. — I did as I was requested, and examined about one half, in Arithmetic. — An exercise in Geography, which consisted in Sailing a ship, closed the school. —

Tuesday Oct. 22nd, 1839 After the usual devotional exercises, Mr P. heard our recitation in Physiology. The subject of this lesson was the proper exercise of the lungs, & the connection between the lungs & other parts of the system. The lessons in Natural Philosophy, was upon the subject of Boiling. — After hearing the lesson in Algebra, Mr P. left the school to attend the Model School, a while. — This time was passed in reviewing the lessons in Bookkeeping, and Mental Philosophy. On his return he attended to these recitations and also to one in Arithmetic, after which the school was dismissed. In the P.M. we recited in Grammar, and then he asked Miss Stodder to go below &

examine the school in Geography. — He returned in season
to hear a Moral Philosophy lesson and the remainder of a
recitation in Geography. —

Wednesday 23d This morn, after the opening of the
school, a lesson in Natural Philosophy on the subject of
Steam was recited. — After this, Mr P. asked some of the
girls to go down stairs, and listen to the exercises. While we
were there, the classes were called, and Reading Books
assigned to them. When we returned to the upper room we
recited in Physiology, and after the exercise Mr Peirce made
some remarks upon Hereditary Disease. — This P.M. Mr P.
handed me a package requesting me to open it and do as
directed within. — I did so, and the scholars all seemed to
be willing, and to wish, to obey the rule, and do as he requested in all things. —

Thursday & Friday [24th and 25th] These days were
passed in going & returning to & from Lynn.[1] On the
morning of the former, with the permission of parents and
teachers, I left Lexington, and arrived in Boston at 10
o'clock A.M., though not in season to take the cars to Lynn
in the forenoon. Passed through Charlestown and very
near Bunker Hill Monument, which was a road that I had
never travelled before. — —

Returned to Lexington at eight, having left Lynn at two
P.M.

Saturday. 26th The first exercise this morn, was in the
Dictionary, and immediately after that the lesson in Enunciation was recited. — At the close of this, Mr P. delivered
his tenth lecture. He said that the daily remarks of the
school-room, and occurrences there, were to be made the
principal means of instruction, but it is best to gather up
those at times and to present them in a collected form. —
The chief object of this lecture, was to correct any erroneous
impressions that might have been made by the last lecture.
— Sympathy must not be a mere passion but an enlightened
sentiment. The teacher must know her duty and perform
it. She must not remit her exertions, until she has brought
her pupils to subjection. It requires patience, perseverance, and kindness continually. Some parents show great

---

[1] Corrected in pencil by Mr. Peirce — "going to & returning from." — Ed.

kindness and love for their children, but do not command
their respect or obedience; this is the way with many
teachers; they have no decision of character, no dignity &
determination. — After the loss of much time to the pupils
placed under the instruction of such teachers, they are
removed from the schools; & parents are dissatisfied because
they have made no improvement. When you go into a new
school, and there meet those, for whom you have never
done anything & who are, therefore, under no obligation to
you & feel no gratitude to you, there must be the expression
of authority and rebuke, as well as of love. The look of
the eye must threaten rebuke, and there are few so hardened
as to withstand it. One young man observed once, that he
felt that he had little authority over his school when he
could not look them into order. What could mere affection
do towards reducing to order the school below? — How long
would it take to make them industrious? One human life
would not be sufficient. They have had kind parents, who
have loved them more than their teachers can, but it has
not made them industrious. — The ground must [be] broken
up and the grain planted, & nourished, before the good fruit
will spring up. The greatest difficulty is insubordination, inattention: it is a scene of continual confusion & talk, in
the seats & out of them. When a class is called it is very
difficult to make them feel, that the question which is put
to their neighbors, should be attended to, by them. The
above is an evil which no amount of love can correct. If it
be asked how we can correct this; the answer shall be by
authority. Let it appear that you mean to be obeyed, and
to have order. It will not be necessary to put on the look
of a tyrant, nor airs of high authority. The example of
Christ, who was meek & lowly, went about doing good, &
when reviled, reviled not again, is a confirmation of this.
Before him all, both old and young bowed and the reason
of this was, as explained in the Scriptures, because he
spake as one having authority. There is a great deal in
having a proper tone. Even a horse can tell whether his
master is afraid of him or not, and in the same way do children tell, whether a teacher can enforce obedience. It is
not in the degree of loudness but in the intonation: a whisper

will sometimes convey more authority than loud speaking.
– – To repeat, some of the principles before stated, which,
although very simple, are very important.

1st Ever be self possessed — be deliberate that you may
not have to annul anything which you say or do. Nothing
tends more to destroy authority, than frequent changes in
rules.

2nd. Give no commands unless you intend that they
shall be obeyed. Follow them up, and see that they *are*
obeyed. The disregard of one, leads to neglect of others. —

3d. Be strictly impartial, — they will respect you more.
I do not mean treat all alike, the industrious & the idle,
but do not exempt one from duty because he is pretty, or
rich, or a good scholar, and exact it of another because he
is homely, poor, & meanly clad.

4th. Be uniform in your requirements. — Because you
have the head-ache today, do not be more rigorous than
yesterday; or because you are in good spirits; suffer them
to do more than at another time. Let it not be said that
the day's disaster may be seen in the morning's face. —
To be uniform, it is necessary to attend to diet. — If you
have transgressed the physical laws to day, the pupils ought
not to suffer tomorrow. —

5th Let your words be few. —

6th. Avoid scolding and fault finding. — It is very dis-
heartening & makes the scholars indifferent whether they
obey or not.

7th Make it a point to speak of the *good*, rather than the
bad. — If you speak of the good deeds of a scholar, you
tell him what you like, & he knows how to please you; but
if, on the contrary you speak of the bad deeds only, you
leave him in the dark, with respect to your wishes. — Capt
Basil Hall relates an account of two captains, the one,
praised the good & said nothing of the bad, the other, seemed
displeased if he found nothing with which to find fault.
The effects of each was very different. The work of the
sailors under one, was done with little spirit; under the
other, nothing was irksome, but all pleasant. —

8th There is much in Mr Abbott's remark — respect
the feelings of the scholars, especially of new ones. Never

speak sarcastically. If your scholars are awkward, it is not their *fault*, but rather their misfortune. It will be difficult to convince them that you are their friend, after you have spoken thus to them. If you censure, give it privately. —

9th If you suspect that your feelings are excited, keep silent.

10th Take care not to speak too often of small things.

11th Put confidence in your scholars. —

12th Induce them to be open & frank —

13th Have but few rules, & those very simple & plain.

Sunday [27th] Mr Cruft preached to day from John the 17th Chap. 24th V. "Father, I will that they also, whom thou hast given me, be with me where I am; &c." This afternoon from the 11th Chap. 35th v. of John, "Jesus wept". The chief subject of the morning sermon was future reunion in Heaven.

[Abstract of sermon omitted.]

.   .   .   .

Monday 28th The school, this morn, commenced at eight, in order to permit Mr P. to pass more time in the model school. — We remained in the Normal School until nine, the time being occupied by a recitation in Physiology. In the M.S. Misses Stodder & Damon & myself assisted. We returned to the N.S. at eleven, and remained until twelve; went in again at one, & returned at 3, to spend two more hours in the N.S. — The exercises of these two hours were Arithmetic & Grammar. —

Tuesday [29th] The recitations of the morn, were N. Philosophy & Physiology. That of Mental Philosophy was deferred until the last hour in the A.M. — I forgot to mention under yesterday's account, that the hour from ten to eleven was devoted to exercises by the pupils, & as long as the present arrangement is adhered to, will be set apart for that purpose. — The lessons of the P.M. were Algebra, which was deferred in the AM. for want of time, Arithmetic, Geography & Moral Philosophy. —

Wednesday [30th] The first hour was devoted to remarks on the subject of Philosophy & Physiology. — The next

two to the Model School & the one remaining to the N.S.
The exercises were the Conversational Exercise & Natural
Philosophy.　Before Mr P. had got up Mr Dodge & a
stranger called whom Mr P. introduced as Mr Wood from
Washington City. —

Saturday 16th Nov.　The time intervening between the
above date, & that of the previous entry, has been passed
in a sick room, part of the time on the bed, & the other
part in needlework, my strength not being sufficient to enable me to pass the time in School.　During the time, I
have received much kindness from the Lexingtonians, the
impression being thus removed, that they are a cold & un-
feeling people. — My teachers also have been very kind;
there is one benefit in sickness at least; it teaches us to feel
grateful, more so than we should perhaps if the same kindness were shown to us in health.　This morning my teacher
presented me with a work, the title of which was "Index
Rerum"; in accepting I suppose I pledged myself to keep
an "Index Rerum", at least I shall so consider it & will
hope that some fifty years hence it may show that life has
not been spent in vain by its owner. — —

We have had during my illness one visiter Mr Lathrop
from the East Village. —

No other events worthy of notice I believe have occurred.
— Friday Nov 1st Mr Wood called. —

This forenoon I remained in school long enough to hear
Mr P's eleventh lecture: the following are some of his
remarks. —

In the ten past lectures, Education has been defined as
the drawing forth of ideas, he has touched upon the qualifications, encouragements & discouragements, of teachers,
the motives to which they should appeal, in their schools. —
In the four last, the principle of premiums & emulation &
fear has been considered. — The conclusion to which he
came, was, that they have great power, but that they are
aids of a doubtful character.　True love & sympathy are
to be the teacher's reliance — He does not say that you
must not appeal to fear at any time: sometimes as in opening
a new school, where the pupils have been under a lax &
inefficient government, it is necessary to resort to it.　Love,

sustained by authority, must be the way of teaching —
Does authority mean, if a pupil does wrong, he is to smart
under the rods of the teacher? Does it mean, power sustained by force? This last is the meaning that Mr Abbott
attaches to it. — The teacher who has not command over
his scholars, must spend his time in keeping order. The
teacher who has not authority wears a frown upon his brow
which counteracts the moral lessons, which he gives. —

The authority which Mr P. means shall be exercised, has
much to do with appeals to the moral feelings: it must
have its foundation in the heart, and be felt by all. — It
is that power which is based on an abhorrence of wrong,
and a desire that all should do well; it is that power exerted
by the teacher of men when on earth, the same power which
was felt, when it is said he spoke with authority, and when
after trying to catch him in his words, they went away
astonished. — It is similar to that which the wicked feel,
in the presence of the good. — It is not to be imitated, but
must be possessed in reality, & make a consistent and constant part of character. — If you cultivate this spirit you
will find it will do more good than the feril (*sic*) or ratan. —
The reason why so much has been said on the subject, is
from a conviction of its importance. Nothing is more
needed than a high standard of government; vain will be
the attempts to go on without order. Without it, speedy
an[d] entire failure must be the effect. — Another subject
to which he called our attention was the art of teaching
which the Germans call didactics (dedacteques), & which
holds an important place in the teacher's profession. It is
parallel with the art of government & of the last importance to the teacher's success. If all is orderly, and nothing
is taught, where are the good effects? Nothing differs more,
the powers of teachers in this respect. One gifted in Language, varies her illustrations according to the subjects &
the capacity of the children: another makes a formal statement, without ever varying it at all & leaves the ideas of the
scholars in "confusion worse confounded." One knows no
way to assist a scholar, but to [do] the work for him: as in
Arithmetic, one will solve the problem for the scholar, while
another, will, by a little reasoning, enable him to do it for

himself. — A teacher may assist a scholar so much, that
they will be unable to assist themselves. The teachers
proper duty, is to present it to the pupil so that he, by his
own exertions, can grasp it. Few naturally possess the art
of teaching but by practice & experiment, every one can
acquire it. A person who thinks himself prepared to teach,
because he has seen others teach, is as much a quack, as a
person who establishes himself as a physician, and has had
the experience of only a few walks through a hospital. —
The art of teaching is not mechanical, but intellectual; it
requires an accurate acquaintance with the subjects taught.
The teacher must know [not only] general principles but
particulars — Language is also very necessary to a teacher,
There is a great difference between those who are just beginning to teach, & those who are experienced. The real
teacher puts her pupils in possession of principles, which
they may apply as they are needed. The old manner of
teaching Arithmetic, furnishes an example of this. — The
rule of Practice, in those Arithmetics was set down under
a separate head, while now, it is sufficient to understand
aliquot parts to know all about it. - - A teacher must be
acquainted with the powers of the mind, and the laws by
which it is regulated, She should have at her command
such languages as will set out the idea clearly, to the pupils'
mind. Study to acquire the art of teaching & the philosophy of the mind. The discerning teacher will discover that
children have curiosity, and she will do all that is possible
to excite it. If you can awaken it, it will surmount many
obstacles. — You may make things so plain, as to destroy
all interest in it. - - - -

Monday 18th This morn, Mr Peirce had many questions
put upon his table. Among the number was one concerning
the length of the year — whether it was the same at the
commencement of time, as now? The decision was, that it
is the same. — The difference in the length of the lives of
the ancients, and those of the present generation, was accounted for, by noticing the numerous exciting topics which
we have that they did not. — As the civilization of the
world advances the calls for the exercise of the powers of

Normal School Building at West Newton, 1844–1853

each individual increase. Another question was, — what is
the length of a generation? — The answer to this was, that
the average time of a persons life, was thirty years. — This
is found by taking an estimate of the population in the world,
& taking the average of the length of their lives. — This
being found, will give the length of a generation. — Another, are there any injurious effects resulting from going
from a warm room to a cold one if we take no cold at the
time? — Ans. It is possible for us to change rooms without
receiving injury, probably, but that generally a slight degree
of injury was done. — Another — Are the writings of the
Apocrypha generally received as making a part of the
Bible? To this question, Mr P. said that he believed they
were not generally so received; because no allusion was
made by Christ or his disciples to them, while there is, in
the New Testament, constant allusion made to the writings
of Moses; the Psalms & other sacred books. – –

The Natural Philosophy lesson was recited, and the
questions in Physiology discussed. The lesson in Book-
keeping was called for, but, owing to my wish to do all that
was possible towards overtaking the class in Natural
Philosophy, I had omitted it. — Mental Philosophy was
recited, and we had an addition to our class, of Misses R & E
Pennell and Miss S. Sparrell. — This morn I have been
into the Model School, and the appearance was much better
than when I left it two weeks ago. — In the afternoon the
exercises were Grammar, Geography & Moral Philosophy;
in the second, I took no part from want of time. — When
I went up from the M. School, found Miss Haskell & Miss
C   Soon after Mr Dodge & Professor Kelley of
Waterville College, Maine. — He could not have taken a
more unfortunate time for his visit, as all of us seemed to
be very dull. —

During my absence from school, Mr P. gave out several
questions to the class in Physiology: the following are the
principal of them. —

First. — When animals are frozen, life is extinct, how is
this explained on the principles of Physiology? There are
some exceptions to this rule, as in the serpent-kind, how is
this explained?

Second — Does an investigation into the laws of matter, explain the phenomena of animal life?

Third. — Is there any danger to animal life in burning completely ignited coal, in close rooms or common wood coal taken from the hearth? And if any, how is it explained?

Fourth — Are the injurious [effects?] of close crowded rooms as great in winter as in summer?

Fifth — Do not people almost universally disobey the laws of their physical natures, that they already understand, and is it reasonable to suppose that any practical good would result from a better acquaintance with them? —

Sixth — Is it not a commonly received opinion that disease and consequent death, are an immediate dispensation of God, independent of any human agency?

Seventh — Is this opinion correct? —

Eighth — If we consider disease & death the natural penalties of the violation of God's established laws, do we diminish the salutary effects of belief in his superintending Providence? —

Ninth — Would it have any practical influence on the community, if they could be generally induced to believe that the preservation of health is so much in their own power as the laws of Physiology show that it is? —

Tenth — Consumptions are frequently said to be brought on by colds. How is this explained by the laws of Physiology?

Eleventh — Do colds necessarily produce a permanent injury to the system or do their effects frequently pass entirely away, leaving the system as sound as ever? —

Twelfth — Will an acquaintance with physiology tend to make us reasonably careful of health or unhappily anxious & over cautious?

The 10th, 11th, & 12th, were answered to day. — The opinion with regard to the 1st was that by exposure, the perspiration was checked & thus the lungs were made to perform more than their usual exercise, & became inflamed, Consumption thus being caused. – – To the 2nd, that an injury done at one time of life, although not immediately perceptible & perhaps not perceptible till some farther transgressions have been made, will aid in reducing the health of our system. — Dr Alcott says, in connection with this subject, that every disease cut off some from the time that we had to live. — To the third that, it was dangerous for two reasons; one was, that the oxygen in the atmosphere was used to support the combustion, & another that carbonic acid gas was disengaged in the process of combustion, and this is incapable of supporting existence. – –

Tuesday [19th] The verses read this morn were upon the subject of Peter's denial of his Lord. At the close of the reading Mr P. remarked upon the subject; he said that it seemed very strange to us, that now when the trying time had come they should be unwilling to remain with him. Friends are dear to us at every time but in seasons of adversity their value is increased. – –

After these remarks, he said he would omit the physiological questions, as he had some remarks nearly allied to the subject. — The remarks were upon the subject of health, & were called forth by the absence of Miss Damon, who has gone home from ill-health which her physician says was produced by the want of proper exercise. — Mr P. as he has repeatedly done before, urged the necessity of taking exercise daily & insisted that the hour from 10 to 11 should be devoted to that purpose. He thought that it would be well for the scholars to take exercise between schools, & not to spend all the time in study. — After one generation has grown wise, they pass away & another comes as unwise as the preceding. Philosophy on the subject of inclined planes, a subject very interesting. The lesson in Bookkeeping was recited, & Mental Philosophy. Grammar, Geography & Orthography occupied the afternoon so that Moral Philosophy was deferred. —

Wednesday 20th This morn a query was answered by Mr P. concerning perspiration, Why do some persons perspire more readily than others, — the answer was, that it was constitutional to some, though sometimes it was the effect of disease. — Another was, were there seasons before the flood? Mr P. said that we knew nothing certainly about it, but that it is probable the same causes were operating before the flood, as now. — The questions in Physiology

were No.'s 1, 2, 3. To number one, it was said that animals
who are called warm blooded part with their heat to surrounding objects; and thus become frozen & consequently
lifeless. While those who are cold blooded remain in a torpid
state during the winter. — The 2nd was answered in the
negative. The third has been mentioned under Monday's
entry. — Lesson in Philosophy was upon Accelerated
motion. — Mr P. by mistaking the hour kept the school
until 11. He, therefore, gave us the long recess between
the hours of 11 & 12. — After school, Mr. P. told the scholars
that he wished them to choose a committee to meet him in
the afternoon, to confer upon *domestic* affairs, rather than
subjects concerning the school. – – This they did, & reported
to the pupils. — This P.M. the wind blows hard & it is
colder than it has been before this season. —

Thursday 21st. This morn seems no warmer than the
preceding evening. — The 4th & 5th questions were debated. Some think the effects of the warm room are more
injurious in the summer & some in the winter. — Mr P.
thought that it was difficult to decide, & said that he had
not thought enough about it, to give an answer. — To the
next question, No 5. the answer was given that the increase
of knowledge would give us a better idea of the connection
existing between the different parts of the system. —
Having acquired this knowledge, it is very evident, that
they will be more unwilling to violate the laws of Physiology. — The lesson in Natural Philosophy was upon the
subject of the Oscillation of the Pendulum. This is very
easy, but the succeeding lesson looks as if it would require
some thought. — Natural History spoke of Vermes or
Worms, but owing to my engagement in the Model School
I was not present at the recitation. The exercises of the
afternoon were Reading, Writing & the application of some
words. The Reading was from the "First Class Reader";
"the description of the Bay of Rio de Janeiro" was the
piece of prose, & "John Gilpin" of Poetry. The risibles of
one or two of the scholars, were affected considerably, upon
which Mr P. remarked that he thought it too stale a piece,
to be a cause for so much mirth – – Miss Ford visited the
school to day. —

Friday 22nd This morning, after the devotional exercises, Mr P. made some remarks upon the preceding day, respecting the story of John Gilpin. He said that he did not think, that, though the story was stale to himself who had lived so many years, it might be comparatively new to us. He then told us, that when the original of it was told to Cowper, he was in a very desponding mood, but it had such an effect upon him that it not only drove away his melancholy, but caused him to laugh all night. — The first question that was debated this morn was the 6th; which was decided in the affirmative. The 7th was taken in connection with & was decided in the negative. Some of the reasons given were, that it would be no use for us to attend to the laws of Physiology, if we were not to be benefited by them. If it was the truth Mr P. observed our greatest good would be obtained by reforming the moral character, and that, on the contrary, we saw many around us who are good, suffering from disease while the most abandoned, enjoy perfect health. — The other question, No. 8 was answered in the negative, — the reason assigned being that the Providence of God was displayed, by showing his creatures how they might save themselves from misery. – – We attended to the lesson in Philosophy, which was a continuation of the subject yesterday, "the oscillation of the pendulum" & *did* require a little thought to keep all the laws in mind, & trace the connection. After this we went into the Model School & having staid two hours returned & recited Natural History; the subject of which lesson was the class "Zoophytes". After the recitation, Mr P. made some remarks upon the subject of Natural History, & concluded by recommending a review of the part that we had been over, & giving us the first Chapter. — Mr P. gave out some questions for debate in Physiology. — 13 — What effects are produced on the skin by friction? — In what diseases may it prove beneficial? — 14 What evils follow a sudden check of perspiration? — 15 State the importance of bathing-rooms in public & private establishments.

16 — What are the two most important functions of the skin? The afternoon exercises were Reading, & Orthöepy. —

The subject of the Reading lesson was "the Chrystal" taken
from the Casket. — The moral of this is very good, & a comparison was made between this & the story of "the whistle",
by Dr Franklin. — Music was omitted for want of time. —

Saturday 23d The devotional exercises this morn, were
from the 15th Chap. 16th verse. In commenting upon it,
Mr P. spoke of the reason why Alexander and Rufus, were
mentioned in the Testament. He said that it was probably because they were well known characters. — There
were many questions placed upon Mr P's. table, & among
them, were the following: 1st When did the 19th century
commence? 2nd Why does the core of an apple freeze
first? 3d Why was the talent given to the one who had
ten talents, rather than to the one who had five? 4th —
Why do some people see the moon so much larger than
others? — 5th Why, when passing between the posts before
the doors in the evening, do we mistake the spaces between
the posts for the posts themselves? 6th If it is true as
phrenologists assert, that the higher the forehead the greater
the intellect; why do we so frequently find people with high
foreheads & little intellect and vice-versa? — The reply to
the first was that much had been said, & much written upon
the subject. Dr Bowditch was applied to for his opinion
upon the subject, but did not decide whether it was in 1800
or 1801. The time when it was discussed, was at the commencement of the 19th century. — Mr P. said that he was
not decided, sometimes he inclined to one opinion and sometimes to another. — If we reckon full 100 then it will not
commence until 1801. – – 2nd The caloric from the core,
passes to the outside, to supply the exhaustion. It is therefore, exhausted from the core first, and freezing ensues.
3d. It could not be given to both, & the object was
answered as well by giving it to the first as to the second.
The object was, to show the unfaithful servant the effects
of his unfaithfulness & we might ask the same question had
it been given to one who had five. —

4th. The difference is chiefly constitutional; perhaps it
is the effect of early education in part. This appearance
is not peculiar to the moon, but it is true of all other objects.
People who see the moon larger see other objects propor-

tionally increased. – – The reason why it is noticed with regard to the moon is because it is a brilliant object & more
conspicuous. —

5th   The spaces between the posts have a dark shade
behind them & therefore appear to be the posts; while the
posts themselves, are light and therefore appear to be
vacancies. — Mr P. said, that he did not call it an optical
illusion, but merely an error of judgement, & that we need
only be deceived once. Quite a compliment to Miss Stodder
and myself, since we always make the mistake when we go
out. — 6th   This is a question leading to a subject on which
it is necessary to say much. — Mr P. said that he would
doubt the truth of the assertion. Sometimes the forehead
is high; but very narrow; in that case, there is a small
quantity of brain: — sometimes the back part is very high,
& therefore it appears low in front, but it is only by comparison. Sometimes the organs of perception as color &
form are protuberant & thus give the forehead a sloping
appearance. — But a really flat and low forehead is seldom
accompanied with much intellect. —

One other question, which I omitted, was "What is the
meaning of the law & the prophets". —

Ans. The law means — the Pentateuch or five books of
Moses: — the prophets — the books succeeding as Jere-
miah & Isaiah. After these had all been answered, we
attended to the lesson in Natural Philosophy which was a
review of the week's recitations. — During the exercise we
received a visit from Miss Damon of Northampton. Returning from the model school, we attended to the exercise
in music, & after that to the debate of the question, "Are
the effects of reading fictitious works pernicious? Only one
voted in the negative — Miss Haskell. The reasons that were
given were, that it weakened the powers of the mind and
thus disabled it from comprehending subjects more abstruse;
that it gives a person a distaste for more solid reading. — If
it be indulged in freely, its effects are comparable to those of
intoxicating drink — the more a person takes the more he
wishes. – – There was only time for the expression of opinions
upon the subject, & therefore, there was no debate. — Mr
P. then commenced his twelfth lecture, but for want of

time, delivered only about the half of it. – – The subject of it, was "the manner of teaching the common branches reading & spelling, arithmetic, & geography. — Some will be those who never attended school before but whatever the age, manage with regard to it. Endeavor to excite their interest and curiosity. The old fashioned way of teaching was to keep all confined and then to go over & over the twenty-six letters, until they have learned them. This is teadious to both teachers & pupils; it begets a dislike to school by the child, and it *has* been the cause of aversion to many, who have suffered much in consequence. What shall be done to correct this? In whatever is done in instruction, discipline, or amusement, have regard to their age. Some you will have who have been taught some things, as reading. — With all your scholars have the exercises short & frequent. — Before you begin to teach them to read, teach them common occurrences, about things around them, about the different trades and acts of life, that they have seen, the fruits & animals. — Teach them the parts and uses of the human body, & upon every subject, give lessons adapted in No. & length, to the capacity of your pupils. It is very important that these things should be attended to, and whether they *have* been, at home or not, make them subjects for school instruction. Let all your instructions be upon visible objects; draw their attention to the world within them, which has been too much neglected, and evils intellectual and moral, are felt all the way on the road of life. Gallaudet's works on the soul are very well adapted to the comprehension of children. The objection sometimes raised, that they cannot understand such subjects is not sound. Attention to their own feelings and thoughts, should be some of the earliest lessons taught to them. May we not have to reflect, when our time of instruction has passed, that we have done nothing towards the moral education of the pupil. Reading is the 1st and principal thing, that requires attention, as no scholar can make much progress, in any other study until he has mastered this. — Mr P. has had little experience in teaching the alphabet of language. The moderns have found out a better way than the old fashioned. If you begin with the letters at all, arrange them in groups according to their resemblance in form & sound, teaching very few at a time, and afterwards teach them in order. It will be necessary that it should be learned in order, by the pupils that they may be able to use the dictionary. With the name & form of the letter, let its force be taught; but it is better that you should begin with words, after the manner of Worcester's primers, used in the Model School. If you take a class to give them the first lesson in reading: First show them a very simple word with which they are all familiar, and also its representation; associate the name with the picture, and have them to speak its name several times. — As the word cat — show them the picture of one, and have them to speak the name several times in connection with it. Then give them pin, & treat the word in the same way, & after these are mastered, (these will be a plenty for one lesson) you may add a third. Have the lessons short & simple, & always of well known words. — The length of the time which must be devoted to these lessons, will be decided by the teacher. — Next take these words & write them into simple sentences, in the reading of these, pay particular attention to articulation. Remember that if you suffer them to pronounce wrong, your successor will have the task of remoulding them. You may say the organization is not complete at this age — but you must do all you can. A good foundation will render the succeeding work comparatively easy. Let them be perfectly familiar with every word in the sentence, or their attention will be absorbed in thinking what the word is, and will thus contract the habit of drawling. —

Take care that they do not repeat by wrote (*sic*) what you think they are reading.

(You *write much, & it is well*. Do not write so *great quantity* as to *insensibly* become less attentive to either *physical* good or to the *manner* or substance of any other concern.)

Sunday–24th. Attended church today, the first time for three Sundays, and heard Mr. Cruft (the proper way of spelling the name) preach in the morning from Hebrews, 13th, 5th, "Be content with such things as ye have."

[Abstract of sermon omitted.]

.   .   .   .

Monday 25th The Physiological questions given out on Friday were answered today, though not so well as usual

[Answers to the questions omitted]

.   .   .   .

The lesson in N. Phil. was upon Gravity & was very interesting. —

Mental Phil. & Book-keeping were also recited in the A.M. The P.M the lessons in Geography, Grammar, & Moral Phil. were recited. —

Tuesday 26th. The first half hour was occupied by Mr P. in making comments upon our journals and giving them out. — The questions in Physiology were —

17 How is the neglect of proper change of clothing injurious? —

18 Why is a warm dry air more healthy than a warm moist one? —

19 When we see a person habitually pale can we judge of his mental habits by observing his countenance? — or on the contrary florid? —

The answer to the first was that it caused inf[l]amation of the skin by keeping the exhalations confined & that they would be again absorbed by the skin. The change of seasons also call for a corresponding change of clothing. — 3rd. Answered in the negative — because the face is sometimes flushed by passion or pale with grief – – The 2nd — Because the exhalations from the body take place more freely when it is dry than when it is moist. – – The Nat. Phil. lesson was upon the subject of Gravity. The other lessons were the same as yesterday morn. — In the afternoon Mr Tidd, & the Misses Howe & Miss Drew called at the school & we soon learned that Miss Drew was to be a scholar. — I neglected to mention that Miss Burdick came yesterday. — The lesson in Geography & on the Globe. That in Moral Philosophy was omitted for want of time. — At the close of the school Mr P. announced his intention of dismissing the school for the rest of the week and wished us to enjoy our Thanksgiving and that it might indeed be made a day for Thanksgiving. —

Sunday 1st Dec. — The first day of winter has come, & instead of the usual weather, it is warm and raining. — Attended church & heard Mr Huntington preach in the morning from the 139th Psalm, 7th verse Whither shall I go from thy Spirit, or whither shall I flee from thy presence. — In the P.M. Romans 12th Chap. 5th v. "So we, being many, are one body in Christ, and every one members one of another". —

Monday, December, 1st. Mr P. spoke of the commencement of our school after the vacation, and expressed his regret at seeing so many of the seats vacant. — The chapter read, was the Third of Luke. — He said that the island now called Malta was anciently called Melita, and was probably the island, on which St. Paul was shipwrecked. The first lesson was in Physiology, when Mr P. gave out the following questions. — Query 21st What are the great causes of mortality among children? — Query 21st Combe's views in regard to cold bathing. — Query 22nd. What permanent injury may the constitution sustain by deficient clothing & how is this brought about & what class of persons most liable to suffer from it.

Query 23d. What is the proper rule in regard to the warmth of clothing? —

Query 24th. Can we with safety depend upon clothing & fire to keep us warm? —

Query 25th In what manner does tightly fitted clothing injure the health? —

Query 26th Explain how sitting with cold feet is liable to injure health. —

[Answers omitted.]

· · · · · · · · · · ·

After the queries were given we attended to N. Philosophy, & then went, into the Model School — At the close of that, returned & recited Mental Phil. & Book keeping. – –

In the P.M while I was in the M.S. the N.S. was visited by Mrs. Trask & Mrs Fisk. — The exercises were in Geography — Globes & Moral Phil. —

Tuesday 2nd The answers given under the head of Monday were, in reality given on this day. — After this Mr P. gave out more for Wednesday —

27th — What is the proper time for making beds? What disposition should be made of clothing on going to bed. —

28th To what two causes must we attribute the pale complexion of those residing in cities. —

29th State concisely the directions for bathing. —

30th If a person is obliged to be exposed to an extreme cold atmosphere, would it be best to go into it directly from a warm room or to cool the body gradually down to the extreme point. —

31st State concisely remarks on vapour bath & how it should be applied. —

32nd Why are sailing, riding on horseback, & bathing useful in diseases of the lungs?

A. When are we most liable to take cold in morning or eve[ng], summer or winter, after a full meal or on an empty stomach? —

The lesson in N. Phil. was recited while I was below. — In the M.S. we had two visiters, Mr Hobbs & Mr Felch, who afterwards visited the N.S. — Mental Philosophy was recited, & also Book-keeping — the latter, not much to the credit of the reciter. – – In the P.M. the exercises were Geography & Grammar. Moral Phil. omitted for want of time. —

Wednesday [3d] This morn the Physiological questions were answered. To the 27th — Not till about noon that the clothes may become perfectly clear of all exhalation which they have imbibed in the night. — The clothes worn by day should be separated and hung up round the room. —

[Answers omitted]

.   .   .   .

The conversational exercise occupied the time after I returned from the M.S. which was satisfactorily performed. – –

Thursday Dec. 5th Before writing an account of the lessons, or rather of the *want* of lessons perhaps it will be best to give the cause of this want. — Last evening, we had a lecture from Mr. Felch the Phrenologist, which commenced at half past six, and continued until ten. It was quite interesting and many of the remarks were very good. — After the lecture was concluded, he examined the heads of many of the scholars. Some of them were described very well & Mr P. thought he "hit the nail on the head" in the description of my character. — It was nothing new, as I have been told before, that my organs of *Self-Esteem*, Love of Approbation, & Mirthfulness, were not no 1. in size. — As the lessons were not learned this morn Mr P. took our queries in N. Phil. — & then I went below. — Had quite a pleasant school & returned up stairs, to do nothing but listen to the class in Algebra. – – Dined, and went into the Model School, to stay until three. After that went to the N.S. and I recited in Enunciation and Music. – – After tea Mr P. called to see us and spoke about the necessity of a strict observance of study hours. — When he went out it was after seven but the remainder of the time was strictly kept.

Friday Dec. 6th This morning, the reading exercise was in the fourth Chap. of Luke — 33d verse. — Mr P. said that the Jews had only one synagogue or temple before their Captivity in Babylon to which they were obliged to go thrice every year. — After this they built temples in different places, though the reason for this is unknown. — The temple where they worshipped was that of Solomon. — He spoke of the opinion common among the Jews, that when a person is sick, he is possessed with some evil spirit, & that although the writers of the Scriptures were better informed, yet they wrote in that language commonly used & best understood by the people, just as a writer of the present day would speak of the rising & setting of the sun. After he had concluded these remarks, he informed us that he should not attend to the regular exercises but should give us something in the form of a lecture, until it was time

to go into the M.S., & should then take the scholars down
there to observe the operations. He commenced by telling
us, that he intended to exhibit to us his manner of teaching
& after that, said that perhaps some were disappointed in
the Model School, & perhaps, in the Normal School also. —
In the commencement of the M.S., he said he might have
committed the charge of arranging & putting into order
the thirty three there collected but he thought or feared,
it would be too severe a task & feared that the *result* might
be a failure. — Another complaint was that there were too
few scholars. — In reply to this he said that he might,
probably, have had 50, instead of thirty scholars, & left
them in the charge of one pupil: some might have succeeded,
but if a failure had been the consequence, all would agree
that he had acted very injudiciously. It was necessary that
the school should be committed to the charge of some one,
& therefore he had placed one as superinten[dent] . . . —
esteeming that the safest way. It may be objected to this
because one scholar can teach well it is not· certain that
she can manage *as* well, or because she can take care of
thirty that she can of fifty. — He compared this case to
the shoe-maker, who has made one pair of boots thoroughly,
& therefore, can make fifty more as well. — The reasons
which he gave for taking this course were three: 1st, he
did not wish to place a burden upon the teachers greater
than they could bear; 2nd, he did not wish to run the risk
of failing, & 3d, he wished those engaged as teachers might
devote some time to their own studies. — He then proceeded to give some of the duties of the superintendent.
She is expected to open the school, give the general lesson, to
see that everything is in good order & proper time. She is
not expected to confine herself to the platform but to be in
every part of the room, passing among the classes, & observing the manner of teaching. — Except in a very palpable
case, it would be best to make any suggestions in private. —
It is the duty of superintendent and assistants, to confer
together and should the latter see anything which they
think would admit of improvement, they should suggest
it to the sup. — The superintendent should be so in every
respect; the scholar having that office one week may be

assistant the next. — "Whatsoever, they bid ye do, that observe & do." She should have her plan which should be made known to her assistants. — The duties of the assistants. — They should receive directions from the sup. & follow them implicitly. It is well for the same scholar to have one class for some time, but not too long, lest she should get into a regular routine of doing things. – – –

Having proceeded, thus far we went below & Mr P. heard the 1st class in Geography and in Arithmetic. These with some remarks occupied the forenoon until eleven, when Mr P advised us all to go and take exercise, thereby to improve the day which was so uncommonly warm for the season. — Most did as he desired & I for one, felt repaid fully for it. — In the P.M. we went into the M.S. at one & Mr P. examined or taught the classes in Reading & Spelling. This occupied the time with the exception of a short recess, until three, & then we went above, to hear the conclusion of Mr P's remarks. — It will not be possible, he said, to put you in the situation of teacher by giving you examples of the manner of teaching. You cannot learn all, until you are in that station yourself. —

There are some things which require particular attention such as the manner of going to and from seats; make it a point to have it done always promptly & orderly, without needless noise. — In going out of school & in coming in especially in recess, care must be taken, or they will make much noise. — The sup. & assistants should be particular with regard to attitude, & holding the book. If you wish to do anything effectually, be constant and uniform. — While hearing a class it is necessary to be Lynx-eyed and Argus-eyed. — Some of the falts (*sic*) which Mr P. has noticed are, want of attention at one end of the class while the other is reciting, the pupils thus becoming inattentive; too much moving in classes, as lifting up of hands, & falling of books. — In Reading he said the classes had done pretty well. Short portions should be assigned to them & frequent reviews should be made by teachers. — In Geography much is to be done by *maps* and teaching the geography of the country immediately around. —

Saturday. 7th This, morn. the devotional exercises

being concluded, Mr P. remarked on the propositions which
were upon his table. One was a petition for a farther explanation of the principle of freezing. He again spoke of the
apple, and then of the water. He explained the reason why
water freezes at the top instead of the bottom first. — He
said that the particles after they were chilled to 40°, arranged themselves in order for freezing. — The lighter
particles are on the top, & therefore the caloric cannot pass
off & the waters freeze. How would you read the fraction
17/22; was another question, to which the reply was 17
twenty seconds. – – He then explained the meaning of the
11th v. 7th Chap. of Matt.[1] – – He said that the Jews were
obliged to support their parents, and that if they wished to
refuse them any thing, they said Corban or a gift, which
meant that the amount for which they asked was to be
given to religious objects. . —

After the remarks were concluded, Mr P. said that it
would be best to take up the debate next that we might
secure the time. Accordingly the question "Is capital
punishment ever justifiable? The debate was quite lengthy,
& when the Yeas Nays, were taken, two only were found in
the affirmative. After we had all expressed our opinion he
said that he thought there were a few cases, in which it was
necessary to resort to it, as in mobs & in self-defence. —
While the debate was going on Mr Wellington of the East
Village came in & appeared to be much entertained. He
also expressed his opinion which coincided with Mr. P's. —

After he had concluded his remarks Mr P. spoke of the
recess & desired us to take exercise. Mr W. then remarked
that he had fifteen hundred scholars under his instruction,
and that he should be unwilling to tell us how many were
deformed in some degree. — This he attributed in part
to the manner of sitting in school, leaning over the desk
but principally to the want of proper exercise. — He recommended battledoor as indoor amusement and skating,
(asking the young ladies, at the same time, not to be shocked
by the proposal) for out-doors. — He said that fifteen years
ago, several young ladies of the first families, practised it,
& it became quite common, after a time. — We all walked

---

[1] Corrected to *Mark*. — Ed.

up the Lincoln road & ascending a hill crossed into the Concord road & returned. Mr P. then read an extract from
Todd's Teacher's Manual, on the necessity of having silence
in the room, when a person is studying. — He then proceeded to give the remainder of the lecture, which he left
unfinished on Saturday, the 23d. The method of teaching
reading by commencing with the words was first recommended by Miss Edgeworth. — In the old way the child
was kept upon the alphabet, which was to him a number of
unconnected sounds, & may justly be considered like string-
ing beads on sand. — Speaking the letters, gives no clue to
pronunciation, as may be seen by taking the parts of the
word physick & pronouncing each letter. After the
schol[ar] has pronounced all the letters in the first syllable
he has no idea of the manner in which it is pronounced. —
It is not best to commence quite yet, with the sounds, but
it is still worse to teach the [scholars] about labials, vowels
& consonant, mutes, &c. Let them put very simple words
into sentences & read them & see that the[y] read naturally.
Take care to question them much, upon what they read.
Mischief is done in schools, by having them to read, what
they do not understand. — Take simple words, & have
them give their ideas of them, as about & with though words
which represent things are easier to define. – – The power
of attention is of more value than the strongest memory,
& a good example of this is to be found in Charles Follen,
whose mother reads to him every night & thus he acquires
the art of being a good listener. Mr P. spoke in very high
terms, of this practice of Mrs. Follen. — In spelling the
words should not be taken from columns, but from the
reading lesson, & care should be taken that unmeaning
syllables as eri, ere, erru, & such combinations of letters
should now be taught them. As soon as possible they should
exercise upon the slate, the object being chiefly to teach
them to write correctly. — Have nothing to do with the
drawling tones or with indistinct utterance, which prevails.
— Many adults even cannot read without a tone. The
fault lies, in having children read what they do not understand, & thus exercising all their powers, in finding out
what the *word* is, instead of thinking of the sense. Let the

words be so simple, that the mind will fall upon the meaning. — Read much to your pupils & have them read to each other thus cultivating the habit of attention. — The exercises closed here as there was no time for reading in the Bible. —

Sunday 8th The minister this morn, was the same that we had last Sunday — Mr Huntington. — The text Romans 8th Chap. 2nd v. "For the law of the Spirit of life in Christ Jesus, hath made me free from the law of sin & death." The discourse was not very interesting to me, probably because it was beyond my comprehension. — The afternoon text was from 1st Corinthians 7th Chap. 29th. "But this I say, Brethren, time is short. — Quite interesting. —

Monday. [9th] For the first time since Thanksgiving, our number were together — or rather those who parted before that time. The physiological questions were first answered.

33d. Explain how confinement to one position occasions in females especially, so much deformity & disease? —

34th. In order that exercise may strengthen, and not reduce the system: what rules are laid down in the fourth chapter?

35th. How does muscular action promote the circulation of the blood & give color to the skin?

36 Is very active exercise either before or after meals injurious & why? —

37th & 38th It is common for persons who are obliged to work hard in preparing a meal to say they have no appetite. How accounted for? —

39th A little boy was asked what kind of a man he would make if he played all the time; he answered "a strong one". Was his answer a philosophical one?

40th Why is it best to eat sparingly while travelling? The first four questions are answered by extracts from Combe. — The 37th & 38th were answered by the pupils, on the principle of active exercise immediately before a meal. Mr P. then suggested that the *smell* of the victuals might have some effect. The 39th was decided to be unphilosophical from principles laid down in Combe. — Immediately after the answers were given, I went below & after calling the school to order, Mr P. came down & heard

Framingham Normal School, 1857

a class in Geography. — The other proceedings were as
usual – – Returned at M [i.e., noon] in season to recite a
part of a lesson in Nat. Phil. Mental Philosophy & Book-
keeping omitted for want of time. — P.M. — Recited the
problem on the globe or rather listened to an explanation
of it. — The day rainy — myself dull & scholars rather
dull too — not the best of lessons. —

Tuesday 10th This morn after reading in the Scriptures
Mr P. made some remarks. — First upon the Publicans;
they were odious to the Jews, because they were tax-
gatherers. — The Scribes were writers of the law. — He
spoke of the saying, putting new wine into old bottles: that
the wine might be compared to old & new opinions — a
person adheres to old customs although he knows the new
are better. – – After the comments, Mr P. gave us our
journals & composition, — saying that he was better pleased
with them than usual. — Went down stairs to call the
school in, & it being ten minutes of nine, occupied the time
in talking with the Modellites about the figures on the face
of the clock. –- Returned at 11 & recited Mental Phil. &
Book-keeping. — The afternoon passed about as usual
Orthography & Moral Phil occupying the time — In the
forenoon Mr P. asked the following questions: "A philosopher said, that when he exercised he did not want an
idea should enter his head, was that a philosopical wish?
On taking the opinion of the school there appeared to be
some diversity but Mr P. thought it only *apparent* and that
we all agreed that it was not philosophical. – –

Wednesday 11th. Mr P. read this morn, from the 6th
Chap. of Luke, and after reading, spoke of a question proposed yesterday in Moral Philosophy. — It was at what
time does the moral power of a child commence? — The
question had been a subject of consideration for the class,
and it seemed to be the general opinion that it commenced
with the intellect. Mr P. said that he agreed with that
opinion, — From this question, he spoke of original de-
pravity, & said that he thought the principles of Physiology & Philosophy shewed plainly, that the child inherited
the predominant traits of character in the parents, & that
he did not think that they were responsible for the defects

thus engendered although it was evident that they did inherit these defects. He said he did not agree with the opinion expressed by a gentleman in his presence, that he felt as guilty for the sins of our first parents, as he should for his own sins, although he was not there. – – He expressed a fear that he might be misunderstood, & said that he did not wish to influence the decision of his pupils, upon the subject. — One query was placed upon the table to this effect; when one part of the brain is destroyed, leaving only one organ, instead of two, to act is that organ strengthened so as to perform the work of two or is the mind weakened? Mr P. said that he thought that the brain acted as one eye would, the other being destroyed, & that philosophers told us that the vision was 1/12 greater by the use of both. — Thus the effect upon the brain would be to strengthen one, although not to make its force (POWER) double. – – The next exercise was in Physiology: answering the following queries given out yesterday. —

41st   The effect of dancing as usually practised; what & why? —

42nd.   Will it do to depend entirely on walking for exercise?

43d.   What other exercise might be practised to advantage, in connection with it? —

44th.   What facts prove that females have suffered more than males, from a violation of physical laws? —

45th.   Mention any practices known to you, which are violations of physical laws?

The 41st & 2d were answered by reference to Combe.

The 43d — trundling the hoop & battledoor were recommended — laughing & swinging the arms, also good.

46th.   That females are more subject to deformity, & to pulmonary affections —

45th.   Too much & too little exercise, food & clothing. Wrong time for exercise & eating, tight dress & not sufficient changes of it. Deficiency in airing beds.

The next subject upon the tapis was a review in N. Phil. which occupied an hour at the close of which, we took the long recess. After that, the class in arithmetic was called. During the exercise Mr Damon called & informed Mr P.

that he had brought his daughter. — This intelligence was joyfully received, of course, & now we are at liberty to speak with her school being over. —

Thursday 12th. The portion of Scripture read this morn was from the 6th Chap. of Luke. After reading, Mr P. made so marks [some remarks] upon the meekness of Christ. — While all around were eloquent in his praise, he was still unaltered. — The first exercise, was in Physiology. —

Question 46th. How do the bones of the head differ from those of the other parts of the system; & what is the advantage? —

Question 47th Does the brain give the form to the scull, or vice versa? What proofs to be adduced? —

48th Is it well to encourage very young children to walk alone? Assign any reasons?

49th Why is it that children so seldom break their bones, notwithstanding their frequent falls.

50th What evils might be expected to follow to children, from overwork and what from the reverse? —

51st. Upon what should we mainly depend for the prevention or cure, of a rickety tendency in children? —

52nd. If the laws of Combe are correct, among what classes should we expect to find the most frequent instances of deformity? What the fact? —

53 & 54th. Why do females exhibit so frequent instances of deformity; and from prevalent customs among females in this country is this likely to increase, or diminish?

[Answers omitted.]

·   ·   ·   ·   ·   ·   ·   ·   ·   ·

After answering these, Mr Peirce made some remarks upon the manner in which the exercise was performed, & then gave out the following

Query 55th Is there reason to believe that the cause of this deformity is generally known?

Query 56th. Will ladies generally, who understand the principles of Physiology, follow them in opposition to fashion? —

[Query] 57th.　State concisely the *general* laws of healthy condition in the bones. —

[Query] 58th.　Defective nutrition is stated to be injurious to the osseous system; what would be the effect of excessive nutrition?

Chap. 7th　59th　What is to be understood by a double circulation of the blood?

Query 60th.　From the structure of the lungs explain how it is that any poisonous effluvia in the air may injure health? —

Query 61st.　Explain how a violation of the first two laws of healthy respiration, may induce consumption? —

After the queries were answered, I was obliged to go below, & therefore missed of the recitation in N. Phil. Returned, but the class were reading therefore had nothing to do. — In the afternoon by Mr P's request the school was to assemble at one. — The intermission was passed in conversation with Mr P., upon domestic affairs — We had previously become so much excited, that the "fountain of tears" was opened by mere recurrence to past events, not as Mr P. implied, by his *words*. — At the close of the conference, we went below, and, on returning at three to the Model School, had time to take part in one exercise, that of Orthography. - -

Friday 13th　The first exercise, this morn, was in Physiology and the answers to the questions which were entered under Thursday's acc't were given. —

Ans 55th　This question was omitted, & therefore received no answer. —

[Ans] 56th　As the laws of physiology are more widely known it is probable that the fashions may alter; but very few would leave fashion for physiology. —

[Ans] 57th　See Combe's Physiology. —

[Ans] 58th　The digestive organs being overtaxed, would perform only a part of their office, & thus a part of the food would be in an improper situation to pass into the blood & the bones would be softened. —

[Ans] 59th　The circulation through the arteries & veins, may be considered as two classes. —

[Ans] 60th　The blood, in its passage through the lungs,

is exposed to the air & thus imbibes and transmits to the
body all impurities which may exist in it? —

[Ans] 61st   The laws are, 1st A sound original state of the
lungs & 2nd a due supply of rich blood to the parts of the
system.

After answering the above Mr P. told us that he wished
to refer to two questions viz, the first answered and the last.
—He thought there was little hope of the generality of people,
as long as the *fashion*, was in opposition to physiology.
With regard to the last, he said that he felt great anxiety
upon the subject,[1] but he feared that few would act upon it.
— The following are the queries for the next lesson. —

Query 62nd.   What influence have strong emotions of the
mind on health as influenced by respiration?

[Query] 63d.   Explain how too closely fitted dress and an
insufficient supply of fresh air, may produce consumption? —

[Query] 64th   Have we reason to believe that there are
any practical *Atheists*, in reference to the first clause in the
last question? —

[Query] 65th   Is it a proof of ignorance, or of a slavish
devotion to fashion, that we so frequently see curtains
around our beds, in our otherwise well furnished apartments? —

[Query] 66th   Should not every one acquainted with
Physiology give the influence of her example? —

[Query] 67th   What objections are there to burning gas
in close rooms? —

[Query] 68th   What arguments can Physiology offer to
those who say they live in habitual violation of its most
prominent laws? —

[Query] 69th   What influence upon young ladies does the
too prevalent notion that delicacy of appearance is one of
the requisites of beauty have upon their modes of life?
Relate any striking illustration which you may know. —

Query 70th   Other conditions being similar, what forms
of the chest in two persons, one subject to chills & cold ex-
tremities, the other suffering no such inconveniences? —

---

[1] Mr. Peirce advocated fresh-air treatment for tubercular patients and separation from other
people. — Ed.

[Query] 71st   In walking for exercise, should hilly or level portions of land be preferred? —

[Query] 72nd.   Should we endeavor to check the laughing crying & shouting of children?

[Query] 73d   In what condition of lungs should reading aloud be avoided? —

Went to the Model School and was there two hours and a half, the latter part of the time engaged in conversation with Mrs Peirce. — The P.M. was passed as usual, the first two hours in the M.S. the last two in N.S. — At the close of the M.S. there was a rap at the door, and a lady asked for Mr P. whom I referred to the room above.   Found there a Miss Fisk of Lincoln & found that Mrs Trask had called. — This eve entered upon a new plan which was to devote the time from six to seven to reading; one reading aloud and the others all listening. — The work with which they commenced, was "Mrs Sigourney's Letters to Young Ladies" – – The preface & 1st letter were read this eve which abound in beautiful language & comparisons.

Saturday 14th   The first exercise was, as usual, reading in the Bible this morn from the 6th Chap of Luke.   The next, was giving out questions in Nat. Phil. for answers.   Most of them related to the figures in the Phil, which were not understood as the construction of the watch, the pulley & wedge. — After the queries were answered, Mr P. made some remarks or suggestions, & left them with the scholars, — About laughing countenances, & improvement of time, & attention to lessons.   The next exercise was in the Bible. Mr P. read the 9th Chap of John, 17th Chap of Acts 22nd & 23d, and 1st Corinthians 13th verse. — One explanation which he made, was a very useful & interesting one to me, as the text had always been obscure — It was in the 17th Chap of Acts 23d verse —, the insc[r]iption upon the altar, "to the unknown God." — The explanation was, that the City of Rome [Athens] was once under the influence of a pestilential disease, & the Romans [Athenians] in their superstition, had erected altars to all their divinities, but still it did not rage with less fury. — They then concluded that there was still some divinity unappeased, who was unknown to them, and therefore erected an altar & placed upon it the inscription, "To the unknown God". — St. Paul passing by, saw it, & made the remarks mentioned in the 23d. — At the close of the last exercise, we took our long recess and returned at half after eleven. Then Mr P. commenced his thirteenth lecture, and continued it until it was so late, that we had no time for our discussion which was to be upon the question, "Is it expedient that the Scriptures should be introduced into schools? —

The subject of the lecture, which was the thirteenth in number, was Reading. — It is more difficult for a child to learn to read, than for a grown person to learn several languages. — Could either teacher or scholar look forward to the future, they would be discouraged. — Go to the work with patience, which nothing can overcome. If you have taught them to read simple sentences, without whining, you have done well & the future work will be easy. — Then they will be able to go on alone without aid, and improve themselves if suitable books are provided. — Have your lesson simple, & short, & various. — The deficiency in books is the greatest difficulty, and those adopted in the Model School are as good as any. — Pierpont's Young Reader & Worcester's Fourth Book, & Abbott's Mount Vernon Reader, are to be preferred to the First Class Book, or to the Young Ladies' Class Book. Porter's Rhetorical Reader contains many valuable hints. The great fault seems to be in bad arrangement of pieces, but it is more easy to find a fault than to mend it. — Give variety as much as possible, thus increasing interest. — At one time let there be a lesson assigned for all the scholars, at another, one paragraph for each of the scholars, at another, one for all to read, letting each one repeat it, & lastly have them to read to each other. — Do not always have them to recite in order, but hear them promiscuously. Sometimes you will attend entirely to reading, at others to questioning. Read to them yourself, and let them correct you, they will feel encouraged to know, that one who is so much their superior does, sometimes fail. — Tell of the errors in pronunciation, inflection &c, but do not let them be interrupted in reading. — Better let them finish the sentence and then correct. — Every one will have something good in their reading & it will be well to call the attention of the class to both faults & perfections. — One reads fast, another, slow, another, omits, another repeats, another fails in inflections. — Call their attention to practise as much more depends on thorough and systematic drilling. Two thorough recitations per week, will affect more than a half dosen imperfect. Take care that it should [not] become a dry lesson. Let every thing, person, character, & date, all be subjects of remark. Do not let them go on through the book, that they may say they have been through it. Call their attention to their own faults and especially to provincialisms which prevail in the neighborhood. Many words of common use, are badly pronounced & the very commonness is the reason why it is not perceived as the words head, catch, tobacco. — This is the course you are to take when you begin with the alphabet. If this was not the case you will have the more difficult task to perform. You will have those who have been instructed badly; there will be much to be done before the good seed can spring up or take root. — In Walker's Elocutionist, Porter's Rhetorical Reader, Bailey's Rhetorical Grammar and also in Parker's Rhetorical Grammar, you will find rules and directions for guidance, in the manner of correcting the faults. — The query how can we become good readers, will next suggest itself. — Reading is the uttering of certain elementary sounds combined to express ideas. — Elementary sounds are the powers of letters. These are made by the muscles of the mouth, which are governed by the same laws as the other muscles. — Exercise them thoroughly and be careful to do it correctly. The chief business is to drill in the elementary sounds until the organs can strike them perfectly. There is no work better calculated to assist, than Russell's Enunciation. — Many common defects in reading, are owing to want of thorough drilling in these forty-two sounds. The difficulty of learning is increased, by knowing that the same letter represents different sounds & different letters the same sounds. — Another point in pronunciation, is the placing of the accent correctly. Custom settles it, and we consult the Lexicon to know how custom decides. Three things are essential to good reading; give the elementary sounds, and syllables distinctly, and accent correctly. Alter the accent and it will make almost a different word; as in the word Agriculture, lay the accent on the last syllable, as the French do, & it will become a different word. In reading speak the words with proper pitch, rate, & force, not too fast, nor set off by regular intervals; pitch depends on the subject, & is to be varied from one degree above a whisper, to shouting and calling. Certain intonations are expressive of emotion; thus grief, pity, incline the voice to the rising, indignation and anger, to the falling. Why, it is not known. The pitch, rate, and force should be nearly what we use in conversation; therefore that, more than all others should be cultivated; but not exclusively, as attention should be paid to the whole compass of the voice. — Exercises should be continued till this power rests as a matter of habit. — Here the business should end. After this fix the mind on the sentiment, and let the soul be filled with it. Think of nothing else; a good reader is not anxious about the tone and inflection, but trusts to habits. — The musician thinks not of the motion of his fingers, neither does the good reader think of the motion of his mouth. He has one rule by which to read and that is read to the sentiment. This is the most important thing. Demosthenes was asked what was most important in good delivery, and replied three times action, action, action; each time increasing the emphasis. Mr P. said if he was asked what was most important to a good reader, he would say READ TO THE SENTIMENT, READ TO THE SENTIMENT, READ TO THE SENTI-MENT. — There should be two sets of exercises in school, one for training and another to show the effects of training. As we here use Russell's Enunciation for the former purpose, and the Fourth Book for the latter. — It is related of Aeschines & of Demosthenes, rival orators, that the Athenians, after hearing the former, went away delighted with his manner; of the latter, that they remembered only what he had said, without knowing anything about his manner. – –

The next lecture will be upon the subject of Spelling and perhaps some additional remarks upon Reading – – – – –

After the lecture, Mr P. read some remarks from a lecture delivered before the American Institute, by a Mr Fosdick. — Spent the afternoon with the exception of a half hour, in writing and the eve in reading & studying—Mr P. called just before study hours, and talked over domestic matters. — The clouds which have so long hung over us, seem to be gradually clearing away, and the clear sky to appear. —

(I think you tax your time too much in writing in your journal.) [Comment of Mr. Peirce]

Sunday Dec. 15th Awoke before day light, and could not refrain from telling Miss Stow, that it snowed. — Had I waited till eve, I should have had no occasion, as all who ventured out to church, were very sensible of it. — We however succeeded admirably in wading, each having only two falls, *all day*. — Such storms seldom visit our island [Nantucket], so that this furnishes a pleasant variety. —

The text of this morn, was from John 13th Chap. 34th v. "A new commandment give I unto you, that ye love one another; as I have loved you, "that ye also love one another." The minister was Mr. Buckingham from Cambridge, a *brother* of the Mr B. mentioned in the first part of my journal. — He left the Divinity School last commencement, and is exceedingly youthful in appearance. — The text in the P.M. was from John 14th 27th "Peace, I leave with you, my peace I give unto you: not as the world giveth, give I unto you. — There were very few in church, & no singers, so that the P.M. service was shortened by the omission of the singing. —

Monday. Dec. 16th The morning dawned, but did not show any abatement of the storm. Everything was white, & looked as if it might be white for some time. — Notwithstanding the severity of the storm, the most of the. pupils were assembled at eight. — The first exercise was in Physiology, in which the questions given out on Friday were answered. —

[Answers omitted.]

.   .   .   .

The questions for the next day were the following:

Query 74th. Chap. 8th   What is the cause of fainting in close ill ventilated rooms?

[Query] 75th State concisely the three conditions of health in the brain? —

Query 76th   Can those who do not sufficiently exercise the brain, expect a long & healthy life? —

[Query] 77th What evil may arise from confining our minds exclusively to one little sphere of occupation as home or school, or from living without any particular or fixed occupation? —

[Query] 78th   What pernicious practises are those liable to fall into who have neglected the proper exercise of the brain? —

[Query] 79th   Is the danger of an insufficiently excited brain well understood in the community? —

[Query] 80th   Explain how it is that precocious children more frequently die than others and that in mature life they are generally surpassed by those once considered as greatly their inferiors? —

[Query] 81st   What error is commonly committed in the treatment of forward & backward children. —

[Query] 82nd   Of what principle does the death of Scott afford an illustration? —

[Query] 83d   Is long & intense thought on one or several subjects, most likely to derange the brain?

[Query] 84th   How may nonomania (*sic*) be accounted for? —

The exercise in Philosophy was upon the Screw, and after I had given an abstract of the lesson, I went below to find how many Modelites I should have. —

Thirteen only had assembled, & they with the determination to make as much complaint of the weather as possible. — Recited a part of the lesson in Mental Philosophy & school closed. – – In the afternoon recited in Orthography & Geography. —

Tuesday Dec. 17th   After the devotional exercises Mr P. said he had many subjects to speak upon. First, the Model School. Mr P. said he considered himself as responsible for the character of the plan. — The success of it will be ours.

The next lesson was in Physiology, the answers to the queries on the preceding page. —

[Answers omitted.]

. . . .

The questions given for the next lesson were,

Question 85th. Why is hard study or labor injurious after eating a full meal? —

[Question] 86th Explain how it is a scholar will learn more in six successive months of education than in the same time by long intermissions. —

[Question] 87th & 88th Are we to understand by what is said on p. 244 that intellect itself is incapable of cultivation & that it is only the powers of manifestation that education can control. —

[Question] 89th Will the moral sentiments be properly trained by enlightening the intellect on moral questions. —

[Question] 90th. If not, how then can we educate feelings of benevolence, reverence, consciousness &c. —

[Question] 91st Have we reason to believe that bodily health will be affected by the training of the intellectual powers and moral sensations as that the powers & sentiments are influenced by the physical condition of the body? —

[Question] 92nd Give any instances to illustrate this. —

[Question] 93d. Why is it that a person in ill health, is benefitted more by a physician in whom he has confidence than by another of equal skill in whom he has less confidence. —

[Question] 94th What benefit can those who are teachers draw from reading Capt Basil Hall's remarks in the last of the 8th Chap.

Went down to the M.S. & staid till it was so late that I could recite only Mental Philosophy. — In the afternoon had serious thoughts of spending the time, after the dismission of the M.S., in the sitting room, rather than to go into the N.S., but repented & went in to recite a lesson on

FRAMINGHAM 1926 — CROCKER HALL

the globes & a part of one in M.Phil. — In the eve we received a present from Mr Baxter of a Young Woman's Guide by Dr Alcott, accompanied by a very pretty note. —

Read a chapter in Mrs Sigourney's work, & then study-hours came. —

December 18th Wednesday In order to secure one conversational exercise Mr P. said that he would commence with it, and accordingly took for his subject the last snow-storm. — He said that we had not had so much snow at one time for many years. — It is a general impression that our climate has changed very much in the last few years. It is true that there has been much alteration & that our winters now are warmer than they were fifty years ago. — It was customary to have cold weather and frequently *sleighing*, at Thanksgiving time, which was in the last of November. *Now* we do not have snow, or steady cold weather, until the last of December. The ancient writers, Virgil & Horace, describe the pleasures of a warm fire, and paint their winters in colours, which, *now*, would best represent our *New England* winters. It is well known, that we never find in Italy, at the present day, weather which would *compare* with our winters, for coldness. — These facts prove, very plainly, that the winters are much warmer than they once were. — There may be two causes for this; 1st the changes going on in the interior of the earth, 2nd the alteration in the face of the country, as it becomes more and more populous. — About one hundred years ago, there was a great snow-storm which receives the appellation of "the great snow storm of New England". The snow was so deep as to cover small houses, and gave the country the appearance of one vast plain. Flocks of cattle were overtaken and buried in it. Some were taken out and found living, at the end of thirty or forty days. At this time, a minister died in Cambridge, and those of Boston and the vicinity, went as was customary to attend the funeral. — The snow was so deep that it took them ten days to complete their journey. In order to convey the corpse to the grave-yard, they had the snow excavated, so that the procession walked under an arch. — That we have less snow now than formerly, may be known from the fact, that we now have no use for the snow shoe which our ancestors wore. — Time would not permit a description of this. Shall we not have it next Wednesday? — Miss Haskell commenced the exercise by relating an anecdote. Miss Stow recited an anecdote of Sheridan. Miss Damon, of two lawyers who were in partnership, and whose names were Catchem & Cheatem. Their sign causing some sport, they determined to have their first names put on which were Isaac & Uriah. The painter not having a board sufficiently long, put only the initials upon it, when it became "I. Catchem & U. Cheatem." Misses Stodder & Drew had an extract from the Vespers of Palermo. — Miss Smith, an anecdote Misses O'Connor & Davis, anecdotes of preachers. Miss Sparrell, the cause of the Trojan War. — Miss E. Pennell, the piece of poetry entitled "Evening Bells." Miss R. Pennell, "A voice from Mt. Auburn" which was very beautiful Miss Ireson a piece of Poetry entitled Lexington. — Miss S. E Locke an anecdote of Peter of Castile. — Miss Burdick, a poem "Who loves me best?" Miss A. Locke, lines composed by Prof. Park at the age of 16, when absent from home. — Miss Harris, anecdote of Fletcher. — Miss Parks gave an account of the colours used by different nations as mourning. — Miss Woodman, Sprague's Address to two Swallows. Miss Swift, a Biographical sketch of Virgil. — After Mr P. had expressed his satisfaction with the exercise, we attended to Physiology, & gave the following

Ans. 85th. It is a law, that no two operate together without one or both are injured. — Hence the rule never exercise the mind or rouse deep feeling after a meal.

Ans. 86th. Repetition is very necessary; as essential to the mind as exercise to the body. —

Ans. 87th & 88th. There seemed to be some difference of opinion, but Mr P. inclined to the affirmative. —

Ans. 89th. Answered in the Negative. —

Ans. 90th By presenting to the child scenes which will call forth these feelings and by giving them power to gratify these feelings. —

Ans. 91st. Answered in the Affirmative. —

Ans. 92nd Numerous instances were given as of people

who had injured themselves by tightness of dress, by over exertion of the brain, & by undue exposure.

Ans to the 99th, written by mistake.

Ans. 93d. Because the physician carries the mind of the patient along with him & he feels no anxiety about the effects of his medicines. —

Ans. 94th. We may learn to rule by persuasion and commendations, rather than by reproof & fault finding. The following questions were given out. —

Query 95th. Combe says bad health may be regarded in three different ways; in which is it commonly regarded?

Query 96th. Is there not a sort of vague, confused, & even contradictory tendency to regard it in all three lights combined?

Query 97th. What have you been in the habit of considering the cause of disease? —

Query 98th If ignorance on this subject is bliss is it not folly to be wise? —

[Query] 99th Mention any instances not cited by Combe, that you may have heard, read, or witnessed, to illustrate the principles of this chapter. —

[Query] 100th Will the pupils who have finished this work of Combe's, feel desirous to regulate their conduct by its precepts? —

The study hours were from the time when we finished our tea, until nearly seven, when many, nine in number, went to the Lecture in the eve. A farther account will be given in the form of Composition. —

December 19th Thursday. — The morning exercise was in Physiology. —

Ans. 95th. In the first light, as sent by Providence for the punishment of sin. —

Ans 96th Answered in the infirmative (*sic*).

Ans 97th A difference of opinion, as might be expected. Some the last, others different at different ages.

Ans 98th. Affirmative. —

Ans 99th Ans. given on p. 170.

Ans 100th Yes. —

The recitation in Natural Philosophy was upon Com-

pound Machinery, and after this we went into the Model
School. The scholars all were very orderly and seemed
determined to do as well as possible. — At the close of the
school, in obedience to my own feelings, as well as to the
wishes of Mr P, — I gave them much commendation, and
they all promised to do as well in the afternoon. The afternoon was not however quite so well. — In the A.M. read an
Abstract of the Introduction & First Chapter of Newman's
Political Economy. — In the P.M. read a lesson in Orthöepy
& punctuated a few sentences. — The school was visited by
Mr Dodge, Dea. Mulliken, Mr Davis & Dr Follen. — In the
eve Miss Sparrell had company, and it made many of us feel,
that we too, should like to see a friend. —

December 20th Friday. — This morn, owing to some un-
accountable cause, the lesson in N. Philosophy, was badly
recited. It was upon the subject of Complex Machinery, —
and was easier than common. — After some remarks from
Mr P., the band of teachers went below & there pursued
their accustomed duties. — Returning to school this morn,
read another Abstract from Political Economy, of the 2nd
Chapter. – – In the P.M. Mr P. informed me, that he expected some company in the Model School. The classes
in Reading were called and immediately after, they had
taken their places, Mr Dodge and Deacon Mulliken entered: they passed the afternoon in school, and the lessons
were somewhat varied, Arithmetic and Geography being
substituted for Writing. — At the close of the school, Mr
Mulliken expressed himself well pleased with the school, &
said that he wished he had come into the school, when it
was first established. One other remark which he made,
was too deep for my comprehension, or rather I was unable
to tell whether it was intended as complimentary or the
reverse. — It was, "that he regretted he did not come into
the Model School before he visited the Normal School.
Why, I do not understand? — Being rather fatigued, I did
not return to the N. School, but passed the time in the
sitting room, writing in my journal. — Mrs. Davis, Miss
Goodwin, & Miss Howe from Boston visited the Normal
School this P.M. —

December. Saturday 21st. The first exercise was in

Philosophy, and was a review of the first part of the book,
as far as the Mechanic Powers. — The young ladies all
exerted themselves, to draw the figures in the lesson. — The
first lesson was well recited, and we next attended to Reading; first, in Abbott's Teacher, then in the New Testament.
The reading exercise was well performed, and after it Mr
P. told us that he should have to borrow some time of
us — & would discharge the debt, when the English paid the
great National debt. — After this exercise, we took the recess, for a few minutes, and returned to listen to the fourteenth lecture. — The subject of it, was Reading. The
art of reading is the correct utterance of written composition. — It not only gives the meaning, but the *force* of the
sentiments, without the help of the eye or arms. It differs
from oratory, and is almost synonymous with elocution.
A young lady can do no better than to confine the eye, and
read without gesticulation. There are two kinds of reading,
grammatical & rhetorical. — The first expresses the sense,
the second expresses the sense, and all we can do with the
voice, without the eye or arm. —

Here, Mr P. read an extract from Milton's Paradise
Lost. The subject is divided into three heads; 1st, suggest
some considerations which give reading claims to attention.
2nd, notice the fact of the great and prevalent deficiency.
3d. Explain how it may be supplied & a good reader formed.
It has a great claim on account of its connection with that
important organ, the human voice, which is the distinctive mark between man and brute. — Think of its power
and importance, as the instrument of human intercourse,
between mind & mind, heart & heart. The art of reading
as a cultivation of this member as a source of entertainment. — It has in many particulars the advantage over
singing. — A gentleman who had a daughter in school,
said he preferred that she should return to him, a good
reader, than an accomplished performer on any instrument. — It is a graceful accomplishment and affords personal amusement. — In the social circle its influence is
very great. — How much one good reader can do in a
family, towards entertaining and improving it. — It is the
foundation of good speaking; & though in this part young

ladies are not particularly interested, yet they must teach those who are to be the orators of the next generation. — All that relates to good articulation, modulation, intonation and enunciation are looked for in good reading as well as in good speaking. — Much more depends on the voice, than we think: this is what Demosthenes & Cicero meant by action. Our young men would do well to cultivate the voice; many of our sermons glow & burn in the closet, but float *as an iceburg*, in the pulpit. He who glows with sacred fervor in private, in the pulpit, is like a statue of marble. Our speakers would do well, if they would spend some of the time, now occupied in searching into abstruse subjects, to the cultivation of the voice. — This art has not received merited attention. — If we have once heard good reading, and probably every one has had that pleasure, at some time, we can contrast it with the common style of speaking which prevails. In our schools it is the first branch taken up and longest continued, & yet it is that in which we are more likly (*sic*) to fail. There is no better place than this for the Genius of reform to commence her work. —

Sunday Dec. 22nd. This day is the anniversary of the landing of the pilgrim fathers, but the minister whom we heard, did not allude to it. — Mr Buckingham preached again, from the texts — Ephesians 6th Chap. 16th verse & P.M.from James 1st Chap. 13th & 14th verses. — "Above all, taking the shield of faith, wherewith ye shall be able to quench all the fiery darts of the wicked." — Blessed is the man that endureth temptation; for when he is tried he shall receive the crown of life" &c. The snow still remains on the ground, and I think seems likely to for the next three months. Spent the eve in reading & study. —

Monday 23d. Owing to the want of *paper* in my journal, I shall make short entries for the remainder of 1839, supposing that a description of our intended excursion to Waltham, will take much space. — This morn, Mr P. made some remarks, and announced the course of studies, which he intends shall be pursued, by Misses Stodder, Burdick & myself. The first new study which he proposed, was Combes Constitution of man. — He mentioned Brigham on Education, as a work which would probably accompany the

above — Simpson, Miss Edgworth, & many treatises on
school-teaching, which are in the library would also be *read*,
and some *studied*. —

The first exercise was concerning the Moving Powers in
Natural Philosophy of course. — It was very easy, as Mr P.
observed, to link together, and I thought was well recited. —
Went into the Model School, & remained till eleven, then
returned, just in season to hear the conclusion of what I
supposed had been an argument, on the sects which divided
Europe, the Nominalists & Realists. — In the P.M. recited only Moral Philosophy, that and N. History being all
the lessons for the P.M. after three. The latter was not
prepared, because I had never learned it, (the class went
over it when I was sick) I had no time between schools to
prepare it. 'Tis very dull, to sit & hear others, in an exercise in which you should participate. —

Tuesday Dec. 24th. This morn, Philosophy came first
upon the tapis; the subject, "Strength of Animals". It
being numerical principally, I was entirely out of my element; my organ of *number* is not so *fully* developed as
Self Esteem. After returning from the Model School recited in Book-keeping & Mental Philosophy. The subject
of the latter, was Imagination. — This was well recited.
In the P.M. felt unable, on account of the head-ache, to
enter the N.School & therefore asked liberty to absent
myself. — It was granted & I passed the hour in studying
Greek; not much better than going into school perhaps but
I felt much *refreshed* by it. —

Heard that Mr P. intends to read to us a letter, stating
the differences between Combe & Wayland, in their views on
Conscience. —

Wednesday Dec. 25th. Christmas day; and the echoing
powers of the house are tried severely, by the repeated
shouts of "A merry Christmas." — Mr P. had his share,
being met by many of his pupils with the wish. — After
reading in the Scriptures and a prayer, Mr P. offered some
remarks upon the day; regarding the uncertainty of the
time, when Christ was born; but said that we had as much
reason & perhaps more to believe that this is the day as
any other. The term merry was not well he thought, be-

cause it conveyed the idea of excessive mirth, and of short-
lived enjoyment; he recommended *happy* as a substitute.
The first exercise was in Arithmetic, during which two
gentlemen, Messrs Locke & Robinson entered. — The next
was in Natural Philosophy, a review of various subjects.
& next our new study, Combe. — This was *tolerably* recited, though it might have been better. — The time for
the long recess came, & after speaking a few words to Mr
Robinson, I went to walk a short distance; the first time
since Sunday, that I have been out. — Res. When I leave
the Model School, to follow the principles of Physiology,
not *now* because 'tis impossible. After recess our number
of visiters increased. Mr Locke left & Messrs Dodge &
brother Mr Stetson Esq & Mr Robinson were present. —
First exercise a few questions in Mental Philosophy, in
which the pupils did *discredit* to themselves. — Next the
Conversational Exercise. — This was not so interesting
as sometimes. — Mr P. commenced by giving an account
of the Snow shoe. The others Poetry & Biographies chiefly.
At the close of it Mr. P. gave us some fatherly advice, about
providing for the physical wants, on the morrow, & took
leave of us for the day. — P.M.

For want of time, did not learn a lesson in Greek, which
I neglected to say we commenced on Monday last. —
Passed the afternoon in writing to my mother and receiving
a call from Mr. Robinson, who does not seem to have altered
much since I was his pupil. In the eve, as there would be
no other time for learning the lessons for Friday, study
hours were strictly observed, & if any thing the room was
stiller than the *school*-room in study. — A new regulation
also was passed; that instead of reading the Scriptures at
half past nine, as has been our practise, they should be read
at the close of study hours. —

Thursday. December 26th. A day which the present
Normalites will probably have cause to remember for
several *years, at least.* — This morn is very delightful, and
all are collected, waiting for the sleigh. — A few moments
more, & we are seated & on our way to Mr. Dodge's to take
a few in addition to the nineteen already there. — We were
joined by Mrs D —, Mrs Trusk & Mr D, & Mrs. P. — After

a pleasant ride, got to Waltham & stopped at the door of
the Central Tavern while the gentlemen made the necessary
arrangements. Thence to the hall, where we found only
one or two. — They slowly assembled, and the time having
come & the president not there, Mr. Dodge said that it was
customary to commence with a prayer & asked Mr Hyde
of Wayland, — This did not strike [me] as very good, perhaps the *manner*, not the *matter*. — The first business
transacted, was the reading of the Constitution. — Mr
Dodge said that it was customary to choose a committee,
for the choice of subjects for debate. — Messrs Peirce, Hyde,
Keith were chosen. A short time in which there was no
business, passed and then Mr P. reported four resolutions,
and fourteen questions or subjects for debate. — (My pencil
& fingers refused to go fast enough to take these). — The
report of the committee concerning the necessity of alteration in the common school system, — Mr Stetson spoke upon
it, & during his remarks Mr Thompson of Charlestown came
in, and took the President's chair. — The report being again
called for, Mr Keith made some remarks giving an abstract
instead of reading the report. Messrs Frost of Concord,
Stetson of Medford, Mr Hyde, Mr Peirce, Mr Barry, of
Framingham, Mr Frothingham of Charlestown, spoke upon
the subject. Next report re-read for the benefit of those
tardy. — A motion was made to choose the officers for the
ensuing year — Moved that a committee of five, be chosen
for the nomination of officers, who retired after appointment. First question on the subject of school examinations,
object, how conducted, & by whom. — Mr Frost spoke
first; thought that the school committee might not be able
to examine on the subjects; that they might not ask the
proper questions; that all would be secured, by having the
committee assign the places where the teacher should examine, without any consultation with the teacher. — Mr
Dodge thought *that not* enough, & that no person was able
to examine teachers, who could not scholars; he asked the
gentlemen present to state the custom in this, in their re-
spective towns. — Mr Barry said that he had been accustomed to examine teachers, but not pupils and should consider the former a far easier task than the latter. He said

that in Framingham, both methods were adopted. — Mr
Peirce agreed with the latter gentleman & gave an example
illustrative. — The committee appointed to choose officers,
now being ready to report, a motion was made, & seconded,
to lay the question upon the table, & listen to the nomination. — It was accepted & the meeting adjourned till two
P.M. — Returned to the hotel and after waiting a half
hour we were summoned to dinner, it being advisable, as the
gentlemen of the party (and I presume some of the ladies)
thought, to attend to the physical as well as the intellectual
wants. — From dinner we went to the Factories for making
cotton, which are worked by the Charles River. We entered
the lower room which was [?] to Carding, the next above
to Spinning, next to Weaving, and next to Dressing. —
The noise of the Machinery was so great, that, at first,
we were unable to hear each other speak. — The poor girls
are now, more an object of my pity than ever before. —
They generally looked very pale, & I should think, according to the principle of Physiology, must suffer much from
lung complaints, on account of the particles of cotton constantly floating in the atmosphere. — Leaving the upper
room, we descended to the basement, to see the water wheel.
— From there to the banks of the river & then back to the
Hall. — On our way Mr P. called our attention to the street
through which we were passing which is level to a great
extent, and is frequently spoken of as Waltham Plain. —
Entering the hall found Mr Norwood Damon speaking.
He was opposed to the examination of the pupils by the
school committee. — Another gentleman, Mr Ripley opposed him. Mr R. offered some arguments; next an unknown person & after him, it was laid upon the table and
the following taken. Can any other means than corporal
punishment & premiums be effectually employed in schools?
Mr Keith said that he approved of corporal punishment
when necessary, but that was very seldom. — He had not
said to his school that he should not use it, but that he did
not. — Mr Stetson said he presumed it had its origin in the
fact that corporals inflicted punishment on the bodies of
recruits. — In later days there has been an advancement in
knowledge. — It has been found that a child has a soul, &

should be governed accordingly. — If he has a soul, then there is a way to move him as a soul, & an important duty is laid upon the teacher. — Mr Muzzey of Cambridgeport said that there were so many handles, he scarcely knew of which to take hold. — The meaning of the word Education suggest many. It is not to put something into the child but to *take*[1] something out, — to lead forth. - - Premiums induce the children to act with reference to the present only. A second objection, they are awarded very unjustly. — He would not say that either corporal punishment or premiums should be expelled as yet, but that they should be resorted lastly. — In the Boston Schools it is still the practise to give premiums of various kinds, and the consequences, beside the unpleasant effects at the time are, that the young lady having obtained the thing desired — a medal — leave their school & studies, & pass the time in reading novels. — Rev. Mr Cobb of Waltham spoke of the evils of laying down codes or laws and affixing punishments to each. — Mr Sweetser of Charlestown said he would go farther than either of the others; he would TELL his scholars that he should not use it. — He now has a school of 400 girls and never resorts to it. He awards premiums for conduct, not for lessons, thus avoiding rivalry. Mr Merrill from Alabama advocated both. Established his arguments, by texts of Scripture, references to Yale, Harvard, & Amherst. Mr Damon asked what you would substitute for them? — Mr Stetson said that he once dislocated his arm & when he next went into the school he told the scholars he could not whip, & he said that he had a better school than before. — Did not remember of having used it since. — Mr P. said it would not make the thing right, if our first institutions used it. — Mr G. from Cambridge thought it might succeed in select, but not in public schools. — Mr Peirce said that he considered the sovereign remedy, to be patient, enlightened, Christian love. — Mr — said, that the teacher must "let patience have her perfect work. — Mr Sweetser said that God had punished himself, but that we could not say he had derogated his power to man. — Mr Frothingham said that he was sorry to hear this point touched upon, as

---

[1] Corrected to "draw" by Mr. Peirce. — Ed.

it was a controverted point in religion — Mr Stetson assented to it — Meeting adjourned, to meet at six in the eve. — We returned to the Hotel, and took some refreshment, after which we were entertained by singing & playing on the guitar by a blind girl. — Returned at six to the Hall and took the settees on one side that all might be together. — Mr Dodge then spoke half an hour, on the subject of Normal Schools, & attempted to remove the errors from the minds of those present, in regard to it. Mr P. spoke next on the same subject & then Mr Mann. The latter alluded to the common jealousy of the Board of Education & said that he had seen no cause for it. — Next, he delivered the following

Lecture. —

The first topic mentioned, was the wants of our community in schools. — In some of the Grecian States children are considered as property, but the state of society is now altered, & our notions vary from those of the feudal ages. – – Many are unwilling to send their children to the public schools, because they are subject so much to the town. — They ask; why is all this interference in schools, the choice of books, times of attendence, &c. The[y] consider the school committee as an obtrusion — They say are not the children our own? — These questions are honestly put, and should be soberly answered. — Children are carried forth by the tide of nature and will soon be men; they will soon have the rights of citizenship, & will become blessings, or curses, to society. — The world receives them as they are and has no option to accept or reject. — The cases from which they draw analogies are very different. In merchandise we pay for an article, and we expect it to be good; if it is not we have a right to return it. — On the contrary after twenty one years from birth society must receive him. — In this state a far larger number of females are employed than males; the proportion being about three to two. — In Prussia, the reverse is true. — They are best for young children. — They have much feeling, & if not exerted it must lie dormant. — In the advancement of civilization, & her duties increase. Is she not fitted to commence

the first work in the Temple of Education? — After a child's
mind has become tough, then let it be subjected to the
firm grasp of a masculine hand. — Why then should woman
put off her form of Seraph, and assume the harsher [ways] of
man? — To be the former of a great mind, is as much greater
as to be Creator, instead of created. — In regard to this
the query is, do teachers require a course of study, to qualify
them? I will not quibble with my adversary, whatever
may be his belief, but imitate those engaged in the ancient
tournaments, who gave their adversaries the advantage
of sun & wind. — At first it almost seems, that a child has
entered the wrong world; but a few revolutions and we see
them in the captive's cell, next dashing themselves about
in a Maniac's confinement. Perhaps he is solving abstruse
problems and contributing to his country's good. — Some
maintain that diversity in education is the cause of all the
difference in people. — But deep as education goes, we do
not arrogate this for it. — This diversity only requires
greater labor in Education, if it were not so, the task would
be comparatively easy. The contrast is not from different
number of faculties but in the power of each. — Every
human body has the same number of muscles, so the soul
has the same powers. — The eye of every person has the
same number of parts, but owing to a difference in its
powers some are far-sighted & others near-sighted Because
of this kindred feeling the same earth is given us. Every
child has dispositions leading to good & evil. You have
properly to guard health that you may sustain them, & the
children themselves, to take care of. — If a young lawyer
come to the town, how he is watched with jealous eyes, &
if trusted at all it is with some case, the results of which are
of trifling importance. It is thus with the physician. — Who
then shall assign a guardian to the child? — The fact that
success depends on practise is shown by the teaching of
brute animals. — Two things are necessary for a teacher;
a knowledge of the properties, qualities & powers of the
mind, and the means of controlling them. A man working
on wood, may mistake it for iron, & by putting it into the
fire reduce it to ashes. — A teacher may make a similar
mistake. — By the powers of intellect he finds his duty.

His lower propensities are his preservation. By social feelings, he is bound to God & man. — The lowest faculties are not to be extirpated, they have their value. — Benevolence, Conscience & Reverence, have the supremacy. — Take the lowest appetites and if he indulge them they may be productive of good or bad. — The desire of acquiring property has good effects; it affords much pleasure & is the parent of frugality & industry; but if carried to too great an extent, much mischief comes from giving to one too much power. — Every one may be so educated, as to perform some duty in life, and every daughter to prepare for those reverses which turn the kitchen up & parlor down. — Every teacher should know by what means the mental faculties may be strengthened & weakened. The powers of the mind as well as body should be exercised for improvement. "Train up a child in the way he should go" is this same principle as train means drill. — Perceptive faculties are cultivated by exercise. — Teacher must constantly exercise the child & teach him accuracy. A person may exercise his faculties, by both useful & useless work. Every teacher should have a tact at explanation, but it is not to be used too often. The teacher should have a care of the health of his pupils. — He should know how to touch the right spring, in the right manner, & at the right time.

During the lecture, we heard our sleigh come to the door, and at half after eight we were all on our way. We got home in an hour, without any essential injury to any one, though Mr Dodge fell several times and was much fatigued. —

Friday 27th Dec. — This morn, the first exercise was in Natural Philosophy — subject Hydrostatics. 2nd Combe's Constitution of man. Went to the Model School and staid till half after eleven, then to the N.S., and recited a lesson in Political Economy, — on the subject of Labor Saving Machines, and was well recited. — In the afternoon at one went again to the M.S. & after that recited in the Globes and in Moral Philosophy. This last was well recited by many of the scholars. — Short entries from necessity. —

Saturday Dec. 28th. After the devotional exercises, the music class was called, and after trying the tenor of one tune, it was nine, & I went to the M.S. to see how many of the scholars had arrived. Owing to the storm, few were there, & I occupied the first half hour, in giving a general lesson. Mr P. then came in, & gave them the first lesson in marching. – – After that Mr P. heard a lesson in Natural Philosophy, & then delivered a lecture, the fifteenth. — The subject of lecture was the third head on Reading, mentioned in the last. — The qualities of a good reader are many, & with the elements all nearly are endowed.—Articulation, enunciation, are requisite and that a person should be free from drawling & precipitancy; his voice should have smoothness & force, compass and variety. — A just conception of the subject is a sine qua non; that we should enter into the feelings. The intonation, inflection, loudness & rapidity should be regulated by the piece he is reading. The whole is included in Shakspeare's; — "Take care not to o'erstep the modesty of nature". — Enunciation & pronunciation are qualities of such importance, as not to be dispensed with. Extract from Russell, showing its importance. — After the power & elementary sound is learned, then go to plain reading, & next to rhetorical. — Read to them yourselves; set them a copy. The fault is, not to make enough pauses rather than too many; they give power to the reading. The fault common to this school is, reading too far without taking breath. Sometimes pauses are used improperly; sometimes they are used for grammatical effect & should be little regarded. Some give the same length to the same pause, but it should depend on the sense. — For training the voice — make selections from the extremes — There are three inflections; the rising used for petitions entreaties, for all tender emotions, & for direct questions. The falling, for command, & for grave matters, requests with strong emotions, terror & exclamations. The subject for discussion was, "Is taking notes better than relying upon memory?" — Yeas — 8 nays — 7.

Sunday 29th Attended church all day. Mr Buckingham preached. — Text A.M. Ecclesiastes 7th Chap. 10th v. — P.M. Matthew 4th Chap. 17th v. —

Monday 30th. This day a new class of teachers go into the Model School, and I resign my place to Miss Stodder. My attachment to the school, is much greater than I could have anticipated from so short a connexion with it. — Exercises of the forenoon — N. Philosophy, Combe's Constitution of man, Book-keeping, in the A.M. & in the P.M. Orthoepy, Nat. History & Moral Philosophy. One gentleman, Mr Tidd, has been in the school all day. — I neglected to say, that this morn we commenced the day by singing a hymn, after the reading of the Scriptures. — The day has not been so fair *as usual* & Mr P. said at the close of the school said that it would take another day to perfect the work. —

Tuesday Dec. 31st. The last day in the year, & the last day of the first six months, of my exile from home. On reflecting upon the pleasant connections formed here, it seems as if it will be nearly as difficult, to part with them as it was to leave our homes, — but we have six months more to enjoy their company, & we will not anticipate trouble. — The exercises were N. Philosophy, Combe, — Mental Philosophy & Book-keeping. In the P.M. Reading in the Dictionary, N. History, M. Philosophy. — In the P.M. Mrs P. called & after a very short recitation in M. Philosophy, school was dismissed. —

And here is the end of the day, of the year, & of my journal, and I will close it with the hope, that when my next is completed it may show some slight improvement in the powers of Composition, and in Chirography. —

[Mary Swift began the second volume of her journal with an original poem, which is reproduced in facsimile in the adjoining cut. The small letters, the slant, and the fineness of the lines are characteristic of girls' penmanship at that time. The work was probably done with a quill pen.

The poem was copied in the journals of other students, under the title, "Dedication of a Journal, by Mary Swift." — ED.]

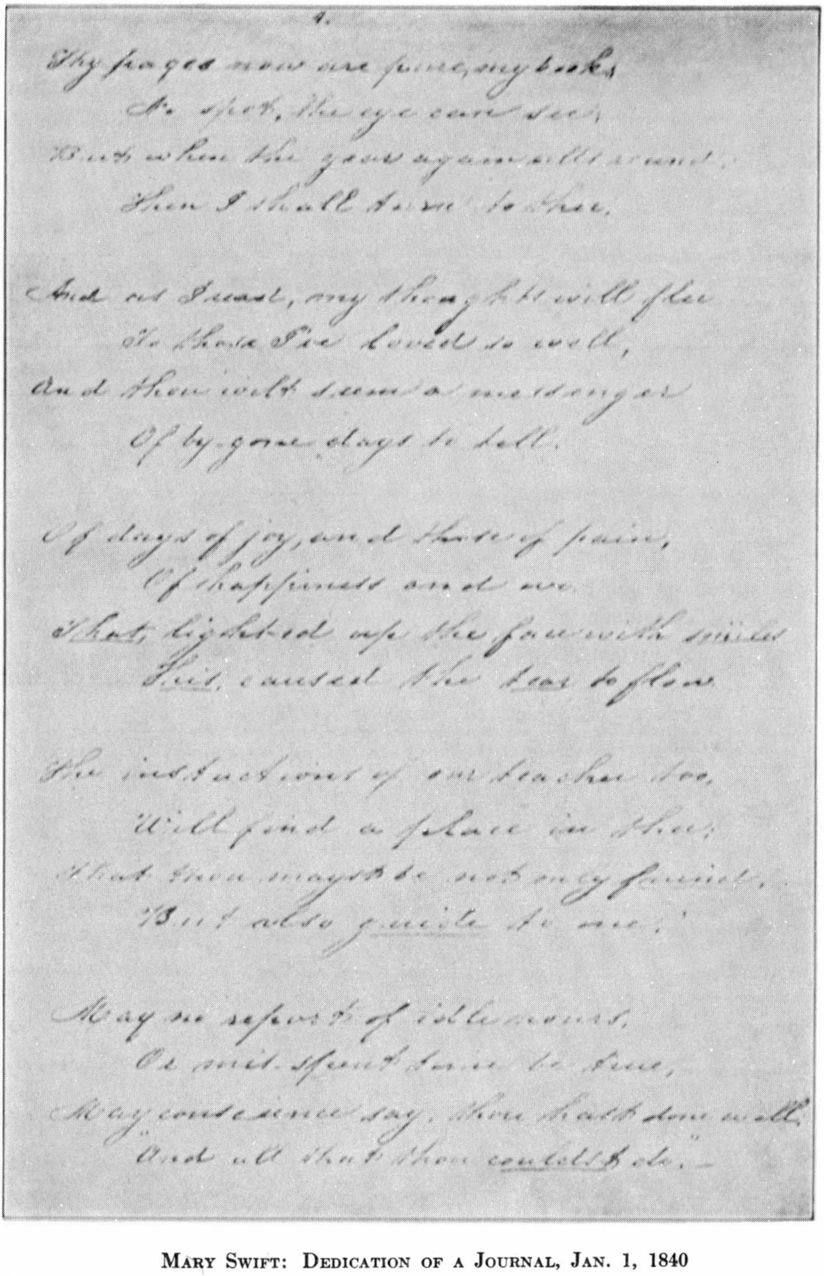

JOURNAL. —

Wednesday, January. 1st. 1840. The first day of the
year, as we were reminded by the repeated shouts of "A
happy new year" "I wish you a happy new year", which
were sounded in our ears, ere we were awake. — The first
exercise was reading from the Scriptures, a part of the
ninetieth Psalm. — The second, some remarks by the
Principal on the opening and closing of the year. — The
following is a short abstract of them. The commencement of a year forms an epoch in human life, and is an
appropriate season for reflection; to review the past and
prepare for what is to come. It is a suitable time to look
at our temporal matters. Though, at present, we may not
be much interested, yet we may be at some future time. A
great part of the alienations, disputes and animadversions,
are caused by omissions. It is important on *our own* account, as well as on *others:* by being omitted, difference of
opinion has been caused, thus making foes, of those who
were once warmest friends. This is important, not merely
for the value of the property: but that peace, love & harmony may be preserved, is of more value than silver or
gold. The new year may lead us to examine our own conduct in the past year. In excitement, we are not so well
prepared to judge of the real nature of an act; in grief and
joy, pleasure and pain, we can not *always* tell what is right.
We should ask, whom have we injured; where have we
spoken an unkind word; where passed by, those whom we
should have assisted; where done too much and where too
little. If we take a sober view, many things will appear in
a different light to us, because we shall be able to view them
impartially. The mariner makes observations sometimes,
to know over what seas he passes, and by what places. —
We are mariners on the great sea of life; then what can be
more proper, than for us to take observations. We enjoy
constantly the means of doing good: we should remember
that there is not a day nor moment but we are watched by
God. We are debtors to society, debtors to our parents
or friends & we should ask, what have we done to discharge

this debt? Have we made one individual happier or better? Have we made that being called MYSELF better? It is a mistake that the young can do no good; it is true, to some extent, that the young are dependent on their guardians, but it is equally true that every station furnishes opportunities. Though our talents be few and our rank obscure, yet we all have our duties. —

Has the weight of our example been uniformly of the right kind? Every one can give a tinge to the surrounding atmosphere. Have we encouraged and supported that which is good, or have we indulged in folly and vice? If we have done good we shall have the hope of doing it for the year to come. Let no one think she has done *nothing*, because she can tell of no great act. — The present is the only time which we possess; then let us make our review now, and if we find that we have been useless, it will excite us to greater exertions. — In looking back upon the past year, we discover many instances of Divine goodness. In periods of excitement, we forget our duties to God, as well as to our friends. If we were to enumerate the blessings of God for one year, how great would be the amount! Many can exclaim with the Psalmist, "thou crownest the year with thy goodness." — It is by his goodness that we are preserved, and now enjoy the blessings of health. — Even through the darkest cloud there shines some solitary star. — In reviewing the past, we should feel grateful to our friends, for perhaps they have been the means of affording us our present happiness. — There is an *indissoluble* connection between virtue and peace. — The History of the past should teach us to moderate our desires. We have suffered much by raising our expectations too high. Often have we anticipated great pleasure, when we have realized nothing. As it is a proper season to examine our temporary affairs, so it is well to form plans by which to make the future better. Is there not some point deficient, some class of duties which have been omitted? Shall we live over the same life that we did the last year? This is an important season for the consideration of our spiritual state. The close of the year reminds of death. A few more mornings and evenings and

the eve of death will shut in upon us. The following would
be a suitable question; are you laying up treasures in heaven
where neither moth nor rust will corrupt? —

The third exercise was Singing a hymn on the Opening &
Close of the year, and the fourth a prayer.

The lesson in Natural Philosophy was on the Weight
and Pressure of fluids; it included a description of the
Hydrostatic or Hydraulic Press. — Mr P. recited the lesson,
and explained the figures on the board, telling us that he
should wish *us* to recite on Saturday. — After the close
of this we had a short recess, & after Arithmetic & Algebra
were recited, a long one. The remainder of the forenoon
was devoted to the Conversational Exercise. — Mr. P
opened it, as usual, by giving us an account of Old Style
and New Style. — This distinction was caused by a mistake
that the ancients made, by calling the year three hundred
and sixty-five days and a fourth. This mistake was corrected
by Pope Gregory of Rome, and at that time, it had amounted
to eleven days. He ordered that this time should be cast
out, and in order to prevent the recurrence of this, he said
that every fourth year, one day should be added, and as
this in process of time, would amount to too much, it should
not be added in the centuries, 1600, 1700, [1800] & 1900
but only in 1600, 2000 &c. that is when the first two figures
denoting the Century are divisible by four it is to be added.
— The next, was by Miss Stodder, & Miss Drew, a dialogue
from Mrs Heman's Vespers of Palermo, next Miss Swift
an anedote of a Minister. — The biography of Empedocles,
by Miss Stow. The remaining were either poetry, or Anecdotes. — During the exercise in Philosophy Dr Haskell of
Ashby visited us, & spent the remainder of the forenoon. —

Thursday January 2nd, 1840. The school was opened
by the customary devotional exercises, and after these Mr.
P. took the school down stairs, to pass the forenoon. The
lessons attended to were Geography and Arithmetic. He
attended to each class separately and was obliged to continue the school till twelve A.M. -— In the afternoon, we
went into the school at one, and remained until four, when
Mr P. dismissed the Normalites and Modelites. The exercises were Reading, and a few remarks upon the subject

of Writing, and closed by Singing "Away to School. The school did not appear to be so orderly as usual, and the lessons not quite so well. Mr. P. expressed himself quite well pleased, and said that he wished more attention paid to the pauses. —

Friday, January 3d. The first exercises of the morning were in Natural Philosophy, an abstract of the first chapter in Combe. The next lesson was in Brigham on Mental Education; which was the first recitation, and, I think, will prove a very interesting study. — Political Economy occupied the remainder of the forenoon. — The exercises in the afternoon were Geography Problems on the Globe, and Moral Philosophy. A pretty happy day, though not quite so much so as sometimes. I omitted to state that this morn Mr P. made some remarks upon the Model School. He said that he thought the girls superior to the boys and that, taken as a whole, perhaps they were in advance of scholars generally of their ages. — The boys on the contrary, were not so far advanced as we generally find them. — He said that he was now entering upon his thirty third year of school teaching, and that, invariably, the girls had excelled the boys in all the schools which he had taught. He said that it was argued by some, that the female mind was brighter in early life, but retrograded afterwards. Mr P. thought that it was because the same advantages were not given to woman, as to men. —

Saturday, January 4th. The school was opened by reading a portion of the Scriptures, singing a hymn, and a prayer. The next exercises were in the Natural Philosophy; a review of Hydrostatics, with a view to the explanation of the figures. In the course of the conversation upon some of them, Mr Bradbury of Framingham called. — The next exercise was in Music; & consisted in practising the tune Winchelsea, in which we were aided by Mr W Bradbury. — The Algebra class were called a few moments, and then we took a recess until eleven. After that we returned to the School-room, and listened to the conclusion of last Saturday's lecture. — He took up the third head, on what principle the art may be acquired, and a good reader formed. — The circumflex accent is next to be noticed; an intonation including both rising & falling. — It may commence with either the rising or the falling. It is used when doubt, ambiguity, hypothesis or irony are expressed. The beauty and force of a sentence can not be brought out, unless attention be paid to intonations. The direct question, it has been said, generally requires the rising, but when great emphasis or feeling is to be expressed the falling is used. — Thus, if you are remonstrating with a person who is [in] the habit of drinking, and say "Will you, in view of all these evils, continue in this course?" you will express it much more strongly if you use the falling. In the repetition of names or addresses, the first requires the rising and the second the falling. The whole art of reading, depends upon reading to the sentiment. — Let the heart feel, and the tongue and organs will speak. —

The monotone is an important tone. It is a fault in ordinary reading, but is introduced with great force, in grave and solemn reading. The following are the common faults in reading. Some have variety, but still are monotonous; they have a uniform emphasis. Others strike on too high a key and run down; some begin too low; some have a tendency to run into the rising, so that they never read a piece on any grave or emphatic subject. — Some say that the remedy of all faults is to read in the natural way or according to our own custom, but the only sure way is Practise.[1] Place yourself under some good teacher, and whatever is your fault give your attention to it. — In reading poetry, do not attempt to make it so; if the author has not made the lines of the right meter do not mar the language to make it so. Let emphasis, accent, & inflection, be correct. There is a slight difficulty in reading proper names, especially in public. When you come to one, do not stop to study upon it, but call it something, whether right or wrong. —

Foreign names must generally be pronounced according to English analogy. Phrases in Latin & French read if you can, but if not, say it is in that language, and that you can not read it.

The subject of the next lecture will be "Spelling". After the lecture, Mr P. called upon us for our debate, and as

---

[1] *S* corrected in pencil to *c*. — Ed.

there were ten minutes left, we occupied it in stating our opinions without much debate. The question was, "Should examinations be conducted exclusively by school-committees? — Ayes 2. Nays 19. Those in the negative, seemed to think that the labor should be divided. —

Good[1]

Sunday, January 5th. Attended church all day, and heard Mr. Buckingham preach. The text in the morning was from 1st Epistle Peter, 2nd Chap. 22nd verse. "Who did no sin, neither was guile found in his mouth." In the afternoon, from John 7th. 17th.

Monday. January 6th. After the usual devotional exercises, Mr. P. remarked to us that the present week was quite an era to us, since it was the last of our second term. — In consideration of this, he thought that it would be best to have a review of the lessons to which we have attended in the last term, and, also, that the bounds of the term might be marked, that perhaps he should give us a day's vacation in the course of the week. —

The class in Combe recited after the class in Arithmetic and then that in Natural Philosophy. Both were recited very well. The Algebra occupied the remainder of the time, until recess. After that, which continued till quarter after eleven, Book-keeping and Mental Philosophy were the subjects of consideration, until twelve. The subject in the latter is Reason and I have heard several speak of it as the best part of the work, but I can feel little interest as yet. — The afternoon exercises were Reading by a portion of the school Orthöepy, (*sic*) Natural History & Moral Philosophy. Quite a good day & very interesting.

Tuesday. January 7th. — This morn our Journals and Compositions were returned, & Mr P. expressed himself pleased with them. He said that he thought they were as good as they had been at any time previous, except at the time when we wrote upon the subject of the debate. — The first exercise was in Combe's Constitution of Man, and second, in Natural Philosophy. The latter was a description of canals and was about the best description, that I have seen in this work. It seems to me that if he had com-

---

[1] Comment in pencil. — Ed.

menced his work with the design of making it as difficult
as possible he would not have been obliged to alter it much.
— The Modelites today numbered only about twelve, the
others having gone to Concord and Bedford for a sleigh-
ride. — The remaining exercises were Book-keeping and
Mental Philosophy. — In the recess, the Misses Roger's
from Billerica came & their parents spent the remainder of
the forenoon in school. — The afternoon exercises were
Dictionary, Natural History and Moral Philosophy. Mr
P. was much unwell, and therefore the recitation in Greek
was omitted. — Hope that his turn has not come now, but
I should think the laws of Physiology were made for *all* of
God's Creatures, *Teachers* as well as scholars. —

Study hours kept strictly without the slightest communication. —

Wednesday January 8th. The anniversary of General
Jackson's victory at New Orleans. One year ago I was returning from the Coffin School, and heard the first salute
fired. Little did I think that I should be in Lexington e'er
another year rolled over my head. —

The first exercise was a review of "Combe's *Constitution*"
which was well performed. The second was in Natural
Philosophy, a review of the first part of the book as far
as Accelerated Motion. Mr P. however, confined his attention to the Introduction and spoke of Geometrical
Figures. — The Algebra Class was called and recited till
ten, and then Mr. P said that he wished to call our attention
to a few remarks upon the manner in which we spend our
recess. — He thinks that the time should be devoted to
exercise chiefly, but that the custom which obtained now,
of passing the time in attemting (*sic*) to study and talk too,
was the worst possible for the mind. —

After this we took our recess until half past eleven, &
then returned to perform our conversational exercise. The
first quarter of an hour was occupied by Mr P., in making
remarks upon the necessity of a proper use of small portions
of time. The conversation was short, lasting only about
one quarter of an hour. Mr P. spoke of Watts and told
the following anecdote. — Some young gentlemen were
travelling and found that they were in the neighborhood

of this great man. Never having seen him, they hastened
to the inn, and were so much surprised at seeing a man
so diminutive in stature, that they could hardly refrain
from laughing in his presence. — W— understanding human
nature and reading their thoughts, went out and wrote in
their carriage, the following stanza.

> Were I so tall to reach the pole,
> And could my hands the ocean span, —
> I must be measured by my soul;
> The mind's the measure of the man.

A similar anecdote is related of Judge Dawes of Boston.
He was one day returning from some meeting, in company
with six of his friends who were all large sized. One of them
endeavored to rally the Judge upon his size, asking him
how he felt among great folks, when he promptly replied,
I feel like four pence half penny among six cents; meaning
that he was of as much value as all of them together. —
Miss Drew spoke a piece of Poetry entitled "the two Spar-
rows", and all the others were *Anecdotes.* —
Study hours observed.
Thursday January 9th. School opened with the usual
devotional exercises. The first recitation was in "Combe"
and was very prompt. — The second was in Natural Philosophy commencing Mechanics and going to Mechanical
Powers. — The class in Arithmetic occupied the remainder
of the forenoon, until recess. — After that time, the class in
Algebra. —
In the afternoon instead of going to school I went to bed,
sick with the head-ache. Whether it was caused by over
or under-exercise, I know not. — Mr P, also sick, and therefore school was dismissed at an early hour.
Friday, January. 10th. — Not being entirely recovered
thought it wiser to pass the forenoon out of the school
room. —
P.M. Intellectual powers in no better condition than in
the forenoon, and as my company would not certainly be
acceptable to any one if I were in an impaired state, I concluded to remain in my room.
Saturday January 11th. — School opened with Reading

from the Scriptures & prayer. The reviews in Natural History and Mental Philosophy were well recited, the former was very prompt: —

Recess occupied a half hour and we then listened to a Lecture from Mr Peirce upon the subject of Spelling. — The fifteenth in the course. — The art of spelling, as connected with school education. The subject divided itself into three heads; 1st the claim of the art to our attention as teachers; 2nd the proper time for children to learn it, and consequently for teachers to teach it; 3d the proper manner of teaching it. — 1st head. Spelling is regarded as holding an humble rank among the branches of school education. Compared with reading, Spelling as an intellectual exercise is subordinate; it calls into exercise a smaller portion of the intellectual faculties. — Still it has its claims.

First, the sense of written composition is much affected by the orthography. There have been instances in which the whole composition was enveloped in darkness by bad spelling. — A commander once wrote to the owners of a ship, an account of an accident which had befallen it but the spelling was so incorrect, that they could only find that the ship had suffered and that it was probable that some lives had been lost, but whose, or where the vessel was, or what the accident was they could not find. Some instances may be given in which the sense is affected. — If I should say our guide led us through a *straight* way, one would infer that the road was not crooked; but if I should spell it *strait* I should be understood that it was a narrow way. —

[Many similar illustrations are omitted.]

. . . .

Second. Correct spelling is important to the permanency of the language, and as scholars and teachers, it should be an object of great concern to us. — The English language, since the days of Queen Elizabeth and of Chaucer has undergone so many changes that it can be read with difficulty. The present diversity is very great and perplexing, and is a great inconvenience to foreigners. Thirdly, it preserves the true etymology of the word and thus aids in ascertaining

their precise meaning. That it is important to preserve
the etymology is shown in the word Oxygen, which is derived from the Greek word ὀξύς, and in transforming it to
English, it becomes oxy, the u being changed to y. —
Chymist is also derived from ξυμοσ, and should be spelled
with y and not i. — In writing words compounded with
ante, care should be taken not to confound it with *anti*. If
we were to write *ante*-diluvian we should mean before the
flood but *anti*-diluvian, one who opposed the doctrine of
the existence of the flood. — *Anti*-Christian, one opposed
to Christ, *ante*-Christian one living before Christ. — Fourth
consideration is, that we are oftener called upon to *spell*
than to read in public. — Very few of all that live are ever
called upon to read in public. — Fifth, Ignorance of spelling
is a source of great embarrassment.   Fine Chirography
accompanied by bad Spelling is like specks upon a fair
surface.   Sixth, influential in forming habits of accuracy,
and thus becomes an intellectual exercise. —

The second division is the proper time for children to
learn it. — It is an exercise depending entirely on observation and memory, and is therefore suited to children at an
early stage of education, as soon as the child has learned to
speak the simplest words. Those who do not learn it in
school, seldom learn it at all. —

The third head, is the best mode of teaching it. Do it
by the eye, and have this to perform some of the offices of
the other senses. — Second, if you use the eye, you will
gain time, you may teach several classes at one time. —
Writing is generally the best way in which they can be
taught. Scholars who have spelled very correctly orally,
miss in writing. It is well to practise differently; sometimes, have one scholar spell a whole word, at another have
one to spell one syllable and pronounce it, at another have
each to give one letter. The last two ways are excellent to
keep up attention. Write sentences introducing words
which are pronounced in the same manner, as mete, meet,
meat and let the pupils spell them in the proper way. —
Exercise them on words of common use, but which are frequently wrongly spelled, as those beginning with in or en
or ending in er or our, ic or ick, tial, tion, trian, tious, cede

and many words of irregular derivation as *cannon* or *canon.* — Matthew [Mather] Byles passing by the King's Chapel when they had just finished the first story, the windows of which were very small, stopped to observe it. — Before he got to his home, he said that he had often heard of the canons of the church but had never seen the port-holes before. — Have them spell the names of places and people. Use books of correct Orthography. There is a difficulty in selecting a standard. Worcester's is here preferred. — After the lecture we had a short debate upon the following question; "Is it proper to make any difference, in our common schools in the discipline and instruction of the males & females? — The most were in the negative. —

In the eve it was decided by a unanimous vote that Sunday eve should be kept, so that this, was spent in domestic labors.

Sunday January 12th. Attended church, as usual all day, and heard two excellent sermons from Mr Parker of Roxbury, a *native* of this town. The text in the morn was taken from Paul's Epistle to the Galatians 2nd Chap. 20th. verse. "Nevertheless I live; yet not *I* live, but Christ liveth in me." The text in the afternoon was from Matthew, 22nd Chap. from the 37th to the 40th verses. The subject was an explanation of the diff. between religion and morality. —

Monday January 13th. This day was set apart for a sort of review, to which we are to invite as many of our friends as we choose. The morning was devoted to the Model School. But few were present, the weather not being very fair. — The scholars, in my opinion, performed as well as could be expected, though Mr P. seemed to be disappointed. In the afternoon, at one, we assembled in the school-room, and were visited by a few friends. The exercises were Grammar — two classes, Problems upon the globe, two classes, Reading, and Natural Philosophy. — The concluding exercise was the reading of some original pieces in Composition, by those of the young Ladies who volunteered in the work; my own part quite made me blush when I compared it with the productions of those around me. Surely my organ of *Self Esteem*, large as it may be, did not perform the work which Phrenologists assign to it; perhaps the task was entirely too great, the chasm between the productions of the girls and my own was too great for it to fill. – –

Monday   Tuesday — 14th. This day is the first of the vacation, and has been devoted to various domestic duties which are neglected, during the time when the school is in session. —

Wednesday, January, 15th. The morning was not very pleasant, but in the forenoon the sun appeared and at half past nine we were all, sixteen in number *in* and *on* a stage coach, going to the dedication of a church recently erected at the East Village. On arriving, we found that the church was not nearly full, and that it was a half hour before the time. When the bell tolled Rev. Mr Pierpont, Rev Mr Stetson, and Rev Mr Ripley. — The 1st exercise was the Voluntary on the piano; the second an Anthem, "Holiness becometh Thine House"; the third Introductory Prayer by Mr Stetson of Medford; the fourth, "Selections from Scripture", read by Mr Pierpont from Boston; the fifth a Hymn by Mrs Follen; the sixth, Prayer of Dedication by Rev. Mr Ripley of Waltham, the seventh an Anthem; the eighth a Sermon by Mr Pierpont, the ninth a hymn by A. Adams; the address to the people by Ralph Waldo Emerson, the Transcendentalist; the eleventh a Hymn by Cowper; the twelfth Concluding Prayer by Rev. Mr Damon; the thirteenth, an Anthem, "Praise ye the Lord"; the fourteenth Benediction by the same. — Returned in the same way as we went and soon after Mr Ware Jr. and Mr Dall, a Sabbath school teacher of Miss Stodder's called. — In the eve the study hours were strictly kept. —

Chapter III

The Third Term, January 16 – April 4, 1840

Thursday. January 16.th. A new scholar, one more added to our number; a Miss Dracut from Kimball (two uncommon names, therefore I have forgotten which is which; but I believe if you reverse them you will have them right.) — The morning exercises were Reading and a prayer. Lessons recited were "Combe's Constitution of Man" Algebra, Arithmetic and Newman's Political Economy. The second class in Algebra was called, and as Mr P. had no time to attend to them, he committed them to my care. — In the afternoon, the exercises were Reading, Orthography Orthöepy, Moral Philosophy and Music. The afternoon was not as good as usual, nor does the opening of the term seem to be very promising. — After tea, Mr P. came up, and heard us recite in Greek, and we then went down to study our lessons for the next day. The study hours were observed until after nine, because the first quarter of an hour was occupied by Miss Drew in reading a communication from Mr P upon the subject of the commencement of the new term. —

Thermometer at 8. A.M. stood at 12° below zero.

Friday January 17th. — The thermometer this morn stands at six degrees below zero. The exercises of the morn were from the Bible, Singing and Prayer. The news which we heard yesterday of the steamboat disaster, and of the death of Professor Follen, was confirmed. I should think that if Mrs Follen's health was no better, the information would probably terminate her existence also. — The usual exercises were performed; Natural Philosophy, the subject of which was Specific Gravity, — Combe's Constitution, Book-keeping, Political Economy and Brigham on Mental Excitement. At the close of school, Mr. P. put the following questions. — Will the young ladies continue the conversational exercise? Will they continue the debates? — For the sake of lessening the incidental expenses, will they take the

care of sweeping the school-room. — In the afternoon the
school was visited by Mr Parks of Lincoln. The exercises
were Reading, Writing Orthography, Punctuation, Moral
Philosophy and Music. — The day has been rather dull,
and a *very gloomy* one to me. Read a letter in the eve,
addressed to Mr P. from Father, and went to bed with the
head-ache.

Saturday, January, 18th. School opened with Reading,
Prayer and Singing. The first Lesson recited was in
Brigham's Mental Excitement. This was not so brisk as
might be, nor as it usually is. Algebra and Arithmetic
occupied the time until recess; (Reading in the Scriptures
I forgot) then we were visited by Mr and Mrs Sherman,
and a widow Mrs Sherman, from Wayland. — The exercises were the debate upon the question, "Is there more
need of educating the faculties, or of communicating information?" – – The pupils all seemed to be united on this
question, all being in favor of the first. – –

The last was the Lecture, the eighteenth in number, upon
the subject of Geography. — This subject claims the attention of schools for several reasons. First, because it
throws light on History and Travels. With how much
more interest do you read these works, when we know where
the places are. — In reading a newspaper, it is also of great
importance. Second, It awakens and gratifies curiosity.
This is illustrated in schools; children love to read and learn
of other places. Perhaps there is nothing which is more
suitable for them, after simple reading. Geography is
happily that study sufficiently intellectual to give them
some exercise, without being too abstruse for them. — The
third use of it is that it is more important at the present
time, than at any previous, on account of the extent of our
commerce and of intercourse. — It is right that it should be
so, because it tends to civilise and Christianise the world.
Every thing that will contribute to the civilisation of the
world claims our attention. — Geography exercises the
faculties of perception, conception, memory, discrimination,
judgement and comparison. — The beginning is founded
upon perception. After we have given him a correct idea
of places, we call upon him to draft a map. He compares

WELLS HALL

MAY HALL

FRAMINGHAM, 1926

countries, their shape, form, and size; he thus uses comparison, discrimination, and judgement, all of which are important faculties, which the teachers should exercise. The cultivation of perception will lead to habits of accuracy. Many mistakes, difficulties, and disputes have been caused by a disagreement upon one small point. If it had no other benefit than to train the powers, and you could imagine everything you taught them, should vanish but that the powers should be cultivated it would be best to teach it in schools. Until recently, it has not been taught in our schools. When first introduced it was taught without maps, by description. — There are two methods in vogue at the present day. One way to begin with generals and to go to particulars. The first lesson would be a general description of the *solar* system; a subject the most abstruse. — Next the map of the world which would be nearly as absurd. Children generally understand particulars. — The second way is to begin with the town in which you live, then to others, and then to states, countries, and the world. Obtain a map of the town, and explain what a map is that it is a picture or representation of the place. Let your map have its boundaries; make them entirely familiar with it, and shew them the places around from some elevation if possible. Next require them to draw a map of it and have them tell the relative position of the countries. Having mastered one town the difficulty will be over; tell them that there are others beyond them and that thus there are a great many all around; finally take the state and teach them its boundaries. Go from one state to another, then to all the states. — How did our first parents get a knowledge of the garden of Eden? Did they look for books to tell of things afar off, or did they examine those around them. The last most certainly. First teach by means of maps and the eye. It is much more sure and observing than the ear. Let them draft it, no matter how crude. — Second Teach them the great and abiding features of nature. The great fault in geographies is to descend too much to the minutiae.

With all your instruction, mingle biographies and histories. Mr P. himself, thinks little of history as studied in schools. When you come to Bunker's Hill, Lake Champlain and such distinguished places, tell them of the history. Avoid details, statistics, and tabular statements. There is a difficulty in obtaining good maps, but you can almost always get good ones of the town an[d] of the world. In this way he begins with what is easy and goes to what is more difficult. Many children are in the situation of the child mentioned by Miss Hamilton who after having answered many questions correctly about Turkey in Asia, was asked where Turkey was. He replied "Out in the yard with the poultry." Three things must be remembered. 1st Teach by maps; 2nd Teach the outlines and not particular places 3d. Begin with the unit, not with millions, with the geography of places around you. — This was the last exercise and school closed. —

Thermometer, this noon, at 14° below zero. —

In the evening a part of the time was devoted to a Society which has been recently formed, the purpose of which is to accomplish some things of a domestic nature, which we are strongly tempted to omit, and at the same time, to cultivate our minds. — This eve we have read three Chapters in "Mrs. Sigourney's Letters to Young Ladies." The Young Ladies seemed to be much pleased, with the appropriation of the time. — We were also favored with the company of Mrs. Peirce, which added much to our enjoyment. — It was agreed last week to devote Sunday evening to study. —

Sunday, January 19th. Attended church to day, and heard Mr Buckingham preach. The sermon of the morning was from the 1st Epistle of Peter. 5. 3. "Neither as being lords over God's heritage, but being ensamples to the flock." A cold house, cold sermon, and very uninteresting. —

In the afternoon James 1, 22. "Be ye doers of the word, and not hearers only." Much more interesting than the morning. — I think it will be an excellent time for me to practise self denial, as I have never before known what it was, to be obliged to think before I went out, whatever the weather might be. Today, my inclination prompted me to go to hear Mr Stetson, who preached a sermon upon the life and character of Dr Follen, at the East Village. — But conscience would have accused me, and I should then have felt conscious of disobeying my parents in which I now feel innocent. —

In the eve we kept study hours an hour and a half, the remaining half hour being unavoidably interrupted by company. —

Monday January 20th. — The exercises of the morning were reading from the Scriptures, and Prayer. — After these were concluded, the class in Arithmetic recited, and then "Combe's Constitution of Man." The latter was very prompt. — Natural Philosophy next required our attention, and was quite an interesting lesson. — The subject of it was the art of flotation and swimming, and also life preservers. Mr. P., in connection with these spoke of Dr. Follen's powers of swimming. He said that in ordinary times he would be able to swim nearly the whole width of Long Island Sound, and this power combined with his self-possession would give him great advantages. His friends still have a hope that he has succeeded in gaining the shore and is still living. But there is one thing to counter-balance, in part, his advantages; viz; his great Benevolence, which would not allow him to take away a bale of cotton, plank or anything which another had, to preserve himself. The ice in the harbors and the coldness of the weather would be another obstacle. —

Algebra and Book-keeping occupied the time until recess; and after it, Mental Philosophy and the Second Class in Algebra.

P. M. Lessons in Reading, Grammar, Orthography, Orthöepy, Natural History and Moral Philosophy. — Mr Peirce remarked that the day had been a very fair one, perhaps a little better than usual.

Study hours *strictly* kept. —

Tuesday, January. 21st. — The weather warm and cloudy, looking as if we might have "a January thaw". — Morning exercises as yesterday, quite well recited. — After the recitation in N. Philosophy Mr P. told us that a Mr Greene of Providence, who had been reported among those destroyed, and for whose body five hundred dollars had been offered, reached Long Island Shore after having been on the water two days and two nights, and walked one mile to a house. When he arrived there he sank senseless, as might have been expected, but was resuscitated. — Efforts are now being made to find others. —

The remainder of the lessons were the same as yesterday in the morning and in the afternoon, with the exception of Natural History, which was omitted for want of time. The lesson in Moral Philosophy was badly recited and was consequently deferred until tomorrow. — Two of the most uninteresting lessons, come on Monday and Tuesday, and which require more time to prepare, than almost any others, viz; N. History and Orthöepy. The former would probably be more tolerable if we could have some ocular demonstrations of things, concerning which we study; but Mr Smellie's descriptives powers are not sufficiently active in this work, to enable me to see the animals described. – – The latter seems much like learning the A–B–C's after one has begun to read sentences. — However I see its utility, and this greatly compensates for the tediousness of the study.—The day upon the whole, has surpassed the last; the lessons having been generally better prepared. — Study hours *duly* observed. —

Wednesday. January 22nd. — School opened with Reading from the Scriptures and remarks, Singing and Prayer. After these were performed, the Dictionary lesson was recited & consisted of the Sounds of the letters, and the rules for Pronunciation of Proper Names. — Then Mr Peirce explained the Natural Philosophy lesson, which was upon the subject of Specific Gravity. — This he made much clearer to me than it ever was before and then gave out some problems involving the principles which we had been over in Hydrostatics. — These will be very interesting, I think, and appear to be easy. — The explanation of these occupied the time until recess. After this we recited a review in Moral Philosophy of the sixth and seventh Chapters. This lesson for some cause unknown to me, is always more difficult to learn thoroughly and to remember when learned, than any other in the course of studies. Generally, I have noticed that when it takes much time to understand the sentiments of a work, they remain fixed more strongly; but this work is an exception. — Conversation omitted.

Thursday. January 23'd. — A storm of rain, the first part of the day, of hail, the second; cloudy, the third. —

For a lesson in Natural Philosophy, we had some problems in Hydrostatics to solve; these occupied all of last evening, and were only accomplished by keeping "Study Hours" from seven until ten. At that hour I was obliged to go to bed, without preparing any lessons in "Combe's Constitution of Man," and "Mental Excitement." This was some thing which I had not done before, since I have been in Lexington, and probably (if I should judge from my feelings) the latter would have been a very suitable subject for my consideration. — Early rising, and diligence have given me an imperfect knowledge of the above lessons, this morn, so that the forenoon passed much better, than I had dared to hope. — Political Economy was recited after recess; Book-keeping deferred, for want of time. — Lessons in the afternoon, were Reading, Writing, Punctuation, Geography, and Problems upon the Globes. —

Study hours kept strictly. —

Friday. January. 24th. Colder than yesterday, but very pleasant. The devotional exercises were Reading from the Scriptures, Singing and Prayer. The question, "what branches are taught in West Point Academy?" was laid upon the table. Mr. P. said the Mathematical Studies were pursued there to a great extent, even farther than in our colleges. — Algebra, *Geometry*, Trigonometry, *Surveying* &c were much attended to. The school is strictly under military discipline. It is examined by a Committee chosen by the President of the United States, once every year. —

Natural Philosophy, Combe's Constitution, Mental Excitement and Political Economy were the forenoon exercises. — The afternoon, Reading, Writing, Punctuation, Geography, Moral Philosophy and Music. —

The day has been a very pleasant one, and quite lively, but I have been *almost* — homesick. Going to retire with the determination to banish such thoughts, as being *worse* than useless, and tomorrow, to be even *more* contented than ever. Study hours observed faithfully.

Saturday. January 25th. — The devotional exercises were as yesterday. Algebra was taken as a morning lesson by most of the school, "Combe's Constitution of Man" by the remainder. Reading in "Abbott's Teacher", was the fore-noon exercise. The subject was Scheming and today on the introduction of new books and plans in schools; I thought that his idea was very good, with regard to the multitude of school books now in existence. After the recess Miss Maria Wellington came into the school, and spent the remainder of the forenoon. — The discussion upon the question, "Is it best to notice individual offences in schools?" lasted about twenty minutes and then Mr P. made some remarks. He thought that it was well to notice or to observe the faults, but it was necessary that no par-tiality should be shown to the older scholars, in a school. There are differences in the temperament of the scholars, which should be regarded as much as possible, without partiality. If you are going to reprove a scholar, it would be well to take some time when he comes to you to get some thing done and speak to him kindly about it. If you know that some thing has been done, but do not know who did the wrong, speak of it publicly, and say that you hope it will be corrected; very likely it will be successful. — He expressed general gratification with the past week.

He then announced to us a piece of intelligence, which he wished us to receive calmly, viz; that he had received a communication from the Secretary and that he intended to come out "to look upon us" on Tuesday; that he had invited Mr G. B. Emerson Dr Howe[1], and some members of the Legislature to accompany him. — Delightful in prospect to be sure, it is to think of the *brilliant* appearance that we shall probably make, before the gentlemen. — 'Tis a pity that we have no stars who, by their light might enlighten the school. "It is *as* it is" and we should be satisfied, I suppose. — Sewing circle met this eve.

Sunday. January 26th. Mr. Buckingham preached again today. — The text in the morning was from Romans 11. 36 "For of him, through him and to him, are all things." The discourse was quite interesting. —

In the afternoon it was from Corinthians 1st 13. 9 "For we

---

[1] Founder of Perkins Institution for the Blind. Mary Swift became a teacher of Laura Bridgman at Perkins Institution. — Ed.

know in part," and was more interesting than the morning. — Have not enjoyed the day much, on account of *a disposition* to cough. — Have passed the time until evening in Reading a French Work. — At seven study hours commenced, and were kept *perfectly* until nine with the exception of a recess at eight of ten minutes. — I think that the most scrupulous person would make no exceptions, to the manner in which they have been observed, for the last two or three weeks. —

Our teacher would be perfectly satisfied with the conduct of "his children" I presume if he could look in upon them during these hours. — We all feel much happier I think by observing *perfectly* the rules, than we did by slightly transgressing them, for our own gratification. —

Monday. January 27th. — 1840. A cloudy morning. — The day was set apart for reviews, and has been devoted chiefly to that purpose. — Natural Philosophy, Bookkeeping & Mental Philosophy were attended to. Owing to a misunderstanding of our teacher's wishes, we did not learn a lesson in "Combe's Constitution." — The afternoon exercises were Enunciation, Natural History, & Moral Philosophy. —

Tuesday February 28th. 1840 The journals were returned, & Mr P. cautioned us upon the subject of going to extremes, in making journal entries. After an hour had passed, Mr Mann, Mr. Emerson, & Dr. Howe, were announced, and the forenoon exercises were commenced. The subjects in N. Philosophy, were chiefly under the head of Hydrostatics & Hydraulics. The gentlemen conversed with the scholars some upon the subjects, and ask a few questions. —

Some of them were the following; which has the greatest Specific Gravity a foot of earth or a foot of solid rock? Miss Pennell replied the *former* which was correct, — Another query: why when a person falls from a great height as the mast head into the sea, does he sink so low as not to rise to the surface again? — One ans. given was, that he acquired so much force in his descent that he fell deep enough for the resistance of the water to more than counterbalance the tendency of the body to rise again. - - Mr. Mann added a second, that it was owing to the cavity of the lungs being filled with air which was very much compressed. — Algebra Class next recited & after that some questions were asked in "Combe's Constitution of Man" & "Brigham's Mental Excitement." The review of the class in Arithmetic closed the morning session. — In the afternoon the school was assembled at the usual hour though the gentlemen with Mr P. were engaged in the Model School for an hour. — When they returned, some questions in Combe's Physiology were put, and then the Reading Exercise was performed. This occupied much time, and after it was accomplished, we listened to some remarks from Mr. Emerson (George B.) — He first alluded to the opinion that it was degrading: he said it was far otherwise: it was ennobling. — If an angel from heaven were to come to this earth, and to take that employment in which he could be most serviceable, he would become a teacher, — and indeed, a greater than an angel, our Savior, came to the earth to teach. — The highest qualifications are necessary for a teacher & even the intellect of Newton would have found sufficient exercise in teaching children. — He expressed his happiness in seeing us so advantageously situated and that the young ladies felt themselves, their privileges and seemed disposed to avail themselves of them to the greatest extent. —

A few remarks from Mr P. & school closed. After school had the pleasure of conversing with Dr. Howe, & of hearing him express his satisfaction with our appearance. — Sick in the eve — for variety's sake. —

Wednesday January 29th. School dismissed for the day. —

Spent the day in my room. —

[Miss Swift was ill and out of school, Jan. 29th to March 2d.]

Thursday January 30th. to Sunday March 1st. Rather a cloudy morning, and the temperature of the atmosphere much lower than that of the last Sunday in February. — Attended church, and heard Mr Parkman of Boston, nephew of Dr. Parkman, preach.

The text of the morning was from the Second Epistle of Peter — 3.9. — The object of the discourse was to remove the impression from the minds of his hearers that God is *angry* with sinners, and to show that anger is on the side of the latter. — In the afternoon from Revelations, 3, 15. "I know thy works that thou art neither cold nor hot: I would thou wert cold or hot." — He applied this text to Unitarians, complaining of their luke-warmness. — In conclusion he said that he might point out faults of other sects, but wisdom teaches us, *first* to correct our own. —

Monday March, 2nd. This morn I received the welcome intelligence that I might return to the boarding house which I left four weeks ago, on account of sickness. — Accordingly, in the afternoon I bent my steps toward the schoolroom and at the opening of the school took my seat with the rest, — but as spectator merely. — *My head* permitted me to remain until recess and then I retired to my room. — In the latter part of the afternoon, the school was visited by Mr. Forbes and the Misses Stetson, from Medford, and Messrs Wellington, Smith, and Lathrop of Lexington. — It being Election Day we were more highly favored than usual. – –

Tuesday. March. 3d. School opened by reading in the Scriptures, from Luke, 22nd Chap. 1–24 — Mr P. was asked to explain Piety which he did in the following manner. It signifies two things, 1st, a dutiful feeling towards God — a filial trust in him and disposition to do his commands; 2nd the feelings which children owe to earthly parents, and corresponding to those which men owe to God though in a less degree. — The journals and themes were returned, and Mr P. proposed that a different course should be adopted, that more time might be given to the afternoon lessons. It was that the morning lessons should be prepared out of school, and thus time would be left in the forenoon for the preparation of the afternoon studies. Remained in school as listener until the long recess, then took a short walk and did not return into school until three in the P.M. — Learned one lesson, in Natural History today but there was not time for the recitation and par consequence it was deferred. —

Wednesday, March 4th. The morning exercises were Reading & Singing, after which some Abstracts in Moral Philosophy were read, and Arithmetical & Algebraical problems performed. The recess commenced at half past ten and after taking a short walk I spent a few moments in the Model School. — In the afternoon had a very pleasant — — — — — to Mr Phinney's, and met with several acquaintances. — The day and visit will not soon I think, be forgotten. — In the eve there was a heavy shower accompanied by thunder and lightning. — The P.M. was oppressively warm. —

Thursday, March 5th. After the usual exercises, Arithmetic, N. Philosophy, "Combe's Constitution of Man," Algebra, "Mental Excitement," & Political Economy were recited, the long recess intervening. — In the afternoon, Geography, Moral Philosophy, Problems upon the Globe and Punctuation, occupied the time.

I am now quite discouraged, and think that it will do little good for me to *attempt* to review the ground passed over by my class for a month. —

'Tis hard to lose time when we *most* need it.

Friday, March. 6th. Entered school in the morning, and remained until recess, when I took a short walk, and returned to try the effects of blistering upon my head, and therefore was unable to attend school in the P.M. —

Saturday, March, 7th. — A delightful *day*, or rather *morning*, for the forenoon proved very windy. — Passed the time until eleven, in the sitting room, and then entered school, to hear the discussions on the question, Is it expedient to continue the discussions? — This was quite spirited, two having been chosen, to take opposite sides, and open the debate. — It was decided in the affirmative and a Resolution was offered by Miss Damon, to the following effect: resolved, that for the future two should be appointed to open the debates, and that they should *never* refuse to perform the duties of their appointment. — It was laid aside, for future discussion. — Mr P. spoke of Arithmetic a few minutes, & alluded to the manner of abbreviating the processes. — School closed. —

P.M. Visited by the Misses Howe & Laura Bridgman. —

Sunday March 8th. Mr Parkman preached to day. In
the forenoon from the third of Colossians the first verse
If ye then be risen with Christ seek those things which are
above; — In the afternoon from Psalms 90,9. "We pass
our days as a tale that is told." It was a practical sermon
and very good. —

Study hours duly observed. —

Monday, March, 9th, — School opened by Reading from
the Scriptures Luke 22–54. In connection with the story
of Peter, Mr Peirce remarked that we had many friends in
prosperity, but *few* remained faithful in adversity. — Some
have been reminded of the uncertainty of life or of its short-
ness, by the swinging of the pendulum. — So Peter in the
61. verse was probably taught more by one look of Christ's
than he knew before; and this was done, by awakening
reflections in his own heart. — Two propositions were placed
upon the desk: one, why is there a storm when the sun
crosses the Line? Mr P. remarked that he doubted the
fact as he had noticed many years when there was no storm
for two weeks *at* that time, nor even for a month. If it was
a fact, he knew of no way to account for it. — The second,
why is the year called the *Julian* year? — Answer: because
Julius made some corrections in the time. — For an account
of these see Encyclopoedia, Art. Style. — After answering
these, Mr P. alluded to some points of order — 1st. In the
opening of the school, it is improper to attend to anything
save the devotional exercises. — These demand the appearance as well as reality, and *reality* as well as appearance, of
attention. — 2nd, The necessity of a thorough preparation
of the morning lessons, that the forenoon may be devoted
to the afternoon studies. — 3d. The Model School. — some
alterations and modifications proposed. — Announced his
intention of visiting it and of teaching some time this week,
perhaps *tomorrow.* Left to the option of the pupils, whether
they remain all the time or a part only. —

First exercises in Natural Philosophy and "Combe's
Constitution of Man." Recited the latter. — My first
recitation in school since the 29th of January. — Algebra,
two classes, Arithmetic two, and Mental Philosophy. — In
the P.M. thought it advisable to take a recess of an hour

and then entered school and recited Grammar & learned
Moral Phil. though I did not recite.

Study hours observed. —

Tuesday.   March.   10th. — Reading in the scriptures,
Singing a Hymn, & Prayer were the first exercises. — Mr P.
commented upon the habit of the Jews, of answering ques-
tions, by saying that they had asserted it in the query. —
Thus in Luke. 22nd. 70th. "Art thou then the Son of God?
And he said unto them, Ye say that I am." —

Mr P. then remarked that probably when we taught, we
should wish to have the obedience to our rules flow from
the heart, the *reality* and not the *appearance*. —

The journals were returned, and the following remarks
made upon them: None were of so high an order as sometimes, and none, so low; there was a greater uniformity
than before for some time. — A good regard to hours had
been shown on the whole. Natural Philosophy upon the
part, Expansion of Bodies by Heat was well recited by
most.   Arithmetic, "Combe's Constitution of Man," Algebra, Mental Philosophy were recited in course. —

In the afternoon, Reading, Grammar, Exercise in Dictionary, and Moral Philosophy, were recited. — The question concerning the word *near*, whether it is an adverb,
preposition or adjective, or in what cases it is so, arose but
was not satisfactorily decided. — Study hours observed. —

Wednesday. March 11th. — The school was opened as
yesterday morn and Mr P. then answered some queries
which were placed upon his table. — First Is it right, when
one person hears another misrepresent something to correct
him in the company of others? It was decided to depend on
circumstances. — Mr P. thought, if in a company you
should hear a misrepresentation of something & you were
not with the group who were conversing upon the subject,
it would not be a proper time to correct it. – – The exercises were "Combe's Constitution of Man," Natural Philosophy, Arithmetic were recited before recess. After this,
two classes in Algebra, Mental Philosophy and Natural
History. —

I neglected to mention that on Saturday Mr P, gave out
two questions for debate, First, Can the pupils of this school,

or of any other literary institution, secure the highest benefits from the institution and mingle freely with the young people of the town in their parties and amusements. 2nd. Can a person be truly polite in the ordinary sense of the word, and be sincere and conscientious? —

Study hours observed. —

Thursday, March, 12th. — Morning exercises, as usual. — Mr. Peirce commented upon the character of Pilate, as displayed when he judged Christ. His course was reprehensible, as an instance of yielding to popularity. To speak Phrenologically, he sacrificed Conscientiousness to Love of Approbation. —

The lesson in Natural Philosophy, was upon the effects of Heat upon different substances, aeriform — liquid — solids, — and was rather more difficult to remember than usual. — "Combe's Constitution of Man" & Algebra occupied the forenoon until recess. — During the latter exercise, Mr Stetson of Lexington and his brother came in, and spent the remainder of the forenoon. The exercises were Political economy, & Brigham's Mental Excitement. —

In the afternoon we were visited by Miss Mary Meriam, Miss Reed and Mrs. – – – –. The exercises were recitations in ancient Geography, Problems upon the Globe, Moral Philosophy, Punctuation.

We can now form some idea, of the difficulty which children experience in committing to memory Geography lessons, which appear so easy to us, by noticing our own progress in A. Geography. —

Friday. — March, 13th. — This day the Model School opened at eight ö clock, and the Normalites attended while Mr P. examined the Modelites. — Many were *in,* the greater part of the day, — but owing to *a diseased head* I was only able to spend about two hours. — Reading & Arithmetic were the subjects then attended to. — In the evening, Miss Smith — (Cousin of Miss Stow) came in the stage with the intention of passing a few days here, and therefore I shall room with Miss Drew for a time. – –

Saturday, March, 14th. — This day Mr P. has gone to Boston, and we have a vacation. — Forenoon passed in domestic employments, social converse, and reading aloud,

the description of Queen Victoria's nuptials. How many
things, which would appear in common people *ridiculous*,
are passed over as things of common occurrence in royalty. —
     P.M. Walked to "Normal Hill," for the first time since
September, and had a good view of the City. - —
     Sunday March, 15th Mr Parkman preached today in
the morning from Luke 8th. 13th "And these have no
root." In the afternoon there was a thick snow-storm, and
few at church. The text was from 1st Peter 4th, 7th. —
"Be ye therefore sober." - - They were both very good —
would that he could stay in Lexington.
     Monday, March, 16th. This morn, Mr P. announced the
new division of the year. — The succeeding one is to commence on the 1st. of May and is to be divided into three
terms of fifteen weeks each. The first vacation is in August,
of three or four weeks, another in January of one week,
another in April of two weeks. — New pupils will be admitted only at the opening of the terms. — The pupils are
obliged to stay one year. — He said that before entering a
school the pupils should ask themselves the question "Do
I wish to teach merely for the sake of gaining a livelihood,
or from love of the employment? — If the former induces
you to adopt this you had better take some other profession. — It is very necessary that the candidates for admission, should be well acquainted with the elementary
branches. — The lesson in Natural Philosophy was omitted
for want of time. — In the long recess, the weather being
very fine, I took a walk on the Burlington Road and afterwards called on Mrs Peirce. —
     In the afternoon, read in Mrs. Hamilton's Letters on
Education for an hour or two, and then went into school. - -
After tea, heard that Mr. Mann and another gentleman
was in town. Soon the intelligence was confirmed, by the
appearance of the aforesaid gentleman and Dr Howe — who
said that they came out to take a ride — and then when
they went away, said that Mr Mann had as much to do in
the evening as ten common men. —
     Do the gentlemen think that we are going to believe every
story, they tell us: — the two parts of the story as people
say don't seem "to hang together well." - - Retired at the

commencement of study hours. — Omitted to mention, that
after the departure of the gentleman, Mr. P. told us that
he expected the Secretary of the Board of Education of
Conn. in company with some others to pass the day with
him. – – This caused a *little* commotion among the scholars.—

Tuesday, March 17th. — This morn the weather is cloudy
and some flakes of snow are falling. — The remark which the
Irishman made "that March never died in debt to winter"
is about to be fulfilled this year. — The weather has probably prevented the anticipated visit of the Sec. — The
morning exercises were in the usual course; the lesson in
Natural Philosophy so long deferred, was *well* recited and
I should think the general character of the day, was *good*. —

Wednesday, March 18th. This day a severe head-ache
prevents me from attending school. — The application of
a blistering plaster, promises a temporary relief however
and I am reminded to "Let patience have her perfect
work" —

Thursday, March 19th. Breakfast rather late this morn,
— and soon after I was seated, received a message from Mr
P. wishing me to go to him; he informed me that Mrs P.
was going to West Cambridge and if I was well would like
to have me go with her. Ere I had time to get up stairs, the
stage was at the door, and with Miss Smith, was soon on
my way. — Returned at noon, in the Harvard Stage after
having called upon Rev Mr Damon. —

Found that two letters had got here before me, and also
the Secretary, Mr Barnard, Mr. Coleman, Superintendent
of the Teacher's Seminary in Andover. Mr Crowel, of
Boston Editor of the Christian Watchman. —

After dinner received a letter from Providence brought
by Mr. Barnard. — Between one and two ö clock, four gentlemen called on Mr. P. and went into the Model School.
Soon all adjourned to the Normal School, the Messrs.
Wheeler, Mr Foster & Mr. Hartwell, all from Lincoln. —
The first exercise was in Reading a description of Childhood
by H. H. White & with Orthoëpy occupied the time till
recess. — At this time the Secretary rose to depart, and
thinking I should lose nothing I left school; contrary to
my expectations he addressed the school, and I was dis-

appointed in not hearing him. — Other gentleman remained
until the close of the school. —

Friday, March, 20th. A stormy day, and a prospect of
being alone. — i.e. destitute of *foreign* company. — The
snow, rain and hail, descend together, and it is real March
weather. — The exercises of the morning & forenoon were
as usual. Mr P announced the decision of the Representatives with regard to us. It was decided that we should
stand, by a majority of sixty-three. — There were three
things opposed to us. — 1st. Sectarianism, — 2nd Expense & 3d Political parties. — He also warned the young
ladies against cherishing false hopes with regard to their
certificates as he should not commit himself in giving them
to those who left. — He added, that if the young ladies begin
to teach and fail, it would be remembered more than three
instances of success. — The forenoon excercises were as
usual. — Brigham, was recited in the afternoon. — Despite
the storm, Mr. Stetson found the way here. — Moral Philosophy was discussed the latter part of the afternoon. Mr
Stetson remarked upon various subjects and at the close of
the school, at the request of Mr P. — made some remarks to
the school. —

He first spoke of his gratification in witnessing the system,
which was so intellectual; of the advantages of it: it was
education not *instruction.* — The discussions of the school
shewed the power of turning the thoughts inward. — There
is a wide difference between education & instruction — it
is as pouring water from one vessel to another in the vain
attempt to fill it. — The former is as the growth of cotton,
but the latter is as piling up the dead material. These will,
at length, be flowers and fruits, but the growth will be *ever-
lasting.* — If you ever turn from this, to a vulgar method,
and bring into the mind what is foreign to it then the growth
will be stopped. Use external things as aids only for developing what is within; —

Education is, according to the meaning of the word, a
drawing forth, a developing of inborn faculties. Instruction is pouring in from without to a passive mind. — We
are in this state when we are hearing lectures. Such a mind
never does any thing worthy of itself. — In a life of thought,

the mind grows; it is then as God designs; we can not spend a day, without advance but go on aspiring to perfection. We should value knowledge, only as it becomes serene wisdom; *thought only* converts knowledge into power: it is thus, theory is converted into practice. — It applies also to *Morals.* Education is more simple than it appears, by being convinced of the manner of putting things into the mind. He said that he was persuaded that we feel it to be the highest privilege to work, and that every one is persuaded that he is to do something. — That we are not all one being but twenty different ones. We must look upon life as a scene of labor and our duty is, to lead others in the path of duty. — We should give our selves to society, to God and daily render ourselves acceptable sacrifices. — He desired that our recollection of this school may be the happiest of our lives; we should convert all our privileges here, to the highest uses — to the acquisition of knowledge of God, of our Savior, and eternal life. —

Mr. P. then spoke a few words in addition. —

He said that those who consider the brightest view of life to be the time spent in luxury, have no enjoyment, compared with those who expect to do good. — In the evening the Sewing Society met and read from the Letters of Mrs Sigourney a part of Benevolence and Self Control. — Misses Locke Davis & Woodman visited us. —

Saturday, March 21st. Today the sun crosses the line, on his way to visit us, and the days and nights are equal. —

The School was opened by Reading, Singing, and Prayer. — The first exercise was in Abbott's Teacher, — the chapter upon the "Reports of Cases," and as it was a very fruitful topic, nearly two hours were spent in discussing the subject of government. — Wayland's case of the management of his child, was introduced. In the long recess, took a walk on the Burlington Road, and returned very much fatigued. — Attended school, that I might see the experiments in Natural Philosophy which Mr P. proposed to try. — First took up the discussion of the question, is it well for the young ladies, members of a literary seminary, to mingle with the people of the town, in their amusements? It seemed to be the opinion of the scholars, that there should be *some* visiting. —

Mr P. tried several experiments and was very successful. —
Magdeburg Cups, — Water spouting from the side of a
vessel at different distances from the base, Pressure of the
Atmosphere — *Archimede's Crew* (screw) and the Communication of motion by the movement of balls —

Sunday, March 22nd. — Heard Mr. Parkman preach from
the 6th chapter 12th verse of John "Gather up the fragments
that remain, that nothing be lost." He applied it in three
ways: 1st to frugality or the goods of this life; 2nd to the
saving of the fragments of time; 3d to moral duties. — In
connection with the second, he said that many put off the
doing of a good work because they had not so many *days*,
hours, or weeks to devote to it, when if they used the fragments of time it might all be accomplished. — If we kept
an account of the number of misimproved moments, and of
those passed in sleep for one day only and then multiply
the amount by three hundred and sixty five, we shall have
the amount for one year. —

Under the third head — he introduced an illustration from
the VIIIth commandment. "Thou shall not steal." — He
said that if a man did not lay hands upon the property
of another he was not said to violate the commandment.
He could incur a debt which he had no expectation of pay-
ing or invest money committed to his charge in wild specu-
lations. —

When he goes to the Scriptures to transplant from them
to his own heart the seeds of virtue why can he not gather
the fragments which are scattered around? — Why in
searching them, does he not treasure up those gems which
most adorn the Christian character? —

Now, if in this discourse there are any fragments which
are worthy of notice, collect them and carry them to your
homes to guide you on the week-day as well as Sabbath.

In the afternoon the text was in Psalms 2. 11. "Serve
the Lord with fear & rejoice with trembling." The subject, was Religious Anxiety. —

Monday, March 23d. School opened by reading from the
Scriptures, Singing and Prayer. — Mr P. remarked that it
was in vain to ask for good, if we did not make corresponding efforts, to obtain it. God is said to provide for the birds

but they must use their wings and bills and other means, to obtain what he has given them. – –

An old rule, and one that still holds true, is, that it is better to prepare Lessons *first* and then if there is any time left, devote it to other matters. —

He then read an extract from the Common School Journal. It was a letter from a child· of twelve years to a cousin, expressing her opinions of premiums and examinations. — Exercise in Natural Philosophy was upon the subject of "Radiation and Conduction of Heat" and was very interesting. — "Combe's Constitution of Man." Arithmetic, and Algebra, were the objects of attention until recess. — Have just learned that I have probably only *three weeks more* to remain in Lexington, and that I am not to study a⁻y in that time. Could I have anticipated this when I came here my efforts for the time that I was allowed to study should have been *redoubled.* —

After recess, one class in Algebra and one in Arithmetic recited. Abercrombie's Mental Philosophy was attended to for a short time; — the subject was *dreaming.* —

P.M. — Entered school at three ö clock: Class in Reading attending to an exercise in Abbott's Teacher. Mr. P. related an Anecdote of a Gentleman who taught the same branches until he could teach them no longer. This was explained by supposing that the powers of his mind were exhausted, and that he had not taken care to keep it active by study. Orthography, Orthöepy, Grammar, Moral Philosophy and Natural History occupied the remainder of the afternoon. — In the exercise in Grammar, Mr. P. related an anecdote of a foreigner who was not familiar with the language and was in danger of drowning. — He cried to the by-standers "I *will* drown you *shall* not help me", thus by changing the sense of the Auxiliaries *shall* & *will*, he entirely perverted his meaning. — The subject of Moral Philosophy was on the "Right of Property and the manner in which it may be acquired." —

Tuesday. March. 24th. — Mr. P. opened the school by reading from the First Chapter of John; Singing & Prayer succeeded it. — He then returned the journals, remarking that he considered them as good, as they had been at any

previous time. He then informed the scholars, that the
Central Public School was to be examined in the P.M. and
that its teacher had sent an invitation to them to attend.
If the pupils wished to attend, it would be necessary to
suspend the school and therefore he asked that we should
consider upon it and *decide upon it,* after the recess. — The
exercises were as yesterday; "Combe's Constitution of
Man," Natural Philosophy upon Electricity, Arithmetic
and Algebra. — After the recess it was a thick snow-storm
and there seemed to be little prospect of weather suitable
for attending an examination. — The young ladies, however,
were desirous to go and voted in favor notwithstanding the
storm. — Miss Damon with Miss Stodder for assistant
concluded to keep the Model School. The question for discussion on Saturday, was decided to be, "Can a person be
truly polite in the ordinary sense of the word and be sincere and conscientious?" — During the discussion upon the
latter subject there was a rap at the door, and Mrs Greene
was announced — who spent the afternoon with me. —

P.M. Young ladies with two exceptions, gone to the
Examination.

Wednesday, March 25th School opened by Reading
Singing & Prayer. — Class in Arithmetic first recited. —
Mr. P. remarked that he should have recommended *first,*
in the Examination yesterday, more performance on the
board, as a better way of exhibiting the knowledge. — He
would also advise us to avoid *leading* questions as they
are no test & the character of the examination must depend
upon others. In making selections, choose such subjects as
are upon a level with their comprehension. — Yesterday
they were put upon pieces from Sterne, which were most
difficult to read. — In most schools, where such pieces are
given, the result will be a failure in nine cases out of ten. —
"Combe's Constitution of Man" and Natural Philosophy
were also recited before the recess. — After it, we listened
to some Reading. — This exercise, in which some of the
young ladies select pieces and read aloud to the school, has,
during my absence, been substituted for the Conversational
Exercise. —

P.M. Spent in domestic employments, Reading, and
Listening to Reading. —

Thursday. March, 26th. — Opening exercises as usual, Reading & Singing. — Natural Philosophy was the first lesson recited. — Some questions were suggested in this recitation by the pupils, with regard to the different kinds of Electricity, and the theories of Franklin and Symmer, which were satisfactorily answered by Mr P. — This occupied much time, "so that" there was little left for the remaining exercises. Arithmetic, "Combe's Constitution of Man," & Algebra. — Recess until 11 + $\frac{1}{4}$.

Visited Mrs Peirce in the recess, and thought it best not to return to the school on account of a *slight headache.* — P.M. Did not go into school, until nearly three, at the close of the reading exercise. Spent the time in reading over the same lesson, that the school were engaged in, problems upon the globe, and Ancient Geography. — During the latter Mr P. remarked that some might be ignorant of the origin of the terms longitude & latitude and thus explained them; viz; Longitude means lengthwise; the longest part of the earth that the ancients knew, was longest from East to West and therefore they gave the name: while the distance from North to South was called Latitude from a Latin word meaning breadth. — Recess of 10 minutes. —

Writing by a part of the school and Geometry occupied the remainder of the afternoon. — During the latter exercise Mr. Norwood Damon visited the school. Session closed, by the exercise in Music. —

Friday, March 27th. — Mr P. read this morn from the 1st chapter of John 35. He alluded to the reply when the two disciples said to Jesus "where dwellest thou"? "Come and see:" — and thought that it was a text fruitful of instruction, especially, when applied to the young. —

"Combe's Constitution of Man" was the first exercise. In Natural Philosophy the Electric Machine was exhibited, and some of the parts explained, no experiments were tried. — Arithmetic and Algebra as usual. —

After the recess, Arithmetic, "Brigham's Mental Excitement" were recited. —

P.M. At two, entered school, and heard the Reading Exercise from Abbott's Teacher, and some remarks by Mr P. and the scholars. After a recess, the class in Ancient Geography recited, & after that in Moral Philosophy.

During this exercise the query arose whether if a person by his will, order his property to be destroyed, it is the duty of his executors to comply. —

Some thought that a person must be insane to do it, & others that he had a right, and also during his existence to squander his property as he pleased. Mr P. said Society thought differently if he had children who would thus be thrown upon others, it has the right to interfere and oblige him to do differently. —

Saturday, March 28th. Mr P. read this morn, the miracle of turning water into Wine at Cana of Galilee. — He remarked upon this. — Some use this as supporting the use of wine, as a drink. But it was not for that (for which)[1] the miracle was wrought; but as we are told in another verse, that he might manifest his glory. He supposed that the assertion that the scriptures *condemned* it, could not be sustained(,) for St. Paul recommends it. — *in a certain instance.*[2] — If you go to them for argument you must take the general benevolence of them. — The precepts in them commanding you to do good as you have opportunity, to be an example in all good, to do to others as you would be done by, — would require abstinence from its use, because his example will not work well to his neighbor. — Some undertake to prove, that the wine used *then*, was the pure juice of the grape, while that now used is adulterated by alcohol. But that the effects were the same, is proved by the frequent references to intoxication in the ancient poets Virgil and Homer.

He then alluded to the *fact* that he heard some inquiring after lessons in the *morning*, that if we were to teach, we should probably consider it as ominous of evil. You will find those scholars will not be among the number, on whom you can *depend* for the reputation of the school. Arithmetic & Algebra were recited, & during that time, I read in Mrs Eliz^th Hamilton's Letters. — Reading the Scriptures and Music occupied the time until recess. During the latter exercise, Mr P. read some theories to explain the use of

---

[1] Corrected to "intent" by Mr. Peirce.
[2] Inserted by Mr. Peirce. — Ed.

Chromatic as applied to the Scale in Music of Flats &
Sharps. — The most reasonable seemed to be that it was used
to signify an embellishment as colors (the word means colors)
serve to embellish. — After the recess, the question "Can
a person be polite in the ordinary acception (*sic*) of the word,
and yet be truly conscientious? — Yeas 10. Nays 9. - -

Mr P. thought that true politeness was consistent in
common life but he doubted it, in what is called fashionable
life. — He thought, that a person who was very conscientious would not find many cases in which it was *necessary*
to prevaricate. — He related an Anecdote of a debating
society in Andover at which a professor was present, and
which was conducted by the students. — It sometimes was
dull and then there were few attended. — On one evening
one of the debaters took the subject, how can we make
these debates interesting and profitable. After he had
spoken, the professor added one more reason. He said this
was a voluntary exercise & if they wished to encourage the
speakers they should not find who was to speak, and the
subjects, but go at all times and show by their presence and
attention the interest necessary.

.Next in order, came the Philosophical Experiments. —
Among them were Barker's Mill, the Pulse Glass, E[x]pan-
sion of Air as it takes place in the bursting of the steam-
engine, Artificial Fountain, the Cup of Bacchus, Expansion
of Air in the Bladder. — These were very successful, and
when they were concluded we found it nearly one. —

Sunday March. 29th. — The morning was stormy, but my
wish to attend church, prevented my keeping at home. Mr.
Parkman preached an excellent sermon, from Deuteronomy
33. 25. — "As thy day, so shall thy strength be."

[Abstract of the sermon omitted.]

.   .   .   .

Monday. March 30th. — Instead of a clear day as we had
anticipated, the morning proved very foggy. —

The school opened as usual. — Reading from the 2nd
Chapter of John, & Singing. Mr P. remarked that the act

of our Savior of driving the people from the temple, gave countenance to corporal punishment. — But though he made a scourge, he may only have used it for the purpose of expelling the beasts. —

Natural Philosophy — a review of Electricity was first recited. — Left school after this, and spent the remainder of the forenoon with Mrs. Peirce. —

P.M. — Entered school at four. The subject under consideration was Grammar. The discussion with regard to active-transitive and active-intransitive verbs was again called up and occupied the time until five when school closed, Moral Philosophy, and Natural History being deferred until the morrow. — —

The afternoon has been very stormy, and the wind high. — It increased in force until ten when by the rocking of the house and bed & the water pouring in at the windows at a moderate rate, I should judge "it blew a hurricane."

Tuesday. March 31st. — The last day of March, and may it be the last wind which we shall feel, for the spring. —

School opened by Reading and Prayer. — The lesson in "Combe's Constitution of Man" which was deferred yesterday morn, was recited. — The second class in Arithmetic, recited and then we took our recess. After this the Classes in Algebra, & first class in Arithmetic performed. — Mental Philosophy was omitted for want of time. — P.M. Reading, Orthography, Grammar, Moral Philosophy and Natural History were recited — the subject of the latter, was the description of Bees. —

In Moral Philosophy, the subject was "the mode in which the right of property may be violated by the Individual." — In connection with this, the question "Can a merchant become rich, and be perfectly honest?" arose, and there was considerable discussion upon it. — Mr. P. said, that he had heard a merchant in one of our cities say, that it was *impossible* for a person if he were honest, to be rich, but he thought that this could not be the case, if the doctrines inculcated by "Combe's Constitution of Man" and the Bible were true. — The hour for closing the school approached, and Mr. P. was obliged to dismiss the discussion

A Certificate

This certifies that from long acquaintance with Miss Mary Swift, both in the Normal School at Lexington, where she has been a pupil, and elsewhere, I have formed a very high esteem of her talent, disposition, and attainments; and I think there is no station in our high school o Academies which she as teacher, would not fill with honor and success.

Lexington. Oct. 9 1840—

C. Peirce Prin. l. N.S.L.—

CERTIFICATE OF PROFICIENCY FOR MARY SWIFT, 1840

to give out some questions in Arithmetic & Algebra for the morrow. —

Wednesday, April 1st. — Commonly called "April Fool's Day." The morning exercises, were in Arithmetic & Algebra — the problems mentioned yesterday:, Mr P. remarked in opening the school, upon the question of honesty in trade & said he wished us to keep it in mind. — He said he intended to be with us but a short time this morn but he wished us to be engaged about the usual time, and then those who were in arrearages might come up with the others. —

School visited by Mr Chamberlain apparatus maker. Miss Damon took the *Chair* after recess and the Session was thus continued until the usual time for its close. —

Thursday, April 2nd. — The exercises of the day about as usual. — Mr. P. at the close of the school announced to us his intention of occupying the remainder of the week in exhibiting apparatus. —

Oh the evils of procrastination! If this had been filled up at the proper time the above mistake would not have been made, — for was not Thursday April 2nd Fast day and did we have a school then, contrary to His Excellency's desire. —

In the morning the young ladies read aloud The Lecturess or Woman's Sphere, which occupied the time until 11 A.M. when we attended church to hear a discourse from Mr Parkman. — After this we *dined* & then listened to some miscellaneous reading while occupied in sewing. — Eve — Study Hours. —

Friday, April 3d. — This morn Mr P. announced his intention of devoting the remainder of the week and longer if necessary, to the exhibition of the Apparatus, which belonged to the school. During this time he wished that the lessons should be prepared as usual though he should not have time to hear all recited. — At nine therefore we repaired to the Model School. — Various experiments in Mechanics & the Exhibition & partial explanation of the Mechanical Powers occupied the forenoon. —

In the afternoon the Apparatus in Hydrostatics was exhibited. — Mr Forbes called to see the school in company with a young lady from Medford. After the exercises had closed I was informed that some one wished to see me, and on entering the sitting room found my uncle W. A. Greene, who had come to escort me to Providence, and intended to leave Lexington the next morning. — After tea walked up to see Miss Clark and obtained Gov. Hancock's Autograph. Passed the eve in conversation with the girls interrupted only by a call from *Mr Tufts.* —

Saturday April 4th. — Rose at five and met the scholars to have a short time more with them, and at half after seven bade Adieu to Lexington feeling a little more sorrow at leaving my Normal Sisters, at the moment than joy at seeing my Cousin. — Our fellow passengers in the stage were not of the *loquacious* order and therefore we did not gain much insight into them. — After a pleasant ride we were left at the Marlboro Hotel in Boston and from there walked to various parts of the city. — On returning found in the room a gentleman in a plain dress (rather uncommon in Boston) whose *forehead* and *eyes* attracted my attention. Ere long my Uncle introduced [me] to him — J. G. Whittier — the Quaker Poet. —

After dinner at about three we rode to the Providence depot and there took cars for that place with about fifty passengers. Arrived in safety and reached my boarding house Mr. John Smith's at six, in season for tea. — Spent the eve at home. —

THE EARLY HISTORY OF
NORMAL SCHOOLS IN
MASSACHUSETTS: DOCUMENTS

JAMES GORDON CARTER
Early Advocate of a State Teachers' Seminary

I

OUTLINE OF AN INSTITUTION FOR THE EDUCATION OF TEACHERS

By JAMES G. CARTER

[This comprehensive and brilliant essay is one of three proposals to establish a state "institution" or "seminary" for the training of teachers, which were published, independently and almost simultaneously, in 1825, by Thomas H. Gallaudet of Connecticut, Walter R. Johnson of Pennsylvania, and James G. Carter of Massachusetts. The three essays are so strikingly similar in their recommendations (though not in their language) as to suggest a common origin. Of course, three men independently thinking over the same problem might well come to the same conclusions; but all three plans are sufficiently like the Prussian "Teachers' Seminaries," as reorganized by the Prussian school law of 1819, to lead to the query whether these institutions were known to the three writers. Johnson alone specifically refers to them.

Carter's essay was first published in the "Boston Patriot," February, 1825. Concerning Carter see pages xxxiv*ff.* of this volume, and the Memoir in Barnard's "American Journal of Education," V, 408.]

[School reforms are impossible without trained teachers.]

It will do but little good for the Legislature of the State to make large appropriations directly for the support of schools, till a judicious expenditure of them can be insured. And in order to this, we must have skillful teachers at hand. It will do but little good to class the children till we have instructors properly prepared to take charge of the classes. It will do absolutely no good to constitute an independent tribunal to decide on the qualifications of teachers, while they have not had the opportunities necessary for coming up to the proper standard. And it will do no good to overlook and report upon their success, when we know beforehand that they have not the means of success. It would be beginning wrong, too, to build houses and to tell your young and inexperienced instructors to teach this or to teach that subject, however desirable a knowledge of such subjects might be, while it is obvious that they cannot know how, properly, to teach any subject. The *science of teaching* — for it must be made a science — is first, in the order of nature, to be inculcated. And it is to this point that the public attention must first be turned, to effect any essential improvement.

[*One may know much, and yet be a poor teacher.*]

And here let me remark upon a distinction in the qualifications of teachers, which has never been practically made; though it seems astonishing that it has so long escaped notice. I allude to the distinction between the possession of knowledge, and the ability to communicate it to other minds. When we are looking for a teacher, we inquire how much he *knows*, not how much he can *communicate;* as if the latter qualification were of no consequence to us. Now it seems to me that parents and children, to say the least, are as much interested in the latter qualification of their instructor as in the former.

Though a teacher cannot communicate more knowledge than he possesses, yet he may possess much, and still be able to impart but little. And the knowledge of Sir Isaac Newton could be of but trifling use to a school, while it was locked up safely in the head of a country schoolmaster. So far as the object of a school or of instruction, therefore, is the acquisition of knowledge, novel as the opinion may seem, it does appear to me that both parents and pupils are even more interested in the part of their teacher's knowledge which they will be likely to get, than in the part which they certainly cannot get.

One great object in the education of teachers which it is so desirable on every account to attain, is to establish an intelligible language of communication between the instructor and his pupil, and enable the former to open his head and his heart, and infuse into the other some of the thoughts and feelings which lie hid there. *Instructors and pupils do not understand each other*. They do not speak the same language. They may use the same words; but this can hardly be called the same language, while they attach to them such very different meanings. We must either, by some magic or supernatural power, bring children at once to comprehend all our abstract and difficult terms, or our teachers must unlearn themselves, and come down to the comprehension of children. One of these alternatives is only difficult, while the other is impossible.

[*The professionally trained teacher must understand. . . .*]

The direct, careful preparation of instructors for the profession of teaching, must surmount this difficulty; and I doubt if there be any other way in which it can be surmounted. When instructors understand their profession, that is, in a word, when they understand the philosophy of the infant mind, what powers are earliest developed, and what studies are best adapted to their development, then it will be time to lay out and subdivide their work into an energetic system of public instruction. Till this step toward a reform, which is preliminary in its very nature, be taken, every other measure must be adopted in the dark; and, therefore, be liable to fail utterly of its intended result. Houses, and funds, and books are all, indeed, important; but they are only the means of enabling the minds of the teachers to act upon the minds of the pupils. And they must, inevitably, fail of their happiest effects, till the minds of the teachers have been prepared to act upon those of their pupils to the greatest advantage.

[*How can teachers be professionally trained? By an institution for that exclusive purpose.*]

If, then, the first step toward a reform in our system of popular education be the scientific preparation of teachers for the free schools, our next inquiry becomes, How can we soonest and most perfectly achieve an object on every account so desirable? The ready and obvious answer is, establish an institution for the very purpose. To my mind, this seems to be the only measure which will insure to the public the attainment of the object. It will be called a new project. Be it so. The concession does not prove that the project is a bad one, or a visionary, or an impracticable one. Our ancestors ventured to do what the world had never done before, in so perfect a manner, when they established the free schools. Let us also do what they have never so well done yet, and establish an institution for the exclusive purpose of preparing instructors for them. This is only a second part, a development or consummation of the plan of our fathers. They foresaw the effect of universal intelligence upon national virtue and happiness; and they projected the means of securing to themselves and to us universal education. They wisely did a new thing under the sun. It has proved to be a good thing. We now enjoy the results of their labors, and we are sensible of the enjoyment. Their posterity have praised them, loudly praised them, for the wisdom of their efforts. Let us, then, with hints from them, project and accomplish another new thing, and confer as great a blessing on those who may come after us. Let us finish the work of our fathers, in regard to popular education, and give to it its full effect. Let us double, for we easily may, the happy influences of an institution which has already attracted so much notice from every part of our country, and drawn after it so many imitations, and send it, thus improved, down to posterity for their admiration.

[Three questions arise concerning the proposed institution.]

If a seminary for the purpose of educating teachers scientifically be essential in order to give the greatest efficacy to our system of popular education, then, in the progress of the discussion, the three following questions arise in the order in which they are stated. By whom should the proposed institution be established? What would be its leading features? And what would be some of the peculiar advantages to the public which would result from it? To answer these several questions at length would require a book; while I have, at present, only leisure to prepare one or two newspaper essays. A few hints, therefore, upon the above three topics are all that I dare profess to give, and more than I fear I can give, either to my own satisfaction or that of those readers who may have become interested in the subject.

[First question: Who shall establish it?   The state.   Why?
  The argument for state control.]

The institution, from its peculiar purpose, must necessarily be both literary and scientific in its character. And
although, with its design constantly in view, we could not
reasonably expect it to add, directly, much to the stock
of what is now called literature, or to enlarge much the
boundaries of what is now called science, yet, from the
very nature of the subject to which it would be devoted,
and upon which it would be employed, it must in its progress
create a kind of literature of its own, and open a new science
somewhat peculiar to itself — the science of the development of the infant mind, and the science of communicating
knowledge from one mind to another while in a different
stage of maturity.   The tendency of the inquiries which
must be carried on, and the discoveries which would be
constantly made, in a seminary for this new purpose, would
be to give efficacy to the pursuits of other literary and scientific institutions.   Its influence, therefore, though indirect,
would be not the less powerful upon the cause of literature
and the sciences generally.   These remarks may seem to
anticipate another part of my subject; but they are introduced here to show that a seminary for the education of
teachers would stand, at least, on as favorable a footing in
relation to the public, as other literary and scientific institutions.   It seems now to be believed that the Legislature
of the State are the rightful proprietors of all public institutions for the diffusion of knowledge.   And if they are of
any, they certainly ought to be of one for such a purpose.
Because there are none in which the public would be more
deeply interested.   There are none which would tend so
much to diffuse knowledge among the whole mass of the
people.   And this, as has been before remarked, is a solemn
duty enjoined upon our government by the constitution
under which they are organized, and from which they derive
their authority.   Besides, it is the first impulse of every
government, operating as quickly and steadily as instinct,
to provide for its own preservation.   And it seems to be
conceded on all hands, by the friends as well as the enemies

of freedom, that a government like our own can only exist among a people generally enlightened; the only question as to the permanency of free institutions being, whether it be possible to make and to keep the whole population of a nation so well educated as the existence of such institutions supposes and requires.

Our government, therefore, are urged by every motive which the constitution can enjoin or self-preservation suggest, to see to it that knowledge is generally diffused among the people. Upon this subject of popular education, a *free* government must be *arbitrary;* for its existence depends upon it. The more ignorant and degraded people are, the less do they feel the want of instruction, and the less will they seek it. And these are the classes of a community which always increase the fastest up to the very point, where the means of subsistence fail. So that if any one class of men, however small, be suffered as a body to remain in ignorance, and to allow their families to grow up without instruction, they will increase in a greater ratio, compared with their numbers, than the more enlightened classes, till they have a preponderance of physical power. And when this preponderance becomes overwhelming, what hinders a revolution and an arbitrary government, by which the mind of a few can control the physical strength of the many?

If this reasoning be correct, a free government must look to it betimes, that popular ignorance does not gain upon them. If it do, there is a thistle in the vineyard of the republic, which will grow and spread itself in every direction, till it cannot be eradicated. The ignorant must be allured to learn by every motive which can be offered to them. And if they will not thus be allured, they must be taken by the strong arm of government and brought out, willing or unwilling, and made to learn, at least, enough to make them peaceable and good citizens. It would be well, indeed, if the possibility could be held out to all of successfully aspiring to responsible stations in society. A faint hope is better than despair. And though only one chance in a thousand be favorable, even that is worth something to stimulate the young to greater efforts, to become worthy of distinction. The few who, under all the disadvantages which adverse circumstances impose, can find their way by untired perseverance to places of trust and influence in the republic, serve to give identity of feeling, of purpose, and pursuit to the whole. They harmonize and bind together all those different and distant classes of the community, between which fretful jealousies naturally subsist.

These are hints, only, at an argument, perhaps unintelligible ones, to establish the principle, that free governments are the proprietors of all literary and scientific institutions, so far as they have the tendency to diffuse knowledge generally among the people. The free schools of Massachusetts, as the most efficient means of accomplishing that object, should therefore be the property and the peculiar care of government. An argument will, at once, be drawn from these principles why they should assume the direction of the schools, so far as to insure to the people over whom they are appointed to preside, competent teachers of them. And as this is the main purpose of the proposed institution, the reasoning seems to be conclusive why they should be its proprietor, or, at least, its patron and protector.

An institution for the education of teachers, as has been before intimated, would form a part, and a very important part, of the free-school system. It would be, moreover, precisely that portion of the system which should be under the direction of the State, whether the others are or not. Because we should thus secure at once, a uniform, intelligent, and independent tribunal for decisions on the qualifications of teachers. Because we should thus relieve the clergy of an invidious task, and insure to the public competent teachers, if such could be found or prepared. An institution for this purpose would become, by its influence on society, and particularly on the young, an engine to sway the public sentiment, the public morals, and the public religion, more powerful than any other in the possession of government. It should, therefore, be responsible immediately to them. And they should carefully overlook it, and prevent its being perverted to other purposes, directly or indirectly, than those for which it is designed. It should be emphatically the State's institution. And its results would soon make it the State's favorite and pride, among other literary and

scientific institutions. The Legislature of the State should,
therefore, establish and build it up, without waiting for
individuals, at great private sacrifices, to accomplish the
work. Such would be the influence of an institution for
the education of teachers; and such is the growing conviction of the strength of early associations and habits, that it
cannot be long before the work will be begun in some form.
If it be not undertaken by the public and for public
purposes, it will be undertaken by individuals for private
purposes.

The people of Massachusetts are able and willing, yea,
more than willing, they are anxious to do something more
for popular education, for the diffusion of knowledge generally. The only questions with them are how and where
can means be applied to the purpose to the greatest advantage. It may safely be submitted, by the friends of
the free schools, to a republican people and their republican
government, which institutions on comparison most deserve
the public bounty; those whose advantages can be enjoyed
but by a few, or those which are open to the whole population; those which have for their main objects good that is
remote, or those whose happy influences are felt at once,
through the whole community. Which institutions deserve
the first consideration, and the most anxious attention of
a popular government, those which will place a few scholars
and philologists upon a level with the Germans in a knowledge of Greek accents, or those which will put our whole
people upon the level of enlightened men in their practical
knowledge of common things? These objects may all be
important to us. But the former will be provided for by
individuals; the latter are the peculiar care of government.

[*Second question: What shall be the leading features of the new
institution? Four important points.*]

The next question, mentioned above, as arising in the
progress of this discussion, was, what would be the leading
features of an institution for the education of teachers. If
the institution were to be founded by the State, upon a
large scale, the following parts would seem to be obviously
essential. 1. An appropriate library, with a philosophical

apparatus. 2. A principal and assistant professor in the different departments. 3. A school for children of different ages, embracing both those desiring a general education, and those designed particularly for teachers. 4. A Board of Commissioners, or an enlightened body of men representing the interests and the wishes of the public.

1. A library should of course be selected with particular reference to the objects of the institution. It would naturally and necessarily contain the approved authors on the science of education in its widest sense. It would embrace works of acknowledged merit in the various branches of literature and science intimately connected with education; such as anatomy and physiology, the philosophy of the human mind and heart, and the philosophy of language.

Physical education forms a very essential part of the subject, and should be thoroughly understood. This branch includes the development of all the organs of the body. And works upon the physiology of children should be added to the library. Books on gymnastics, containing directions for particular exercises adapted to the development of the several organs, belong to the library of the accomplished instructor, as well as to that of the surgeon. Indeed, if the former properly use them, they will enable him to give a firmness to the parts of the body which may, perhaps, supersede the necessity of the interference of the latter to set them right in manhood.

The philosophy of the infant mind must be understood by the instructor before much progress can be made in the science of education; for a principal branch of the science consists in forming the mind. And the skill of the teacher in this department is chiefly to be seen in his judicious adaptation of means to the development of the intellectual faculties. Every book, therefore, which would aid in an analysis of the youthful mind, should be placed in the library of the proposed institution.

The human heart, the philosophy of its passions and its affections, must be studied by those who expect to influence those passions, and form those affections. This branch of the subject includes the government of children, especially in the earliest stages of their discipline. The success of the

teacher here depends upon the good judgment with which
he arranges and presents to his pupils the motives that will
soonest move them, and most permanently influence their
actions. The mistaken or wicked principles of parents
and instructors, in this department of education, have, no
doubt, perverted the dispositions of many hopeful children.
If successful experience has been recorded, it should be
brought to the assistance of those who must otherwise act
without experience.

Lastly, the study of the philosophy of language would be
essential to the scientific teacher. The term language is
not here understood to mean a class of words called Greek,
or another class of words called Latin, or even that class of
words which we call English. It means something more
general, and something which can hardly be defined. It
embraces all the means we use to excite in the minds of
others the ideas which we have already in our own minds.
These, whatever they are, are included in the general defini-
tion of language. This is a great desideratum in our systems
of education. We do not possess a language by which we
can produce *precisely* the idea in a pupil which we have in
our own mind, and which we wish to excite in his. And
impatient and precipitate teachers quite often quarrel with
their pupils, because they do not arrive at the same conclusions with themselves, when, if they could but look into
their minds, they would find that the ideas with which they
begin to reason, or which enter into their processes of
reasoning, are altogether different. Every book or fact,
therefore, which would do any thing to supply this desideratum, or enable the teacher better to understand precisely
the idea which he excites in the mind of his pupils, should
be collected in the instructor's library.

2. The institution should have its principal and its assistant professors. The government and instruction of a
seminary for the education of teachers would be among the
most responsible situations which could be assigned to men
in literary or scientific pursuits. As many of the objects of
the institution would be new, so the duties of its instructors
would also be new. No commanding minds have gone
before precisely in the proposed course, and struck out a

path which others may easily follow. There are no *rules* laid down for the direction of those who will not think upon, or who cannot understand the subject. Men must, therefore, be brought to the task who have the ability to observe accurately and to discriminate nicely. They must also collect the results of what experience they can from books and from others, in order to enable themselves to form some general principles for the direction of their pupils, who will go abroad to carry their improvements to others. It is not supposed for a moment that all who may receive instruction at the proposed institution with the intention of becoming teachers, will necessarily be made thereby adepts in the science, any more than it is believed that all who happen to reside four years within the walls of a college are necessarily made expert in the mysteries of syllogisms and the calculus. But having seen correct general principles of education successfully reduced to practice, they may, at least, become *artists* in the profession, and be able to teach pretty well upon a system, the philosophy of which they cannot thoroughly comprehend.

3. A school of children and youth of different ages and pursuing different branches of study would form an essential part of the institution. In the early stages of the education of children, the discipline should consist almost wholly of such exercises as serve to develop the different faculties and strengthen all the powers of the mind. And in the subsequent education of youth, when the discipline comes to consist partly in the development of the mind, and partly in the communication of knowledge, the course of instruction would be the same, whether the pupil were destined to be a teacher or not. The objects of the institution do not, therefore, become peculiar till after the pupil has acquired a certain degree of freedom and strength of mind; nor till after he has made the acquisition of the requisite amount of knowledge for the profession of teacher. Though a pupil would necessarily imbibe a good deal of clearness and method in his intellectual exercises by submitting the direction of them to a skillful instructor, the study of the science of teaching cannot properly begin till he changes relations with those about him; and, instead of following a course

prescribed by another, and exhibiting the powers of his own mind without an effort to take cognizance of them, he assumes to look down upon humbler minds, to direct their movements, and to detect and classify the phenomena of their subtle workings.

After the young candidate for an instructor, therefore, has acquired sufficient knowledge for directing those exercises and teaching those branches which he wishes to profess, he must then begin his labors under the scrutinizing eyes of one who will note his mistakes of government and faults of instruction, and correct them. The experienced and skillful professor of the science will observe how the mind of the young teacher acts upon that of the learner. He will see how far and how perfectly they understand each other, and which is at fault if they do not understand each other at all. If the more inexperienced teacher should attempt to force upon the mind of a child an idea or a process of reasoning for which it was not in a proper state, he would be checked at once, and told of his fault; and thus, perhaps, the pupil would be spared a disgust for a particular study, or an aversion to all study. As our earliest experience would in this manner be under the direction of those wiser than ourselves, it would the more easily be classed under general principles for our direction afterward. This part of the necessary course in an institution for the education of teachers might be much aided by lectures. Children exhibit such and such intellectual phenomena; the scientific professor of education can explain those phenomena, and tell from what they arise. If they are favorable, he can direct how they are to be encouraged and turned to account in the development and formation of the mind. If they are unfavorable, he can explain by what means they are to be overcome or corrected. Seeing intellectual results, he can trace them, even through complicated circumstances, to their causes: or, knowing the causes and circumstances, he can predict the result that will follow them. Thus every day's experience would be carefully examined, and made to limit or extend the comprehension of the general principles of the science. Is there any other process or method than this to arrive at a philosophical system of education? If any occurs to other minds, it is to be hoped that the public may soon have the benefit of it.

4. The fourth branch, which I mentioned above as constituting an important part of an institution for the education of teachers, was a Board of Commissioners. Although they would, probably, have but little to do with the immediate government and instruction of the institution, they would be valuable to it by representing the wishes of the community, and by bringing it more perfectly in contact with the public interests. Besides, it must occur to every one, that in the general management of such an establishment, many of the transactions would require characters and talents very different from those that would, generally, be found in the principal or professors. Men might easily be found who would lecture to admiration, and yet be wholly incompetent to assume the general direction of the establishment. The professors, too, would always want assistance and authority in determining what acquisitions should be required for admission into the institution, and what proficiency should be deemed essential in the candidates before leaving it to assume the business of teaching. Upon what principles shall the school be collected? How shall the privilege of attending as new learners in the science of education be settled upon applications from different parts of the State or country? These and many similar questions would render a body of men, distinct from the professors, important to the institution. Many decisions, too, must necessarily be made, affecting individual and private interests. This would be an invidious duty, and the instructors should be relieved from it as far as possible. It is confidently believed that the peculiar advantages to be enjoyed at such an institution by children and youth generally, as well as by those designed for teachers, would command a price sufficient to defray nearly the whole expenses of the establishment. If not so, then might not each town send one or more young men to the institution to be properly educated for instructors, and require them in return to teach their public schools to liquidate the expense? All these means, however, are subjects for future consideration, and are to be devised after the utility of the institution has been demonstrated.

*[Third question: What are the advantages to the public of such
an institution? General advantages: Better teachers;
consequently better schools and better citizens.]*

The peculiar advantages of an institution for the education of teachers would be far too numerous and too important
to be either embraced or enforced in the space which remains
for this topic. A few, therefore, of the most obvious ones
are all that can here be alluded to. One advantage, and a
very certain one, would be to raise the character of teachers
generally; and consequently, in the same degree, the character of the schools which they teach. Let us pause, for a
moment, to consider to what an extent we are interested in
every thing which affects our system of public instruction;
and hence derive a motive, before we pass on, to enforce
attention to every suggestion for improvement in it.

There were in the district of Massachusetts, according to
the census of 1820, five hundred and twenty-three thousand
one hundred and fifty-nine souls. Of this number, two hundred and forty-one thousand seven hundred and eleven
were under the age of eighteen years. The numbers have
since been much augmented. If the population has increased
only as fast since the last census as it did between the
census of 1810 and that of 1820, there are now, in round
numbers, about two hundred and fifty thousand children
and youth in Massachusetts under the age of eighteen years.
This, it will be perceived, amounts to almost one-half of the
whole number of souls. If we take from the older those
between the ages of eighteen and twenty-one, and add them
to the younger part of the population, we shall find at least
half, and probably more than half of the whole, under
twenty-one years.

These are all flexible subjects of education, in its most
comprehensive sense; though they are not all within the
influence of that part of it which can be easily controlled by
legislation, or indeed by any means except by an enlightened
public opinion. A few of this great number have left the
schools and all direct means of education, and entered upon
the active business of life. And a portion of the younger
part of them are yet subjects only for domestic education.

But after these deductions from the two extremes, it will not be extravagant to state, that one-third of the whole population are of a suitable age, have opportunity, and do actually attend school some portion of the year. In Massa-chusetts we have not the means of knowing accurately the numbers of children and youth who attend our schools; because we have no system of returns to any public author-ity, by which such facts can be ascertained. But I am confirmed in the belief that the above is not an extravagant estimate, by two circumstances. One of them is, several towns have been carefully examined, and this is about the proportion of the population found in their schools. And the other is, official documents and acknowledged authorities from the neighboring State of Connecticut inform us that one-third of the population attend their free schools a part of the year. And probably the same would be found to be true of New York, as well as of the remainder of the New England States.

These are statistical facts. Others may reason upon them and draw what conclusions they can, about immigration, the future prospects of New England, her comparative influence in the Union, and the facilities she affords for a *manufacturing district*. They have been introduced here because they suggest motives stronger than any others, to enforce attention to our means of popular education. One-third of our whole population are now at that period of life when their principles and characters are rapidly forming. Habits, both moral and intellectual, are taking their direc-tion, and acquiring the strength of age. In all this, the schools must have a deep influence. Both the degree and the kind of influence are, to a certain extent, within our control, and consequently depend upon our efforts. In twenty years, and surely twenty years are not beyond the ken of a tolerably clear-sighted politician, this part of our population will succeed to most of the responsible places and relations of their fathers. They must receive all that we have to leave for them. They must take our names, and attach to them honor or infamy. They must possess our fortunes, to preserve or disperse them. And they must inherit our free institutions, to improve, pervert, or destroy them. Here, then, are the strongest political motives, as well as paternal affection, urging upon us attention to all the means of forming correctly the characters of those who are to receive from us our choicest blessings. And what means within our control can be devised more efficient for this purpose, than those primary seminaries for instruction, where the mass of the people must receive several years of their education? Find, if they are to be found, or create, if they are not now to be found, a class of teachers *well skilled* in their profession, and put them into all our free schools. What an effect would soon be produced in their condition! And what a renovating influence these same schools would soon have upon the character of the whole people who have access to them!

[*Third question (continued). Special advantages of the proposed institution?* (1) *A science of education will develop from the facts collected in the library and from observation in the model school. This will be used to improve the common schools.* (2) *Teachers will organize into a more distinct profession.* (3) *Many advantages which cannot now be foreseen will arise.*]

But these are general advantages of a good class of teachers. I promised to speak of the peculiar advantages of the proposed institution to produce them. The library, collected with particular reference to the objects of the institution, would contain the *facts* of the science of education scattered along in the history of the world. Facts are the materials of philosophy. And we cannot philosophize, safely, till we have an extensive stock before us. The library would naturally collect, not only those phenomena relating to the subject which have already been observed, but also the records of those which must be daily passing before our eyes. Books connected with and collateral to the science will be as important to the purposes of the institution as those professedly written upon the subject. And frequently they will be found to be much more so. Because the former contain the facts and the phenomena, while the latter have only an author's reasoning and conclusions upon them. And the authors who have written upon education, with very few exceptions, have reasoned speciously, but from very limited and imperfect inductions. So that their conclusions, though they may be correct, as far as they had the necessary means of making them so, are liable to fail, totally, when reduced to practice under circumstances a little different from those from which the principles have been formed. We want more experience before we begin to reason at large and to draw sweeping conclusions on the subject. And our library would be chiefly valuable as containing that experience, or the results of it, accurately and authentically recorded.

But the conclusions of writers on the subject, though received and repeated by every body, are not binding and beyond question, till we know that the facts from which they reasoned are *all* which can affect the principles that they deduce from them. And to believe that the experience of two thousand years, embracing the present age, which is so full of phenomena of all kinds, has not added something to our means of a copious and safe induction to principles of education, requires a stretch of credulity with which my mind is not gifted. It will be safer, as a general rule, to assume that they teach us what to avoid, rather than what to imitate.

When we have collected the means of reasoning correctly, which books can afford, and added to them the living materials of philosophy, which will be constantly exhibited in the school which is to form a part of the institution, we are to place all these before instructors of discriminating minds, who are able and willing to *observe* as well as to reason. We are, then, to turn the public attention toward them in good earnest, and let them see that something is expected from them. There is a moral certainty, under such circumstances, that the expectation will be gratified. When the public attention is turned toward any subject, all the ardent and discriminating minds act in concert. And like the rays of the sun converged to a point by a lens, they act with an intensity which must produce an effect.

It would be a natural result of the proposed institution to organize the teachers into a more distinct profession, and to raise the general standard of their intellectual attainments. It would therefore concentrate and give energy and direction to exertions and inquiries, which are now comparatively wasted for want of such direction. No one, indeed, can now foresee, precisely, what effect would be produced upon our systems of education and principles of instruction by subjecting them to such an ordeal. To foretell the improvements that would be made, would be to make them, and supersede the necessity of an institution for the purpose. Though the necessity would still remain for some similar means to propagate them among the people. But if our principles of education, and particularly our principles of government and instruction, are not already perfect, we may confidently expect improvements, though we may not know, precisely, in what they will consist.

Many persons knew twenty years ago that steam was expansive. But who foresaw the degree to which its expansion could be raised, or the purposes to which it could be applied? Public attention was turned to the subject in earnest, and we now see vessels moving in every direction by its power. It was known long since that light wood would float, and water run down hill. But who foresaw, twenty years ago, the present state of our internal improvement by means of canals? Public attention and powerful minds were directed to the subject, and we now see boats ascending and descending our mountains, and traversing our continent in every direction. Those who were before almost our antipodes, have now, by the facilities of communication, become our neighbors. The most intrepid prophet would hardly have dared, even ten years ago, to predict the present state of our manufactories. This has all been done, because it could be done, and many minds were turned to the subject, and resolved that it should be done. All these are in many respects analogous cases, and go to show that we do not always know how near to us important improvements are; and that it is only necessary to direct the public attention to a subject in order to insure some inventions in it.

A great variety of other peculiar advantages to the public, it occurs to me, must arise from an institution for the education of teachers. But I have confined myself to those only which seemed to be the most striking and important.

All others will be found to be involved, in a great degree, or wholly, in those which I have stated. And although to enumerate them might add some new motives for attention to the subject, they could not strengthen much the argument in favor of an institution somewhat like that which has been above described. I must now take my leave of the subject for the present; my only regrets being that I have not had ability to do more justice to the several topics which I have discussed, nor time to do more justice to my own views of them.

II

MEMORIAL OF THE AMERICAN INSTITUTE OF INSTRUCTION TO THE LEGISLATURE OF MASSACHUSETTS ON NORMAL SCHOOLS[1]

(Submitted January, 1837)

To THE HONORABLE THE LEGISLATURE
OF THE COMMONWEALTH OF MASSACHUSETTS.

The Memorial of the Directors of the American Institute of Instruction, praying that provision may be made for the better preparation of the teachers of the schools of the Commonwealth, respectfully showeth:

That there is, throughout the Commonwealth, a great want of well-qualified teachers:

That this is felt in all the schools, of all classes, but especially in the most important and numerous class, the district schools:

That wherever, in any town, exertion has been made to improve these schools, it has been met and baffled by the want of good teachers; that they have been sought for in vain; the highest salaries have been offered, to no purpose; that they *are not to be found* in sufficient numbers to supply the demand: —

That their place is supplied by persons exceedingly incompetent, in *many* respects; by young men, in the course of their studies, teaching from necessity, and often with a strong dislike for the pursuit; by mechanics and others wanting present employment; and by persons who, having failed in other callings, take to teaching as a last resort, with no qualifications for it, and no desire of continuing in it longer than they are obliged by an absolute necessity: —

That those among this number who have a natural fitness for the work, now gain the experience, without which no one, whatever his gifts, can become a good teacher, by the sacrifice, winter after winter, of the time and advancement of the children of the schools of the Commonwealth:

---

[1] Henry Barnard: Normal Schools, pp. 85*ff.*

FRAMINGHAM, 1926 — CYRUS PEIRCE HALL

That every school is now liable to have a winter's session wasted by the unskillful attempts of an instructor, making his first experiments in teaching: By the close of the season, he may have gained some insight into the mystery, may have hit upon some tolerable method of discipline, may have grown somewhat familiar with the books used and with the character of the children; and, if he could go on in the same school for successive years, might become a profitable teacher: but whatever he may have gained *himself*, from his experiments, he will have failed too entirely of meeting the just expectations of the district, to leave him any hope of being engaged for a second term: He accordingly looks elsewhere for the next season, and the district receives another master, to have the existing regulations set aside, and to undergo another series of experiments: We do not state the fact too strongly, when we say, that *the time, capacities, and opportunities of thousands of the children are now sacrificed, winter after winter,* to the preparation of teachers, who, after this enormous sacrifice, are, notwithstanding, often very wretchedly prepared:

That many times, no preparation is even aimed at: that such is the known demand for teachers of every kind, with or without qualifications, that candidates present themselves for the employment, and committees, in despair of finding better, employ them, who have no degree of fitness for the work: that committees are obliged to employ, to take charge of their children, men to whose incompetency they would reluctantly commit their farms or their workshops:

That the reaction of this deplorable incompetency of the teachers, upon the minds of the committees, is hardly less to be deplored, hardly less alarming, as it threatens to continue the evil and render it perpetual: Finding they cannot get suitable teachers at any price, they naturally apportion the salary to the value of the service rendered, and the consequence is, that, in many places, the wages of a teacher are below those given in the humblest of the mechanic arts; and instances are known, of persons of tolerable qualifications as teachers, declining to quit, for a season, some of the least gainful of the trades, on the ground of the lowness of the teachers' pay.

We merely state these facts, without enlarging upon them, as they have already too great and melancholy a notoriety. We but add our voice to the deep tone of grief and complaint which sounds from every part of the State.

We are not surprised at this condition of the teachers. We should be surprised if it were much otherwise.

Most of the winter schools are taught for about three months in the year; the summer not far beyond four. They are, therefore, of necessity, taught, and must continue to be taught, by persons who, for two-thirds or three-fourths of the year, have other pursuits, in qualifying themselves for which they have spent the usual period, and which, of course, they look upon as the main business of their lives. They cannot be expected to make great exertions and expensive preparation for the work of teaching, in which the standard is so low, and for which they are so poorly paid.

Whatever desire they might have, it would be almost in vain. There are now no places suited to give them the instruction they need.

For every other profession requiring a knowledge of the principles of science and the conclusions of experience, there are special schools and colleges, with learned and able professors, and ample apparatus. For the preparation of the teachers, there is almost none. In every other art ministering to the wants and conveniences of men, masters may be found ready to impart whatsoever of skill they have to the willing apprentice; and the usage of society justly requires that years should be spent under the eye of an adept, to gain the requisite ability. An apprentice to a schoolmaster is known only in tradition.

We respectfully maintain that it ought not so to be: so much of the intelligence and character, the welfare and immediate and future happiness of all the citizens, now and hereafter, depends on the condition of the common schools, that it is of necessity a matter of the dearest interest to all of the present generation; that the common education is to such a degree the palladium of our liberties, and the good condition of the common schools, in which that education is chiefly obtained, so vitally important to the *stability* of our State, to our very *existence* as a *free* State, that it is the most proper subject for legislation, and calls loudly for legislative provision and protection. The common schools ought to be raised to their proper place; and this can only be done by the better education of the teachers.

We maintain that provision ought to be made by the *State* for the education of teachers; *because,* while their education is so important to the State, their condition generally is such as to put a suitable education entirely beyond their reach; *because,* by no other means is it likely that a system shall be introduced, which shall prevent the immense annual loss of time to the schools, from a change of teachers; and *because,* the qualifications of a first-rate teacher are such as cannot be gained but by giving a considerable time wholly to the work of preparation.

.   .   .   .

Now it is known to your memorialists that a very large number of those, of both sexes, who now teach the summer and the winter schools, are, *to a mournful degree,* wanting in all these qualifications. Far from being able to avail themselves of opportunities of communicating knowledge on various subjects, they are grossly ignorant of what they are called on to teach. They are often without experience in managing a school; they have no skill in communicating. Instead of being able to stimulate and guide to all that is noble and excellent, they are, not seldom, persons of such doubtful respectability and refinement of character, that no one would think, for a moment, of holding them up as models to their pupils. In short, they know not *what* to teach, nor *how* to teach, nor in *what spirit* to teach, nor what is the nature of *those* they undertake to *lead,* nor what they are *themselves,* who stand forward to lead them.

Your memorialists believe that these are evils *of portentous moment* to the future welfare of the people of this Commonwealth, and that, while they bear heavily on all, they bear especially and with disproportioned weight upon the poorer districts in the scattered population of the country towns. The wealthy are less directly affected by them, as they can send their children from home to the better schools in other places. The large towns are not affected in the same degree, as their density of population enables them to employ teachers through the year, at salaries which command somewhat higher qualifications.

We believe that you have it in your power to adopt such measures as shall forthwith diminish these evils, and at last remove them; and that this can only be done by providing for the better preparation of teachers.

We therefore pray you to consider the expediency of instituting, for the special instruction of teachers, one or more seminaries, either standing independently, or in connection with institutions already existing; as you shall, in your wisdom, think best.

We also beg leave to state what we conceive to be essential to such a seminary.

1. There should be a professor or professors, of piety, of irreproachable character and good education, and of tried ability and skill in teaching.

2. A library, not necessarily large, but well chosen, of books on subjects to be taught, and on the art of teaching.

3. School-rooms, well situated, and arranged, heated, ventilated, and furnished, in the manner best approved by experienced teachers.

4. A select apparatus of globes, maps, and other instruments most useful for illustration.

5. A situation such that a school may be connected with the seminary, accessible by a sufficient number of children, to give the variety of an ordinary district school.

·   ·   ·   ·   ·   ·   ·   ·   ·   ·   ·

Establish a seminary wherever you please, and it will be immediately resorted to. We trust too confidently in that desire of excellence which seems to be an element in our New England character, to doubt that any young man, who, looking forward, sees that he shall have occasion to teach a school every winter for ten years, will avail himself of any means within his reach, of preparation for the work. Give him the opportunity, and he cannot fail to be essentially benefited by his attendance at the seminary, if it be but for a *single month*.

In the first place, he will see there an example of right ordering and management of a school; the spirit of which he may immediately imbibe, and can never after be at a loss, as to a *model* of management, or in doubt as to its *importance*.

In the second place, by listening to the teaching of another, he will be convinced of the necessity of preparation, as he will see that success depends on thorough knowledge and a direct action of the teacher's own mind. This alone would be a great point, as many a schoolmaster hears reading and spelling, and looks over writing and arithmetic, without ever attempting to give any instruction or explanation, or even thinking them necessary.

In the third place, he will see put in practice methods of teaching; and though he may, on reflection, conclude that none of them are exactly suited to his own mind, he will see the value of method, and will never after proceed as he would have done, if he had never seen methodical teaching at all.

In the next place, he will have new light thrown upon the whole work of education, by being made to perceive that its great end is not mechanically to communicate ability in certain operations, but to draw forth and exercise the whole powers of the physical, intellectual, and moral being.

He will, moreover, hardly fail to observe the importance of the *manners* of an instructor, and how far it depends on himself to give a tone of cheerfulness and alacrity to his school.

In the last place, if the right spirit prevail at the seminary, he will be prepared to enter upon his office with an exalted sense of its importance and responsibility — not as a poor drudge, performing a loathsome office for a miserable stipend, but as a delegate of the authority of *parents* and the *State*, to form men to the *high duties of citizens* and the *infinite destinies of immortality*, answerable to them, their country, and their God for the righteous discharge of his duties.

. . . .

Let him now enter the district school. He has a definite idea of what arrangements he is to make, what course he is to pursue, what he is to take hold of first. He knows that he is himself to teach, he knows *what* to teach, and, in some measure, *how he is to set about it*. He feels how much he has to do to prepare himself, and how much depends on his self-preparation. He has some conception of the duties and responsibilities of his office. At the end of a single season, he will, we venture to say, be a better teacher than he could have been after half a dozen, had he not availed himself of the experience of others. He will hardly fail to seek future occasions to draw more largely at the same fountain.

. . . .

For the elevation of the public schools to the high rank which they ought to hold in a community, whose most precious patrimony is their liberty, and the intelligence, knowledge, and virtue on which alone it can rest, we urge our prayer. We speak boldly, for we seek no private end. We speak in the name and behalf of those who cannot appear before you to urge their own suit, the sons and daughters of the present race, and of all, of every race and class of coming generations in all future times.

For the directors of the American Institute of Instruction. George B. Emerson; S. R. Hall; W. J. Adams; D. Kimball; E. A. Andrews; B. Greenleaf; N. Cleveland, *Committee.*

EDMUND DWIGHT

Benefactor of State Normal Schools
Member of the Massachusetts Board of Education

III

HISTORY, REGULATIONS AND CURRICULUM OF THE FIRST NORMAL SCHOOLS: NARRATIVE AND DOCUMENTS [1]

[By HORACE MANN]

The interesting subject of schools for the qualification of Teachers attracted the attention of the members of the Board of Education, at an early day after they were organized. It was an object which, at that time, they felt a strong desire, but possessed no means, of accomplishing. There was reason to fear that they would have to await the slow process of a revolution in public sentiment; — a process, which is always materially retarded, when an appropriation of moneys is foreseen to be a consequence of conversion to a new opinion. But at this unpromising moment, a philanthropic gentleman, — Edmund Dwight, Esq. of this city, — authorized the Secretary of the Board of Education to communicate to the Legislature a proposition, that he would place at the disposal of the Board, the sum of ten thousand dollars, to be expended in the qualification of Teachers of common schools, on condition that the Legislature would place an equal sum in the same hands to be appropriated to the same purpose. On the 12th of March, 1838, this proposition was communicated to the two Houses, by the Secretary, in a letter of which the following is a copy: —

"*To the President of the Senate, and the Speaker of the House of Representatives*

GENTLEMEN,

"Private munificence has placed conditionally at my disposal, the sum of Ten Thousand Dollars, to promote the cause of Popular Education in Massachusetts.

"The condition is, that the Commonwealth will contribute the same amount from unappropriated funds, in aid of the

---

[1] This collection is printed in the " Common School Journal," Feb. 1, 1839.

same cause; — both sums to be drawn upon equally, as needed, and to be disbursed under the direction of the Board of Education, in qualifying Teachers of our Common Schools.

"As the proposal contemplates that the State, in its collective capacity, shall do no more than is here proffered to be done from private means, and as, with a high and enlightened disregard of all local, party and sectional views, it comprehends the whole of the rising generation in its philanthropic plan, I cannot refrain from earnestly soliciting for it the favorable regards of the Legislature.

Very respectfully,

HORACE MANN,

Secretary of the Board of Education.

"Boston, March 12th, 1838."

This communication was referred to a Joint Committee, who, on the 22d of March, made the following Report, accompanied by a Resolve: —

"In House of Representatives, 22d March, 1838.

"The Joint Committee, to whom were referred the communication of the Hon. Horace Mann, Secretary of the Board of Education, relative to a fund for the promotion of the cause of popular education in this Commonwealth, and also the memorial of the Nantucket County Association for the promotion of education, and the improvement of schools, and also the petition and memorial of the inhabitants of the town of Nantucket, on the same subject, having duly considered the matters therein embraced, respectfully

REPORT

That the highest interest in Massachusetts is, and will always continue to be, the just and equal instruction of all her citizens, so far as the circumstances of each individual will permit it to be imparted; that her chief glory, for two hundred years, has been the extent to which this instruction was diffused, the result of the provident legislation, to promote the common cause, and secure the perpetuity of the common interest; that, for many years, a well-grounded apprehension has been entertained, of the neglect of our common town schools by large portions of our community, and of the comparative degradation to which these institutions might fall from such neglect; that the friends of universal education, have long looked to the Legislature, for the establishment of one or more seminaries devoted to the purpose of supplying qualified teachers, for the town and district schools, by whose action alone other judicious provisions of law could be carried into full effect; that at various times, the deliberation of both branches of the General Court, has been bestowed upon this, among other subjects, most intimately relating to the benefit of the rising generation and of all generations to come, particularly when the provision for instruction of school teachers was specially urged on their consideration, in 1827, by the message of the Governor, and a report thereupon, accompanied by a bill, was submitted by the chairman, now a member of the Congress of the United States, following out to their fair conclusions, the suggestion of the Executive, and the forcible essays of a distinguished advocate of this institution at great length, published and widely promulgated; that, although much has been done within two or three years, for the encouragement of our town schools by positive enactment, and more by the liberal spirit, newly awakened, in our several communities, yet the number of competent teachers is found, by universal experience, so far inadequate to supply the demand for them, as to be the principal obstacle to improvement, and the greatest deficiency of our republic; that we can hardly expect, as in the memorials from Nantucket is suggested, to remove this deficiency even in a partial degree, much less to realize the completion of the felicitous system of our free schools, without adopting means for more uniform modes of tuition and government in them, without better observing the rules of prudence in the selection of our common books, the unlimited diversity of which is complained of throughout the State, and that these benefits may reasonably be expected to follow from no other course than a well-devised scheme in full operation, for the education of teachers; that the announcement, in the communication recently received from the Secretary of the Board of Education, of that private munificence, which offers ten thousand dollars to this Commonwealth, for removal of this general want, at least in the adoption of initiatory measures of remedy, is received by us, with peculiar pleasure, and, in order that the General Court may consummate this good, by carrying forward the benevolent object of the unknown benefactor, the committee conclude, with recommending the passage of the subjoined resolutions.

All which is respectfully submitted,

JAMES SAVAGE, per order.

RESOLVES RELATIVE TO QUALIFYING TEACHERS FOR COMMON SCHOOLS

Whereas, by letter from the Honorable Horace Mann, Secretary of the Board of Education, addressed, on the 12th March current, to the President of the Senate, and the Speaker of the House of Representatives, it appears, that private munificence has placed at his disposal, the sum of ten thousand dollars, to promote the cause of popular education in Massachusetts, on condition that the Commonwealth will contribute, from unappropriated funds, the same amount in aid of the same cause, the two sums to be drawn upon equally from time to time, as needed, and to be disbursed under the direction of the Board of Education in qualifying Teachers for our Common Schools; therefore,

Resolved, That his Excellency the Governor be, and he is hereby authorized and requested, by and with the advice and consent of the Council, to draw his warrant upon the Treasurer of the Commonwealth, in favor of the Board of Education, for the sum of ten thousand dollars, in such instalments and at such times, as said Board may request: *provided*, said Board, in their request, shall certify, that the Secretary of said Board has placed at their disposal an amount equal to that for which such application may by them be made; both sums to be expended, under the direction of said Board, in qualifying teachers for the Common Schools in Massachusetts.

Resolved, That the Board of Education shall render an

annual account of the manner in which said moneys have been by them expended.

This Resolve, after having passed both Houses, almost unanimously, was approved by the Governor on the 19th of April, — a fact in regard to the date, which those, who are curious in coincidences, may hereafter remember.

The Board was now possessed of the sum of twenty thousand dollars; but how inadequate is such a sum towards supplying the wants of a State, in which, during the preceding year, there had been employed in the *public* schools, *twenty-three hundred and seventy* male, and *thirty-five hundred and ninety-one* female, teachers.

Here such questions as these arose; "Shall the Board concentrate its efforts and expend its funds upon a single school?" "Shall they attempt to engraft a department for the qualification of teachers, upon academies in different parts of the State?" "Shall they attempt to obtain the coöperation of public spirited individuals, and establish private institutions, in the centres of convenient sections of the Commonwealth?" Perhaps no one of these suggestions was so decidedly superior to the others, as to preclude all difference of opinion on their relative eligibility. The questions were to be decided, not less on a comparison of the weight of objections against each, than on the arguments in favor. If but one were established, its success could be known but to the citizens of a small part of the Commonwealth; and it was desirable that an experiment, in which the whole people had a direct interest, should be tried in presence of the whole people. If existing academies were selected and a new department engrafted upon them, this department would be but a secondary interest in the school; — the teachers would not be selected, so much with reference to the incident, as to the principal object; and as the course of instruction, proper to qualify teachers, must be essentially different from a common academical course, it would be impossible for any preceptor duly to superintend both. Let there be one department of business for one man and make him responsible for its success, is a good maxim, when it can be applied. The proposition to establish as many as three schools, one at some convenient place for the North-eastern part of the State, another for the middle or Western section, and a third for the South-eastern,

seemed, on the whole, to be most eligible. But an insuper-
able objection to this course, so far as it regarded the means
of the Board, was a "plentiful lack" of supplies. The
expenditure of twenty thousand dollars could hardly have
given the Board ownership of three adequate and sufficient
establishments for the intended purpose; and even if it
could, all the means intrusted to them for educating teachers,
would have been exhausted in acquiring a place to carry on
the work. Fine buildings, excellent locations, the Board
might have; but how, without funds, could the schools be
afterwards sustained? What teacher would assume the
risk of being remunerated for his services by the amount of
tuition? The teachers of all such schools would have to be
elected as honorary members, with liberty to reside elsewhere and attend to their own employments.

But might not something be expected from individual
liberality, from local aid? Were there not men, residing in
different sections of the Commonwealth, who had deeply
pondered the subject of educating a free people in such a
manner that they would be worthy of freedom and able to
maintain it; were there not men, who saw, how, like a
moulder's hand, human institutions give shape to human
character; men, who thought more of the intellectual and
moral condition in which they should leave their children,
than of the length of their inventory of chattels and of
lands; who foresaw that the general condition of the future
society, in which those children were to reside, ranked a
thousand times higher in importance, than the amount of
their patrimony?

Upon this thought, the Board caused due notice to be
given to the friends of education in all parts of the Commonwealth, that until the whole fund in their hands should
become pledged, they would undertake to establish, in any
place, unobjectionable in point of locality, a school for the
qualification of teachers, and would sustain the same for
the space of three years, provided that suitable buildings,
fixtures and furniture, together with the means of carrying
on such school, (exclusive of the compensation of the
teachers of the school,) could be obtained from private
liberality and placed under the control of the Board.

In the course of the last season, offers, substantially com-
plying with this proposition, were made to the Board from
seven different towns in the State. Other towns also made
generous propositions to the Board, with a view to become

partakers of the bounty, which public and private liberality had placed at its control. Such a spirit of generosity, emanating from so many different points, could hardly have been anticipated. It is encouragement for the present; it is an augury of good for the future. The interests of education will not languish, confided to men animated by such a spirit.

To arrange preliminaries, correspondence and many visits to different places, in order to compare their relative eligibility, became necessary. This has rendered some delay inevitable. In a work, where the guide of no precedent could be obtained, where almost the whole ground was to be explored for the first time, great caution was the first requisite, otherwise, far more time might be lost in retracing steps incautiously taken, than would be consumed by previous and full deliberation, in projecting the true course to be pursued. In this country, we have no institutions of the kind, which can safely be adopted as a model. And the political and social differences between us and the European nations, where schools for the qualification of teachers have been founded, are so numerous and fundamental, that a transcript of their systems, without material modifications, would threaten failure, if adopted by us.

After an anxious comparison of all practicable plans, and a careful consideration of all the arguments preferred by different applicants, the Board decided to proceed so far as to establish, at least three schools, to be located respectively either in the North-eastern, the South-eastern, or the middle or Western sections of the State, and to be so located as to admit of a subsequent increase of the number, without interfering with those already established.

On a combined view of the offer and the situation, the town of Lexington was selected for the North-eastern division of the State; no other town being more favorably situated, or giving so much weight to its other claims by the liberality of its donation. Two substantial offers have been made from Worcester county; one from the town of Barre and another from that of Lancaster; and one of great generosity from New Salem, in the county of Franklin. No offer of assistance was received from any place in the State, further West, than the town of New Salem. On a careful comparison of all the circumstances, bearing upon the relative eligibility of these three places, the Board decided in favor of the town of Barre. The location of the third Normal School awaits the action of the friends of education, in the Western, or in the South-eastern part of the State.

[*Meaning of the Term Normal School*]

It may be proper here to say a word in regard to the appellation, by which these institutions are to be designated and known. The term *Normal Schools* has for some time been familiar to the literary men of this country. In Prussia, where schools for the qualification of teachers have long been in successful operation, they are universally known by the epithet, *Normal*. France, having copied, to some extent, the Prussian system, has borrowed the name, by which the distinguishing feature of that system is known. [An error of fact. The name, Normal School (*école normale*) appears to have originated in France. The extent of its use in Prussia is doubtful. — Ed.] A *Normal School* signifies a school, where *the rules of practice and the principles of guidance and direction in the various departments of Education*, are taught. The name is short, descriptive from its etymology, and in no danger of being misunderstood or misapplied.

[*Purpose of the Normal Schools*]

The most material point, in regard to the Normal Schools, relates to the course of instruction to be therein pursued. The elements for a decision of this question are found in the existing wants of our community. We want improved teachers for the Common Schools, where the mass of the children must look for all the aids of education, they will ever enjoy. In the Common School, whether it be better or poorer, the great majority of the future members of the State, — those who are to form its society and uphold or overthrow its institutions, — are to obtain the principal part of all the education, they will ever receive. Others, of different fortunes, will have superior advantages. But whosoever cares most for the greatest number will look first to the welfare of the Common Schools. In establishing the regulations for the Normal Schools, and the course of studies to be pursued therein, the idea has not for a moment been lost sight of by the Board, that they are designed to improve the education of the great body of the people. We proceed to state some of the leading rules in the code, by which they will be governed.

Admission

As a prerequisite to admission, candidates must declare it to be their intention to qualify themselves to become school teachers. If males, they must have attained the age of *seventeen* years complete, and of *sixteen*, if females; and must be free from any disease or infirmity, which would unfit them for the office of teachers. They must undergo an examination and prove themselves to be well versed in orthography, reading, writing, English grammar, geography and arithmetic. They must furnish satisfactory evidence of good intellectual capacity and of high moral character and principles. Examinations for admission will take place at the commencement of each academic year, and oftener at the discretion and convenience of the Visiters and the Principal.

Term of Study

The *minimum* of the term of study is fixed at one year. If application have been assiduous and proficiency good, the pupil may receive, at the expiration of that time, a certificate of qualification.

Course of Study

The studies first to be attended to, in the Normal Schools, are those which the law requires to be taught in the district schools, viz. orthography, reading, writing, English grammar, geography and arithmetic. When these are thoroughly mastered, those of a higher order will be progressively taken.

Any person wishing to remain at the school more than one year, in order to increase his qualifications for teaching a public school, may do so, having first obtained the consent of the Principal; and therefore a further course of study is marked out. The whole course, properly arranged, is as follows:

1. Orthography, Reading, Grammar, Composition and Rhetoric, Logic.

2. Writing, Drawing.

3. Arithmetic, mental and written, Algebra, Geometry, Book-keeping, Navigation, Surveying.

4. Geography, ancient and modern, with Chronology, Statistics and General History.

5. Physiology.

6. Mental Philosophy.

7. Music.

8. Constitution and History of Massachusetts and of the United States.

9. Natural Philosophy and Astronomy.

10. Natural History.

11. The principles of Piety and Morality, common to all sects of Christians.

12. THE SCIENCE AND ART OF TEACHING, WITH REFERENCE TO ALL THE ABOVE NAMED STUDIES.

A portion of the Scriptures shall be read daily, in every Normal School.

A selection from the above course of studies will be made for those who are to remain at the School but one year, according to the particular kind of school, it may be their intention to teach.

Visiters

Each Normal School will be under the immediate inspection of Visiters, who are, in all cases, to be chosen from the Board, except that the Secretary of the Board shall be competent to serve as one of said Visiters.

Instructers

The Board will appoint for each School a Principal Instructer, who shall direct and conduct the whole business of government and instruction, subject to the rules of the Board and the supervision of the Visiters.

At all examinations, the Principal shall attend and take such part therein, as the Visiters may assign to him; and he shall make reports to them, at such times and on such points, as they may require.

The Visiters will appoint the assistant Instructers, when authorized and directed to do so by the Board. The assistants will perform such duties, as the Principal may assign to them.

To each Normal School, an Experimental or Model School will be attached, where the pupils of the Normal

School can apply the knowledge, which they acquire in the science of teaching, to practice.

For aught that can be now foreseen, the first system of Normal Schools, properly so called, to be founded in this country, will be established in Massachusetts. Strong indications are given, however, that other States, emulating this noble example, will soon enter upon the career of furnishing higher and more efficient means for the education of the rising generation; — thus providing new guaranties for the permanency of their institutions, and adopting the most direct course to make a wiser, a better and a happier people.

IV

ATTACK ON NORMAL SCHOOLS IN THE LEGISLATURE OF 1840

In a speech at Bridgewater in 1846 Mann gave the following account of the attempt to abolish the normal schools in 1840, a few months after the beginning at Lexington and before the opening of Bridgewater:

It is well known that in the winter session of the Legislature of 1840 a powerful attack was made, in the House of Representatives, upon the Board of Education, the Normal Schools, and all the improvements which had then been commenced, and which have since produced such beneficent and abundant fruits. It was proposed to abolish the Board of Education, and go back to the condition of things in 1837. It was proposed to abolish the Normal Schools, and to throw back with indignity, into the hands of Mr. Dwight, the money he had given for their support.

That attack combined all the elements of opposition which selfishness and intolerance had created, — whether latent or patent. It availed itself of the argument of expense. It appealed invidiously to the pride of teachers. It menaced Prussian despotism as the natural consequence of imitating Prussia in preparing teachers for schools. It fomented political partisanship. It invoked religious bigotry. It united them all into one phalanx, animated by various motives, but intent upon a single object.

The Committee of the Legislature on Education presented a majority and a minority report. The former argued that the establishment of the Board of Education and the Normal Schools were attempts to "Prussianize" education in Massachusetts and a menace to local self government. The minority effectually disposed of this argument by showing that no such centralization of power in educational matters was possible under the law. The sections of these reports dealing with Normal Schools follow:

FRAMINGHAM, 1926 — HORACE MANN HALL

I. COMMITTEE OF THE LEGISLATURE ON EDUCATION: MAJORITY REPORT, AGAINST NORMAL SCHOOLS, 1840

Another project, imitated from France and Prussia, and set on foot under the superintendence of the Board of Education, is the establishment of Normal schools. Your Committee approach this subject with some delicacy, inasmuch as one half the expense of the two Normal schools already established has been sustained by private munificence. If, however, no benefit, in proportion to the money spent, is derived from these schools, it is our duty, as legislators, in justice not only to the Commonwealth but to the private donor, to discontinue the project. Comparing the two Normal Schools already established with the academies and high schools of the Commonwealth, they do not appear to your Committee to present any peculiar or distinguishing advantages.

Academies and high schools cost the Commonwealth nothing; and they are fully adequate, in the opinion of your Committee, to furnish a competent supply of teachers. In years past, they have not only supplied our own schools with competent teachers, but have annually furnished hundreds to the West and the South. There is a high degree of competition existing between these academies, which is the best guaranty for excellence. It is insisted by the Board, however, that the art of teaching is a peculiar art, which is particularly and exclusively taught at Normal Schools; but it appears to your Committee, that every person, who has himself undergone a process of instruction, must acquire, by that very process, the art of instructing others. This certainly will be the case with every person of intelligence; if intelligence be wanting, no system of instruction can supply its place. An intelligent mechanic, who has learned his trade, is competent, by that very fact, to instruct others in it; and needs no Normal School to teach him the art of teaching his apprentices.

Considering that our district schools are kept, on an average, for only three or four months in the year, it is obviously impossible, and perhaps it is not desirable, that the business of keeping these schools should become a distinct and separate profession, which the establishment of Normal Schools seems to anticipate.

Even if these schools did furnish any peculiar and distinguishing advantages, we have no adequate security that the teachers, thus taught at the public expense, will remain in the Commonwealth; and it seems hardly just that Massachusetts, in the present state of her finances, should be called upon to educate, at her own cost, teachers for the rest of the Union.

If it be true, that the teachers of any of our district schools are insufficiently qualified for the task, the difficulty originates, as it appears to your Committee, not in any deficiency of the means of obtaining ample qualifications, but in insufficiency of compensation. Those districts, which are inclined to pay competent wages, can at all times be supplied with competent teachers; and the want of means or inclination to pay an adequate salary is not a want which Normal Schools have any tendency to supply.

From the number of scholars who have hitherto attended the Normal Schools, established by the Board of Education, it does not appear that any want of such institutions is seriously felt. The number of pupils falls far short of the average number in our academies and high schools.

It may be suggested, that to abolish these Normal Schools, when they have been in operation for so short a time, is not to give the experiment a fair trial. But the objections of your Committee, as will appear from the considerations above submitted, are of a general and fundamental nature; and they do not consider it advisable to persevere in an experiment, of the inutility of which they are perfectly satisfied. In fact, these schools do not appear to your Committee to have any stronger claims on the public treasury, for an appropriation of two thousand dollars a year, than many of our academies and high schools.

Should the Normal Schools be discontinued by the Legislature, it is but just and reasonable, in the opinion of your Committee, that the sums, advanced by the individual who has generously contributed to the support of those schools, should be refunded; which might be done, by an appropriation of probably five or six hundred dollars, in addition to the money not yet expended, in the hands of the treasurer of the fund.

The Secretary of the Board of Education stated, in his argument before your Committee on the subject of Normal Schools, that engagements with the teachers of those schools and other parties interested, had been entered into for a term of three years; and he argued, that it would be improper for the Legislature to disturb these contracts. With respect to these contracts, your Committee are decidedly of opinion, that they ought never to have been made, except with the express understanding of a liability to be rescinded or modified, at the pleasure of the Legislature. If, however, they have been otherwise made, and if any individuals shall appear to have any reasonable claim to be remunerated for any disappointment, occasioned by discontinuing the schools, the Legislature have the power to make such remuneration; and your Committee believe, that the sooner such a settlement is made, the better, — inasmuch as an increase in the number of the schools, as contemplated by the Board, would increase the difficulty and cost of such a settlement.

In conclusion, the idea of the State controlling Education, whether by establishing a central Board, by allowing that Board to sanction a particular Library, or by organizing Normal Schools, seems to your Committee a great departure from the uniform spirit of our institutions, — a dangerous precedent, and an interference with a matter more properly belonging to those hands, to which our ancestors wisely intrusted it. It is greatly to be feared, that any attempt, to form all our schools and all our teachers upon one model, would destroy all competition, all emulation, and even the spirit of improvement itself. When a large number of teachers and school committees are all aiming at improvement, as is doubtless the case, to a great extent, in this Commonwealth, improvements seem much more likely to be found out and carried into practice, than when the chief right of experimenting is vested in a central Board.

With these views, your Committee have come to the conclusion, that the interests of our Common Schools would rest upon a safer and more solid foundation, if the Board of Education and the Normal Schools were abolished.

II. MINORITY REPORT IN FAVOR OF NORMAL SCHOOLS

[The minority of the legislative Committee on Education were not permitted to see the majority report until it was handed in. However, they delivered a shattering reply to the charges that the Board of Education would "Prussianize" the schools by showing that under the law the Board could do none of the things feared. They then proceeded to discuss the Normal Schools as follows:]

On the subject of the Normal Schools, the undersigned feel obliged to enter into some details. By the donation of an individual, and a public grant to an equal amount, the sum of twenty thousand dollars was placed at the disposal of the Board, subject to only one condition, that it should be expended in qualifying teachers for our Common Schools. By the very terms, both of the private gift and the public grant, they were to have the entire control of it, as to the time and manner in which it should be expended, the number of schools, course of study, &c. The Report of the Board in 1839, informed the public of the course proposed. Three schools, at least, were to be established, for three years, each, in different parts of the State. As the money was not sufficient to provide for buildings, the Board made known that they would establish them at suitable places, as soon as they should receive the requisite assistance. Citizens from the county of Plymouth, and from several towns in other parts of the State, came forward with their offers. That from Plymouth county was among the first. When the citizens of that county inquired of the Board, on what terms they would establish a school within its limits, they passed the following resolve: "*Resolved*, That this Board will establish a school for the education of school teachers, at a point to be hereafter selected, within the

county of Plymouth, and provide suitable teachers therefor, for a time not less than three years, so soon as suitable
buildings, fixtures, and furniture, and the means of carrying
on the school, (exclusive of the compensation of teachers,)
shall be provided and placed under the control of the
Board."

Proposals substantially alike being made by many towns
in different parts of the State, the Board selected Lexington
and Barre as the most eligible places for the two other
schools. The citizens of Lexington procured a lease and
placed at the disposal of the Board a good academical building and boarding-house, for the term of three years, and
raised by contribution the sum of a thousand dollars, to be
expended in library, apparatus, &c., for the benefit of the
school. The Board leased the boarding-house for the accommodation of pupils. They engaged Cyrus Pierce, Esq.,
then the teacher of a public school in Nantucket, where he
was receiving fourteen hundred dollars a year, to become
Principal of this school. Mr. Pierce left Nantucket, at a
pecuniary loss, and removed with his family to Lexington.
The school has been open, about eight months. Two letters
from distinguished teachers, annexed to this Report, will
show what we believe to be its true character.[1]

The town of Barre voted to offer the Board, for the term
of three years, a spacious apartment in its town hall; and
individuals raised by subscription fourteen hundred dollars,
to pay the rent of a boarding-house, for three years, to purchase library, apparatus, &c. The boarding-house has been
let, for the term of three years, for the accommodation of
the school. The Rev. Professor Newman, of Bowdoin College, Maine, and for several years acting President of that
institution, was engaged as Principal. He has disposed of
his property in Maine, and removed with his family to
Barre. The school has been open, six months.

The friends of Common-School education in Plymouth
county, with a spirit worthy the descendants of the pilgrims,
projected their plan on a still more liberal scale. Towns in
their corporate capacity, and private individuals, have together contributed the sum of ten thousand dollars, for the

---

[1] See the letters of Samuel G. Howe and George B. Emerson, pp. 271, 274.

erection of buildings, and other necessary expenses. An act of incorporation was given them, last winter, upon the faith of which they have thus far proceeded. A committee of gentlemen, residing out of the county, had already agreed on a day for going thither and selecting a site for the school, when the Report of our Committee was made.

The majority of our Committee propose, in one short bill, to violate all these contracts, — to break their faith with the generous donor of ten thousand dollars, to turn out the boarding-house keepers, to disperse the pupils, and discharge the teachers of the schools, and to annul a charter under which, at much expense and labor, the sum of ten thousand dollars has been raised.

For a period of two hundred years preceding the liberal donation of Mr. Dwight, nothing was given by wealthy individuals, so far as we can learn, for the general benefit of the Common Schools of our State. Hundreds of thousands of dollars have been given to colleges. Academies have been liberally endowed. But, before this donation, the bounty of the rich had never been expended for the benefit of the whole people; and this first sum ever given to promote the great cause of common education, it is now proposed to treat with contempt, and cast back into the face of the generous donor. Let this benefaction be thus contemned, and far distant is the day when any one else will expose himself to be treated in a similar way.

The Committee speak of our Normal Schools as possessing no advantages for qualifying teachers, above what are possessed by our academies and high schools. We cannot suppose that they have formed this opinion from having visited them. The two letters, before referred to, contain the opinions of men who speak that which they know. With their testimony before the public, it is not necessary for us to enlarge on this subject.

Whatever objection any one might have had to the establishment of the Board and the Normal Schools, originally, yet, since they have been created and organized, it seems but right that they should have a fair trial. Let the experiment be tried, and not broken off as soon as begun. It has not yet had that trial. A change in public sentiment cannot be effected at once. Any new proposition, however valuable, may meet with opposition, at first. If the Board and Normal Schools are abolished now, they cannot be said to have failed. They will have fallen, prematurely, by the hand which should have sustained them. Men who desire to see the whole people educated in the manner that the citizens of a free republic ought to be, that rational and immortal beings ought to be, will not be satisfied, until measures, which they deem important to effect their favorite object, have been fairly tested.

The undersigned would not have extended these remarks to so great a length, were they not deeply impressed with the importance of the subject to which they relate. We only ask of the Legislature a dispassionate consideration of the subject before us. We only ask, that they will not disappoint the cherished hopes of those who are laboring in the great and good work of the intellectual and moral improvement of man.

III. LETTER FROM DR. SAMUEL G. HOWE, DIRECTOR OF THE INSTITUTION FOR THE BLIND, AT SOUTH BOSTON[1]

South Boston, March 9, 1840

MR. GREENE,

SIR, — I have received your note, in which you ask my opinion of the Normal School at Lexington, and I cheerfully comply with your request.

I can express my opinion the more confidently, because I have more than once visited the School; because I have examined the pupils, in their various branches of study; and because I have had other opportunities of knowing the principles of the system of instruction.

In common with others, I entertained some theoretical objections to Normal Schools as carried on by European governments, for I have personally witnessed the serious abuses to which they are subject, in Prussia; but none of those objections can apply to the establishment at Lexington.

---

[1] "Common School Journal," Vol. 2, p. 238.

It has been in my power to examine many schools, in this country, and in various parts of the world; but I am free to declare, that, in my opinion, the best school I ever saw, in this or any other country, is the Normal School at Lexington.

The discipline of the School is perfect; the pupils regard their teacher with profound respect, yet tender affection; their interest in their studies is deep and constant; their attainments are of a high order; and they thoroughly *understand* every subject, as far as they go.

But not for these things do I give this School the preference; for others in this country and in Europe may equal it, in these respects; but I prefer it, because the system of instruction is truly philosophical; because it is based upon the principal that the young mind hungers and thirsts for knowledge, as the body, does for food; because it makes the pupils not merely recipients of knowledge, but calls all their faculties into operation to *attain it themselves;* and finally, because relying upon the higher and nobler parts of the pupil's nature, it rejects all addresses to bodily fears, and all appeals to selfish feelings.

I have said, sir, that the pupils were thoroughly acquainted with the various branches of an English education, as far as they advanced in them, and that they bore well a very severe examination. But this is faint praise; for a teacher may cause a class to make very great *intellectual* attainments, by pursuing a system which, nevertheless, is ruinous to the moral nature of his pupils. But, at the Lexington School, the moral nature is as much cultivated as the intellectual, and the training of each goes on at the same time.

There is one point of view, however, in which this School particularly interested me, and in which it presented a beautiful moral spectacle, the memory of which will dwell long in my mind; it was the fact, that every pupil seemed impressed with a deep sense of the importance of the calling which she was to follow; they seemed to feel that at least the temporal weal or wo of hundreds of human beings might be dependent upon the fidelity with which they should perform their duty as teachers. Consequently, every one was desirous of becoming acquainted with the philosophy of mind; and they received such excellent instruction, that they seemed to understand the various springs and incentives to action, which exist in a child's bosom.

To me, sir, it was delightful, to see that they were becoming acquainted with the nature of the children's mind, *before* they undertook to manage them; and that they would not, like other teachers, have to learn, at the children's expense.

Perhaps, sir, you, like myself, may have *suffered*, in boyhood, under some usher, who was learning his trade, by experimenting upon you, as the barber's apprentice learns to shave, upon the chins of his master's less favored customers; and if you have ever been a teacher, you may look back with bitter regret upon the course you followed, during the first years of your practice.

Some of the very best teachers, I have ever known, have confessed, that, when they commenced, they had no more idea of the real nature of their employment, than a cabin boy has of navigation. Would not the merchant be called mad, who should give the direction of his vessel to a young man who had never been at sea, and who knew none of the ropes of the ship? But is it not greater madness to commit a school to one who knows nothing of the springs of action in the human mind, and who may cause moral shipwreck and destruction to all under his charge?

But this is a subject so completely set at rest in the mind of every enlightened philanthropist, that it would be a work of supererogation to urge any more considerations upon you.

I will only repeat to you, what I have said to others, that if, instead of the twenty-five teachers who will go out from the Normal School of Lexington, there could go out, over the length and breadth of Massachusetts, five hundred, like them, to take charge of the rising generation, that generation would have more reason to bless us, than if we should cover the whole State with rail-roads, like a spider's web, and bring physical comforts to every man's door, and leave an overflowing treasury to divide its surplus among all the citizens.

With much respect, truly yours,

SAMUEL G. HOWE.

To THOMAS A. GREENE, Esq.

IV. LETTER FROM GEORGE B. EMERSON, ESQ., FORMERLY PRINCIPAL OF THE BOSTON HIGH SCHOOL, AND NOW TEACHER OF A SCHOOL FOR YOUNG LADIES [1]

Boston, March 9, 1840

DEAR SIR: — I very much regretted that you could not have joined us in the visit, to which you refer, in your note of this morning, to the Normal School at Lexington. I spent the day with more pleasure than I ever received from a similar examination.

I had, as you know, high expectations of the effect of special instruction, in the preparation of teachers. But what I saw far surpassed what I had expected. The kind of instruction given as to the preparation to be made by a teacher, the branches to be taught, the methods of teaching, and the modes of influencing and governing pupils, were such as might have been expected from a long, enlightened, and well-directed experience. But the facility, with which these were communicated, surprised me, and the interest in the pursuit, which I found to have been excited, was such as I never before witnessed.

The establishment consists of two departments, the proper Normal School, made up of the future teachers, and the Model School, containing children from the neighborhood, to be instructed according to the most approved methods.

In the former, there were about twenty-four young ladies,

---

[1] "Common School Journal," Vol. 2, p. 236.

of from sixteen to twenty-four years of age, coming from almost as many different kinds [of] schools, and having therefore experience of almost as many different modes of teaching and governing. This School had been in operation, but little more than half a year, and several of the young ladies had been there, only a few weeks. Yet I am confident, from what I saw of their modes of teaching, that those individuals will show the effects of those few words of special instruction, all the remainder of their lives. They can never teach in the blind and lifeless way in which thousands of elementary schools are taught.

And, if the spirit which I saw exhibited may be taken as an indication of the influence which would be exerted in a longer course, I will say, without hesitation, that so amply qualified teachers are not now to be found in the elementary schools of the State, as would be formed, among the individuals now at the School, by a full course of instruction, such as is designed.

In the Normal School, the object *seemed* to be, — for I have had no opportunity of learning what *are* the intentions of the Principal, — first, to give great thoroughness in those branches which are of the greatest importance in the common elementary schools, such as Reading, Writing, Arithmetic, etc.; next, to add those studies which would give an acquaintance with the minds and characters of children, just as, in an agricultural school, we should expect to see communicated an acquaintance with plants, and the nature of soils; and, lastly, to give some knowledge of those principles of science on which children are most inquisitive, and with which, therefore, a well-qualified teacher's mind should be amply stored.

These all were admirably-well taught; and, what was still better, the pupils seemed to have imbibed, in a most remarkable degree, the zeal and earnestness which are so essential to success in a teacher, and which yet are so uncommon. This was evidenced, by the readiness of their answers, the clearness of their explanations and the interest with which they engaged in the discussions, and still more by the life that had been communicated to the Model School below.

In this latter, which may be considered as the test of the
success with which the operations of the upper School are
managed, I listened, with still greater interest, to the manner in which questions were put and answered, the object
of which was to excite the attention of the children to the
meaning of what they were reading.   There was nothing of
the listlessness of manner and monotony of tone, which are
so often observed, and often so inevitable, in Common
Schools.   The same was observable in the answers given to
questions on the elements of geography, and on grammar;
very thorough instruction had evidently been given.   The
children had been made clearly to comprehend what they
had been taught.   Yet they occasionally made mistakes;
enough to show that their own minds were at work, and, of
course, sometimes going wrong.

In this School, the great objects in view seemed to be, to
ascertain and impart the best modes of teaching the art of
reading intelligently, distinctly, and naturally; of communicating the elements of grammar, arithmetic, and geography; of bringing the mind into complete and cheerful
activity, in making these acquisitions; of acquiring the art
of governing, by gentleness, and without resort to violence;
and of imparting the love of order, quiet, and regularity.
In all these respects, the success had already been signal.

The Model School is only under the general superintendence of the master.   For the greater part of the time it is
left to the care of the young ladies, who all have the charge
of it, in turn.   I have never before seen little children so
completely under the right influence of their teachers, —
so fully awake; I never saw so little of mere mechanical
teaching, or greater activity of the faculties of the mind.

I have mentioned some of the advantages of continuing
this process of preparing teachers.   It would be easy to
enlarge upon them.

Great benefits have been experienced from meetings of
teachers for mutual consultation.   The Normal School has
all the advantages of a continued meeting, with the opportunity of testing, at once, all suggestions made.

It is usually the case, that a teacher is familiarly acquainted with only one mode of managing a school.   This

may be a bad one. Others may suggest themselves to him; but it would be altogether impracticable for him to test their excellence. But in the Normal School he has an opportunity of becoming acquainted with a great variety of methods, and taking from among them that which he most approves.

I can hardly express to you the great satisfaction which I derived from this visit. The only draw-back was an apprehension, lest, from the entire devotion of the teacher, and the intense interest excited in the pupils, the health of both should suffer.

If there is any danger that this most valuable establishment should be discontinued, I would recommend to you to take the earliest opportunity to make it a visit, or you will lose a pleasure which may not again be presented.

I am very truly yours,

GEORGE B. EMERSON.

To THOMAS A. GREENE, Esq.

V

WHAT PEIRCE AIMED TO ACCOMPLISH

LETTER TO HENRY BARNARD, 1851

"DEAR SIR: — You ask me 'what I aimed to accomplish, and would aim to accomplish now, with my past experience before me, in a Normal School.'

I answer briefly, that it was my aim, and it would be my aim again, to make better teachers, and especially, better teachers for our common schools; so that those primary seminaries, on which so many depend for their education, might answer, in a higher degree, the end of their institution. Yes, to make better teachers; teachers who would understand, and do their business better; teachers, who should know more of the nature of children, of youthful developments, more of the subjects to be taught, and more of the true methods of teaching; who would teach more philosophically, more in harmony with the natural development of the young mind, with a truer regard to the order and connection in which the different branches of knowledge should be presented to it, and, of course, more successfully.

Again, I felt that there was a call for a truer government, a higher training and discipline, in our schools; that the appeal to the rod, to a sense of shame and fear of bodily pain, so prevalent in them, had a tendency to make children mean, secretive, and vengeful, instead of high-minded, truthful, and generous; and I wished to see them in the hands of teachers, who could understand the higher and purer motives of action, as gratitude, generous affection, sense of duty, by which children should be influenced, and under which their whole character should be formed.

In short, I was desirous of putting our schools into the hands of those who would make them places in which children could learn, not only to read, and write, and spell, and cipher, but gain information on various other topics, (as

SILVER VASE PRESENTED TO CYRUS PEIRCE, JULY 26, 1848

accounts, civil institutions, natural history, physiology, political economy, &c.) which would be useful to them in after life, and have all their faculties, (physical, intellectual and moral) trained in such harmony and proportion, as would result in the highest formation of character. This is what I supposed the object of Normal Schools to be. Such was my object.

[Do teachers need training?]

But in accepting the charge of the first American Institution of this kind, I did not act in the belief that there were no good teachers, or good schools among us; or that I was more wise, more fit to teach, than all my fellows. On the contrary, I knew that there were, both within and without Massachusetts, excellent schools, and not a few of them, and teachers wiser than myself; yet my conviction was strong, that the ratio of such schools to the whole number of schools were small; and that the teachers in them, for the most part, had grown up to be what they were, from long observation, and through the discipline of an experience painful to themselves, and more painful to their pupils.

It was my impression also, that a majority of those engaged in school-keeping, taught few branches, and those imperfectly, that they possessed little fitness for their business, did not understand well, either the nature of children or the subjects they professed to teach, and had little skill in the art of teaching or governing schools. I could not think it possible for them, therefore, to make their instructions very intelligible, interesting, or profitable to their pupils, or present to them the motives best adapted to secure good lessons and good conduct, or, in a word, adopt such a course of training as would result in a sound development of the faculties, and the sure formation of a good character.

I admitted that a skill and power to do all this might be acquired by trial, if teachers continued in their business long enough; but while teachers were thus learning, I was sure that pupils must be suffering. In the process of time, a man may find out by experiment, (trial), how to tan hides and convert them into leather. But most likely the time would be long, and he would spoil many before he got through. It would be far better for him, we know, to get some knowledge of Chemistry, and spend a little time in his neighbor's tannery, before he sets up for himself. In the same way the farmer may learn what trees, and fruits, and seeds, are best suited to particular soils, and climates, and modes of culture, but it must be by a needless outlay of time and labor, and the incurring of much loss. If wise, he would first learn the principles and facts which agricultural experiments have already established, and then commence operations. So the more I considered the subject, the more the conviction grew upon my mind, that by a judicious course of study, and of discipline, teachers may be prepared to enter on their work, not only with the hope, but almost with the assurance of success.

[*Are there principles of education?*]

I did not then, I do not now, (at least in the fullest extent of it,) assent to the doctrine so often expressed in one form or another, that there are no general principles to be recognized in education; no general methods to be followed in the art of teaching; that all depends upon the individual teacher; that every principle, motive and method, must owe its power to the skill with which it is applied; that what is true, and good, and useful in the hands of one, may be quite the reverse in the hands of another; and of course, that every man must invent his own methods of teaching and governing, it being impossible successfully to adopt those of another. To me it seemed that education had claims to be regarded as a science, being based on immutable principles, of which the practical teacher, though he may modify them to meet the change of ever-varying circumstances, can never lose sight.

[*What are these principles?*]

That the educator should watch the operations of nature, the development of the mind, discipline those faculties whose activities first appear, and teach that knowledge first, which the child can most easily comprehend, viz., that which comes in through the senses, rather than through reason and the imagination; that true education demands, or rather implies the training, strengthening, and perfecting of all the faculties by means of the especial exercise of each; that in teaching, we must begin with what is simple and known, and go on by easy steps to what is complex and unknown; that for true progress and lasting results, it were better for the attention to be concentrated on a few studies, and for a considerable time, than to be divided among many, changing from one to another at short intervals; that in training children we must concede a special recognition to the principle of curiosity, a love of knowledge, and so present truth as to keep this principle in proper action; that the pleasure of acquiring, and the advantage of possessing knowledge, may be made, and should be made, a sufficient stimulus to sustain wholesome exertion without resorting to emulation, or medals, or any rewards other than those which are the natural fruits of industry and attainment; that for securing order and obedience, there are better ways than to depend solely or chiefly upon the rod, or appeals to fear; that much may be done by way of prevention of evil; that gentle means should always first be tried; that undue attention is given to intellectual training in our schools, to the neglect of physical and moral; that the training of the faculties is more important than the communication of knowledge; that the discipline, the instruction of the school-room, should better subserve the interests of real life, than it now does; — these are some of the principles, truths, facts, in education, susceptible, I think, of the clearest demonstration, and pretty generally admitted now, by all enlightened educators.

[The principles of teaching suggest reform of the old methods of teaching the common branches.]

The old method of teaching Arithmetic, for instance, by taking up some printed treatise and solving abstract questions consisting of large numbers, working blindly by what must appear to the pupil arbitrary rules, would now be regarded as less philosophical, less in conformity to mental development, than the more modern way of beginning with mental Arithmetic, using practical questions, which involve small numbers, and explaining the reason of every step as you go along.

So in the study of Grammar, no Normal teacher, whether a graduate or not, of a Normal School, would require his pupils to commit the whole text-book to memory, before looking at the nature of words, and their application in the structure of sentences. Almost all have found out that memorizing the Grammar-book, and the exercise of parsing, do very little toward giving one a knowledge of the English la guage.

Neither is it learning Geography, to read over and commit to memory, statistics of the length and breadth of countries, their boundaries, latitude and longitude, &c., &c., without map or globe, or any visible illustration, as was once the practice. Nor does the somewhat modern addition of maps and globes much help the process, unless the scholar, by a previous acquaintance with objects in the outer world, has been prepared to use them. The shading for mountains, and black lines for rivers on maps, will be of little use to a child who has not already some idea of a mountain and a river.

And the teacher who should attempt to teach reading by requiring a child to repeat from day to day, and from month to month, the whole alphabet, until he is familiar with all the letters, as was the fashion in former days, would deserve to lose his place and be sent himself to school. Could anything be more injudicious? Is it not more in harmony with nature's work, to begin with simple, significant words, or rather sentences, taking care always to select such as are easy and intelligible, as well as short? Or, if letters be taken first, should they not be formed into small groups, on some principle of association, and be combined with some visible object?

Surely, the different methods of teaching the branches above-mentioned, are not all equally good. Teaching is based on immutable principles, and may be regarded as an art.

[*How Peirce attempted to teach the art of teaching.*]

Nearly thirty years' experience in the business of teaching, I thought, had given me some acquaintance with its true principles and processes, and I deemed it no presumption to believe that I could teach them to others. This I attempted to do in the Normal School at Lexington; 1st. didactically, i.e. by precept, in the form of familiar conversations and lectures; 2nd. by giving every day, and continually, in my own manner of teaching, an exemplification of my theory; 3rd. by requiring my pupils to teach each other in my presence, the things which I had taught them; and 4th. by means of the Model School, where, under my general supervision, the Normal pupils had an opportunity, both to prove and improve their skill in teaching and managing schools. At all our recitations, (the modes of which were very various,) and in other connections, there was allowed the greatest freedom of inquiry and remark, and principles, modes, processes, every thing indeed relating to school-keeping, was discussed. The thoughts and opinions of each one were thus made the property of the whole, and there was infused into all hearts a deeper and deeper interest in the teachers' calling. In this way the Normal School became a kind of standing Teachers' Institute.

But for a particular account of my manner and processes at the Normal School, allow me to refer you to a letter which I had the honor, at your request, to address to you from Lexington, Jan. 1, 1841, and which was published in the Common School Journal, both of Connecticut and Massachusetts, (vol. 3.) [See pages l–lviii above for this account. See also Mary Swift's Journal, *passim*, for detailed examples.]

What success attended my labors, I must leave to others to say. I acknowledge, it was far from being satisfactory to myself. Still the experiment convinced me that Normal Schools may be made a powerful auxiliary to the cause of education. A thorough training in them, I am persuaded, will do much toward supplying the want of experience. It will make the teachers' work easier, surer, better. I have reason to believe that Normal pupils are much indebted for whatever of fitness they possess for teaching, to the Normal School. They uniformly profess so to feel. I have, moreover, made diligent inquiry in regard to their success, and it is no exaggeration to say, that it has been manifestly great. Strong testimonials to the success of many of the early graduates of the Lexington (now W. Newton) Normal School, were published with the 8th Report of the late Secretary of the Board of Education, and may be found in the 7th vol. of the Massachusetts Common School Journal.

[*Do we need professional schools for teachers?*]

But it is sometimes asked, (and the inquiry deserves an answer,) Allowing that teaching is an art, and that teachers may be trained for their business, have we not High Schools and Academies, in which the various school branches are well taught? May not teachers in them be prepared for their work? Where is the need then of a distinct order of Seminaries for training teachers? I admit we have Academies, High Schools, and other schools, furnished with competent teachers, in which is excellent teaching; but at the time of the establishment of the Normal Schools in Massachusetts, there was not, to my knowledge, any first-rate institution exclusively devoted to training teachers for our common schools; neither do I think there is now any, except the Normal Schools. And teachers can not be prepared for their work anywhere else, so well as in seminaries exclusively devoted to this object. The art of teaching must be made the great, the paramount, the only concern. It must not come in as subservient to, or merely collateral with any thing else whatever. And again, a Teachers' Seminary should have annexed to it, or rather as an integral part of it, a model, or experimental school for practice.

Were I to be placed in a Normal School again, the only difference in my aim would be to give more attention to the development of the faculties, to the spirit and motives by which a teacher should be moved, to physical and moral education, to the inculcation of good principles and good manners.

[Conclusion: What the professionally-trained teacher should be able to do.]

In conclusion, allow me to recapitulate. It was my aim, and it would be my aim again, in a Normal School, to raise up for our common schools especially, a better class of teachers, — teachers who would not only teach more and better than those already in the field, but who would govern better; teachers, who would teach in harmony with the laws of juvenile development, who would secure diligent study and good lessons and sure progress, without a resort to emulation and premiums, and good order from higher motives than the fear of the rod or bodily pain; teachers, who could not only instruct well in the common branches, as reading, writing, arithmetic, &c., but give valuable information on a variety of topics, such as accounts, history, civil institutions, political economy, and physiology; bring into action the various powers of children, and prepare them for the duties of practical life; teachers, whose whole influence on their pupils, direct and indirect, should be good, tending to make them, not only good readers, geographers, grammarians, arithmeticians, &c., but good scholars, good children, obedient, kind, respectful, mannerly, truthful; and in due time, virtuous, useful citizens, kind neighbors, high-minded, noble, pious men and women. And this I attempted to do by inculcating the truth in the art of teaching and governing, — the truth in all things; and by giving them a living example of it in my own practice."

[CYRUS PEIRCE]

BIBLIOGRAPHY

BIBLIOGRAPHY

AGNEW, WALTER D. The Administration of Professional Schools for Teachers, 1924.

ALBREE, JOHN. Charles Brooks and his Work for Normal Schools, 1906.

AMERICAN INSTITUTE OF INSTRUCTION, LECTURES AND PROCEEDINGS, 1830–1850.

AMERICAN ANNALS OF EDUCATION, 1830–.

AMERICAN JOURNAL OF EDUCATION, 1826–1830.

AMERICAN JOURNAL OF EDUCATION (Henry Barnard), 1855–. s.v. Biographical Sketches: Brooks, C.; Carter, James G.; Dwight, Edmund; Emerson, G. B.; Gallaudet, T. H.; Hall, S. R.; Johnson, Walter R.; Mann, H.; May, S. J.; Peirce, C.; Perkins, T. H.; Stowe, C. E.; Tillinghast, N.; Wadsworth, J.; Woodbridge, Wm. C. s.v. Normal Schools.

BARNARD, HENRY. Normal Schools, 1851.

BURTON, WARREN. The District School as It Was, 1833.

CARTER, JAMES GORDON. Essays upon Popular Education, Containing a Particular Examination of the Schools of Massachusetts, and an Outline of an Institution for the Education of Teachers, 1826.

—— Letters to the Hon. William Prescott, LL.D., on the Free Schools of New England, with Remarks upon the Principles of Instruction, 1824.

COMMON SCHOOL JOURNAL, edited by Horace Mann, 1837–1848.

COUSIN, VICTOR. Rapport sur l'état de l'instruction publique dans quelques pays de l'Allemagne, et particulièrement en Prusse, 1833.

EVERETT, EDWARD. Address on Normal Schools, Am. Jour. Ed. (Barnard) II, 494.

—— Papers, 1836–1840, Mass. Hist. Soc.

MANN, HORACE. Life and Works, by Mary P. Mann, Vols. 1–5, 1865, 1891.

—— Papers, 1837–1849, Mass. Hist. Soc.

MASSACHUSETTS BOARD OF EDUCATION:
Abstract of the Massachusetts School Returns, 1837–1850.
Annual Report, 1837–1850.
Minutes, 1837–1849.

MASSACHUSETTS GENERAL COURT:
Acts and Resolves, 1780–1850.
House of Representatives, Documents, 1826–1850.
Senate, Documents, 1826–1850.

NORMAL SCHOOL, BRIDGEWATER. History and Alumni Record, by A. G. Boyden, 1876.

NORMAL SCHOOL, LEXINGTON-FRAMINGHAM. Catalogue, 1839–1846.
Historical Sketches, 1914.
Journal of the Model School, 1840–1846.
Journal of the Normal School, 1844–.
Journal of Cyrus Peirce, 1839–1841.
Journal of Mary Swift, 1839–1840.
Records of the First Class, 1903.

RANDOLPH, E. D. The Professional Treatment of Subject-Matter, 1924.

RANTOUL, ROBERT, Jr. Memoirs, Speeches and Writings, edited by Luther Hamilton, 1854.

STEINER, BERNARD C. Life of Henry Barnard, 1919.

INDEX

INDEX